D1090882

All of my words
If not well put
Nor well taken
Are well meant.

       11 Jan 1949
       Coney On The Lowland Sea

Woody Guthrie

SONGS AND ART • WORDS AND WISDOM

BY NORA GUTHRIE AND ROBERT SANTELLI

VOICE OF THE PEOPLE

CHRONICLE BOOKS
SAN FRANCISCO

The Joy of writing words down has flowed me over.

(30)

Copyright © 2021 by Nora Guthrie. All rights reserved. No part of this book may be reproduced in any form without written permission from the publisher.

All words and art by Woody Guthrie copyright © Woody Guthrie Publications, Inc. All rights reserved.

Library of Congress Cataloging-in-Publication Data
Names: Guthrie, Woody, 1912-1967, author, artist. | Guthrie, Nora, writer of supplementary textual content. | Santelli, Robert, writer of supplementary textual content. | Guthrie, Woody, 1912-1967. Lyrics. Selections. | Guthrie, Woody, 1912-1967. Diaries. Selections. | Guthrie, Woody, 1912-1967. Drawings. Selections.
Title: Woody Guthrie : songs and art * words and wisdom / [curated by] Nora Guthrie and Robert Santelli.
Other titles: Woody Guthrie (Chronicle Books)
Description: San Francisco : Chronicle Books, 2021.
Identifiers: LCCN 2021020496 | ISBN 9781797211787 (hardcover)
Subjects: LCSH: Guthrie, Woody, 1912-1967. | Guthrie, Woody, 1912-1967--Portraits. | Guthrie, Woody, 1912-1967--Notebooks, sketchbooks, etc.
Classification: LCC ML410.G978 A25 2021 | DDC 782.42162/130092--dc23
LC record available at https://lccn.loc.gov/2021020496

Manufactured in China.

Design by Jon Glick.
Pages 338 to 339 constitute a continuation of the copyright page.

10 9 8 7 6 5 4 3 2 1
Chronicle books and gifts are available at special quantity discounts to corporations, professional associations, literacy programs, and other organizations. For details and discount information, please contact our premiums department at corporatesales@chroniclebooks.com or at 1-800-759-0190.

Chronicle Books LLC
680 Second Street
San Francisco, California 94107
www.chroniclebooks.com

PAGES 1 & 3: New York City, 1943.

Contents

OCTOBER 1942	NOVEMBER 1942	DECEMBER 1942

NOVEMBER
19
THURSDAY

WRITING:
Tracks behind
a leaky mind

Welcome to Mermaid Avenue

NORA GUTHRIE

I was born on Mermaid Avenue in Coney Island, Brooklyn. The corner store was the center of the world in our neighborhood; everyone could find something they needed, from the morning's first newspaper to a late afternoon cup of coffee. It was a terminal for everyone who lived within ten blocks, where they bumped into each other to share an impromptu conversation or gossip. My father was a regular.

As little kids, we went there often for the milkshakes. There was a soda fountain lined with about eight green leather-topped stools that twirled, which was just about as much fun as a kid could have in those days. As Dick, the owner, made our shake (which seemed to take forever to prepare), my brothers and I would spin each other 'round and around. When the milkshake was ready, Dick poured it into three small glasses, one for each of us. As I sipped my shake, I would spin more slowly, taking it all in.

Neighbors, delivery men, mailmen, and passersby appeared and disappeared. All shapes, sizes, colors, languages. They stopped to pick up one of the dozens of newspapers that sat on a stand on the sidewalk; they carried groceries from the fruit stand and butcher shop next door.

Through that plate glass window, decorated with "soda," "news," and "cigarettes" signs, I watched as they strolled down West 37th Street to Surf Avenue and to the beach and boardwalk, or sat on their stoop cooling off.

Toward the back of the store, there were a few Formica lunch tables with chairs for the older people. The pay phone inside the wooden booth with a folding glass-paneled door would ring for anyone on the block who didn't have a home phone. The shelves were lined with school supplies—(marble composition notebooks, pens, and pencils) and art supplies (delicious new crayons, glue, scissors, construction paper, small jars of finger paints, watercolor paints, and cheap brushes). A different shelf had supplies for the grown-ups: onionskin typing paper, accounting ledgers, wrapping paper.

In the late '40s and '50s, this was where my father loved to be. And although he wasn't known to spin on the stools, he too was taking it all in. Often, it's where he sat and wrote in his notebooks and diaries. Why did he write so many of his essays in composition books? Well, because they were there, at Dick's.

Why did he write the ode "Ain't You Sam"? Because Sam worked in the store and answered the calls from that phone booth, swept up the sawdust from the floor, and put out the newspapers every morning on the sidewalk. "Child Sitting" (page 284) is about Woody spending the day with his three-year-old daughter, Cathy Ann, who is stuck at home with a cold, using up all the art supplies from Dick's store.

But that's just one corner store in one town.

During my father's life, he nestled into many places, corners where he could inconspicuously watch and listen and learn, be it a boxcar en route somewhere, a migrant workers' campfire at night, or an artist's loft in New York City.

Many of the lyrics, notes, and essays in this book come from my father's diaries and notebooks. Some might be very familiar, but many are unknown and were never intended for publication. Many were notes to himself, perhaps fodder for future lyrics, novels, articles. Or words just to let off steam or to remember something that happened on a street or subway.

My mother often said that he loved the feeling of pencil or pen on paper, that writing in itself was a physically sensuous experience.

The surge of his writings is astounding, and the sheer amount of words often overwhelming. They cover the most seemingly inconsequential event, person, or thought, to the most historic, dramatic, or esoteric. You could say that nothing in the existing universe was safe from his accounting. He freely witnessed every-thing and set it down without an inner, or outer, editor.

He often rambled through his thought process to come to a conclusion or state a belief using any and all available tools: pen, ink, pencil, crayon, type-writer, paintbrush, watercolor. In addition to writing lyrics, he used cartoons, poems, jokes or quips, one-liners—anything to help excavate his ideas. Twenty pages in a notebook filled with words, drawings, or watercolors would lead him to some final insight. At last, perhaps, a song was born, an essay written, or a letter sent.

When I think of my life, I remember my stool-spinning days at our corner store, pausing here or there for a longer look or spinning quickly when nothing much seemed to be happening. But it's also how I went about looking at my father's life and curating this book. I want you to get a bigger picture of what his life was like—all 360 degrees of it. And though I did the curating, he'll do most of the talking.

I also wanted to connect his life with the people around us now. After all, most of the ideas in this book are not uniquely his own private property. They come and go with each generation, with fresh names and faces that speak in that day's tongues. Bob and I invited a few of them here, to stand side by side with my father's thoughts..

Finally, my hope is that this book feels more like a daily almanac rather than a scholarly work. I want you to open to any page, on any day, and find something that will make you smile or think or be inspired in some way. That's been my approach for the past thirty years working with his archive, and believe me, it works.

I often wondered, if my father hadn't been hospitalized with Huntington's disease in my younger years, how would he have raised me, day to day? What would he have told me, where would he have taken me, what would he have wanted to show me? I guess this book is the answer to that question. It's the people, the places, the feelings, the teachings. I have chosen what to me are some of his clearest thoughts and some of the conclusions he came to at the end of all his rambling, the ones that I have personally connected to and found to be helpful. But my guess is that they might also be meaningful to many other people. I don't represent him as an icon, a hero, or even a folk singer, but as a man who acquired some smarts along the way that he shared with his daughter and many others.

Sometimes a good father throws a baseball in the backyard with his kids. Sometimes he writes down songs for them to sing. All good. As it turns out, for me, even though he was debilitated with Huntington's for most of my childhood, he was, and still is, quite a father. He gave me thoughts to think about, history to hear about, and people to know about. All because he left me, and you, with these tracks behind a leaky mind.

Take it easy,
But take it.
Woody Guthrie

Introduction

ROBERT SANTELLI

Woody Guthrie's heyday was a long time ago. Why should we read about him today? Why listen to his music? Why should we care? I wish Woody was merely a once-relevant relic of his age, and his songs simply historical markers of an America working out its flaws. But the sad truth is that so much of what Woody wrote about—racism, economic inequality, the un-American treatment of immigrants, war, corruption from capitalism gone wild—is still very much with us today.

Woody and his words are still relevant and necessary here and now. We might shake our heads and wonder: How could this be? Woody's songs don't supply answers, but they do point the way to where the answers are hidden, deep in the nation's soul.

Woody came from common stock in uncommon times. Born in Oklahoma in 1912, five years after the territory became a state, young Guthrie witnessed explosive economic growth all around him. Oil, "black gold" as they called it, gushed out of newly constructed rigs and wells all over Oklahoma. Some people got rich. Some lost everything.

The Guthrie family didn't enjoy the fruits of Oklahoma's oil boom. Instead, Woody—named Woodrow Wilson Guthrie after the soon-to-be president—saw his father hold a variety of jobs, all the while clinging to a dusty mirage of the American Dream. Woody's mother succumbed to what was then thought insanity but was actually a rare fatal neurological disorder, Huntington's chorea, today known simply as Huntington's disease. It would be the same disease, incurable then, incurable now, that would do Woody in, slowly but surely, stealing every last bit of his creative juices. Finally, in 1967, Huntington's would end his life.

From early on, Woody loved to read and paint; he had an insatiable curiosity and a gift for writing. He also loved music, especially the Carter Family and the blues of the Black laborers he came to know. Woody learned

Los Angeles, CA, 1939.

to play guitar, harmonica, and a bit of banjo and joined a country string band or two before he realized he could write his own songs and play and sing them himself—and in doing so, work out the many ideas that streamed through his brain most every day.

It's hard to say when, exactly, Woody realized that a song could be more than entertainment—it could carry a powerful message, change a darkened mind, tell an essential truth. But once he did, the result was a raging river of songs that aimed to alter the bad deals and bad luck that people, especially poor people, suffered in their lives. He was their champion, and his songs would be his most vital means of fighting for their rights.

Woody Guthrie became a man-of-the-people philosopher. He was also a political analyst, a keen observer of America and all its trials and tribulations, and a folk-singing sage whose way with words could make you laugh or cry or feel compelled to act.

Woody gave voice to the many who were barely surviving the Great Depression. Later, he wrote songs that rallied Americans against fascism in World War II. He flirted with a couple of other -isms, namely socialism and communism. But when asked if he was a card-carrying member of the Communist Party, he simply shrugged and said that he'd "been in the red all his life," preferring to identify himself as a "common-ist."

Along his journey, Woody wrote songs, sometimes two or three in a day. He would read an article in the newspaper that moved him, and that afternoon he'd write a song about it. And that evening, he'd sing it somewhere. You could teach a college course on the life and times of the working man in the 1930s just by assigning Woody Guthrie songs as the syllabus. There was simply no stopping him in his prime.

But he wrote songs about pretty much everything: politics, personal relationships, prairies, mountains, islands, the man in the mill, the woman in the home, babies, big shots, baseball players, fascists, communists, capitalists, socialists, picking fruit, playing for unions, being on the radio, sleeping in the subway, sex, love, California, Coney Island, America.

If he didn't write a song, he wrote a letter or a poem or a list. Or he painted a picture, or sketched one, or jotted down something in one of his many notebooks, which were neater and more organized than he ever was. That shaggy head of hair of his hardly saw a comb, and he never much cared for clothes that were pressed or clean. He roamed and he rambled from one place to the next. Home life and domesticity were not his specialties, though he enjoyed being a father. Hopping freights, hitchhiking, and walking were the ways he usually got to where he was going, which was usually wherever the spirit moved him.

He played his songs on street corners and in union halls, in bars and local living rooms. He made his way to California, where the difference between the haves and have-nots shook him to his bones, and then across the country to New York City, where left-wing intellectuals celebrated him as authentically "Okie." It was there he met the famous folklorist Alan Lomax and a young Harvard dropout turned folk singer named Pete Seeger, two men who recognized Guthrie's genius and sought to stay connected to it—and him—their entire lives.

Woody wrote more than three thousand songs, and new ones still pop up now and then, more than a half century later. He was a man with a guitar and a head full of ideas. When one of those ideas was satisfied in song, it seemed as if another five took its place. Guthrie was determined to chronicle seemingly everything he saw, heard, and felt, everyplace he went, and everyone he met. This book is proof of that.

For some, it's a chance to reconnect with an old friend. For others, it's the opportunity to get to know an important and enduring new voice. If you believe in an America that holds itself to the highest ideals, then whoever you are and wherever you come from, you're in the right place. Woody Guthrie, an American Original, will show you the way home.

1-39

Woody,

Pvt. W. W. (Woody) Guthrie
A.S.N.; 42234634

I got a few hundred more ballads
where this one come from

What do you think?
Give me a call, or drop a line.
Me and my harp and guitar are
hot and ready.

Yours truly,
Woody Guthrie

Woody Guthrie

Back in that cave was a funeral held
Fifty jillion come sung for Buzzy Bill;
were gonna phone that Judge to th' end of his trail
For killin' Dee mocracy & Buzzy Buzzy Bill.

Woody Guthrie the Older
August 15th 1949
Coney Island, N.Y.C.

by
Woody Guthrie

I always liked this one better
than the people that heard it.

Typed up
& changed

Woody Guthrie

***If you were I, I would try.
May 28th, 1947;

Woody Guthrie

Take it easy
But take it

woody

Good books put songs in
my head. Ants is next
pants and my feet to
itchin' — for the big
Peoples Highway

30

Woody Guthrie
13 of Jan 1949
Feeding Joady Ben

30

Woody Guthrie

W.W. Woody Guthrie,
49 Murdock Court, Apt 1J,
Beach Haven At Brighton,
Brooklyn, 23, New York.

**************RECOPIED AT HOME 5-3-46 WG*****
Exactly Two Years after I wrote it. Funny.
****

W.W. Woody Guthrie

*an outlaw song
by Woody Guthrie

I love you

I love you

I love you

I love you

Woody Guthrie

Woody Guthrie
August 3, 1948
Coney In this ocean
Drinkin' hot Tea.

Woody

WOODY K.F.V.D.
338 SO. WESTERN - L.A.

Yours truly,
W.W. (Woody) Guthrie
October 25th 1940,
New York City, N.Y,
31 East 21 Street,
Top floor —

FINISH
LATER

END

"Biggest thing
words & music by me Woody Guthrie

TAKE UP Words
for SPIRITUAL
Album

ORIG.
WOODY KFVD
4-39 to L.A.

original Song
Woody Guthrie
3-11-41 L.A.

** I MADE UP THIS SONG TO HAVE SOMETHING
TO SING WHEN I GOT JOBS AROUND AT CHURCHES OF
ALL THE DIFFERENT FAITHS. WG. *******

Woody W. Guthrie
november 7th, 1946
new York City,
new York State.

my
seal

Thanks
the down

This song made up by Woody Guthrie
3520 Mermaid Avenue, Brooklyn, 24, NY.?
March the Fifth, wife in town working,
Daughter in nursery school, jug dry,
temperature warmer. A March wind is
marching down along the ocean looking
at the wreckage that washed in last night

Woody Guthrie

Same As Ever
Woody G

Wrote up and sung, fiddled, and danced out
for Arlo Dybuck's Brother Joady, (Come with Ol
Jacky Frostifer, and with the big freeze, that
blowed down on New York out of the Texas Panhan
dle on a Christmas Nighte, 1849, I mean, 1984,
no, dammitall, 1498, $14.99 --- $19.48))))))))
W.G.
(The feller on the Fone))).

ALL I GUESS FOR THIS TIME

Woody & Tribe
Woody Guthrie

30

all for you
Woody

CHAPTER ONE

Self Portrait

*Poems
Ballads
Thoughts
Ideas
dreams
Visions
and midnight battles

by me
Woody Guthrie*

Woody typically signed his name at the bottom of his lyrics, added a date and location, and often included anecdotes and commentary. He titled and indexed many of his notebooks. His lyrics and notebook entries serve as a diary offering a record of his daily thoughts and feelings and documenting his travels.

Beluthahatchee, FL, 1951.

I am a changer
A constant changer
I have to be or die
Because
whatever stops changing
Is dead. And I am alive.

SELF PORTRAIT

Woody Guthrie

Clara, doll and Woody, Nov. 1913

LEFT: Woody's parents, Charley and Nora Belle Guthrie.

RIGHT: Woody's sister Clara Guthrie with infant Woody and doll in carriage, November 1913.

It was in the quicksands and muds of the river's rising, the wind that blew and whipped from east to west in a spit second, the lightning that splintered the barn loft, the snakey tailed cyclone, prairie cloudbursts, the months of fiery drought that crippled the leaves, in the timber fires, prairie fires that took more than it could build back, in the fights of the men against all of these, that I was born. . .

In The Oklahoma Hills Where
I Was Born

typed

Punctuate

Many a year has come and gone
Since I wandered from my home
In those Oklahoma hills where I was born
Many a page of Life has turned
Many a lesson I have learned
And I feel like in those hills I still belong.

Way down yonder in my Indian Nation
Ride my pony over the reservation
Make a cowboy life my occupation
In the Oklahoma Hills where I was born.

Now my dreams turn back a page
To the land of the great Osage
Chicasaw, Choctaw, Cherokee, Creek, and Seminole,
Where the Black oil rolls and flows
And the snow white cotton grows
In the Oklahoma hills where I was born.   (Chorus)

And as I stand here today
I'm a many a mile away
From the place I rode my pony through the draw
Where the oak and black jack trees
Kiss that happy prairie breeze
In the Oklahoma hills where I was born.   (Chorus)

Words & music
Written by –
W.W. (Woody) Guthrie

"I was born and raised in the state of Oklahoma, called the land of the five civilized Indian tribes; Chickasaw, Choctaw, Cherokee, Creek and Seminole. At the time that I was born, in the year 1912, my father was a sort of a hard, fist fighting Woodrow Wilson Democrat. So, Woodrow Wilson was nominated that same year, and at the age of about four or five years old, a long time before I was in school, I remember my dad used to teach me little political speeches and rhymes.

And I'd climb up in a hay wagon around at all the political meetings and rallies they had on the streets, and I'd make my little speeches. And it might be that I've turned out now that where I don't believe the speeches anymore and make speeches just the opposite. But that was a pretty early age to be standing up in a hay wagon, barefooted, several years before I ever thought of going to school. I must have been four or five or six years old . . .

But when I first started remembering anything about the town, I remembered that my life had been a sort of typical cowboy. I had a horse, I had two, three horses, we had several bird dogs and several prize hogs and several prize cattle and several prize horses. My life was more or less wrapped up in all of that just like any other kids." (Interview, 1949)

OPPOSITE: Woody's father, Charley Guthrie, working in a dry goods store in Castle, OK, and posing with hunting dogs, horses, and a prize bull.

Papa - clerking in Castle Okla.

Papa & hunting dogs Okemah, Okla.

Called Hardtime

Papa & Called "Hardtime"

WHEN I WAS A LITTLE BOY
Woody Guthrie

When I was a little boy,
First, I had to grow;
Then I had to guess;
And then I had to know;
                    First I played marbles;
                    And, I next played ball;
          But I had to study fighting most of all,
                    Most of all;
          And I had to study fighting most of all.

When I was a little boy,
Next, I had to see;
Then I had to feel;
Even tried to steal;
                    Learned I had to eat;
                    Had to learn to work;
          But I had to study fighting most of all,
                    Most of all;
          And I had to study fighting most of all.

When I was a little boy,
I had to get bigger;
Had to get wider;
Had to get longer;
                    Had to throw some rocks;
                    Had to learn to run;
          But I had to study fighting most of all,
                    Most of all;
          And I had to study fighting most of all.

                    ****

woody guthrie

[My grandma] had one of the first phonographs in [Okfuskee] county. The first notes of so-called civilized music echoed in the holler trees along Buckeye Creek and in the leaves of the sumac and the green June corn from out the screen door of the Tanner house. The Negroes made up songs and sung around the new Tanner place every day of its building up. Indians walked the back trails and rooty rut roads, sang, cursed, chanted blessings and poison words out at the white man. This and the shirt staining fistfights that broke out around the house parties and dances, the foamy ponied outlaws, and the screaks of greasy wheeled buggies and wagons, newly-oiled trigger springs, the first oil scouting crowds that had commenced to drift out from back East, South, West and up North, their hurts, greeds, fears, this was the big song I heard all around me.

copied
into big
wg

WAY OVER YONDER IN THE MINOR KEY
Woody Guthrie

Ain't nobody that can sing like me
  Way over yonder in the minor key
  Way over yonder in the minor key
Ain't nobody that can sing like me.

    I lived in a place called Okfuskee
    I had a little girl in a holler tree
    I said, Little Girl, it's plain to see
    Ain't nobody that can sing like me.

Chorus:

    She said it's hard for me to see
    How one little boy got so uglee
    Yes, my Little Girly, that might be,
    But there ain't nobody that can sing like me.

Chorus:

    We walked down by the Buckeye Creek
    To see the Frog eat the Goggle Eyed Bee
    To hear that west wind whistle to the east
    There ain't nobody that can sing like me.

Chorus:

    Oh my little Girly will you let me see
    Way over yonder where the wind blows free
    Nobody can see in our holler tree
    And there ain't nobody that can sing like me.

Chorus:

    Her mama cut a switch from a cherry tree
    And laid it onto she and me
    It stung lots worse than a hive of bees
    But there ain't nobody that can sing like me.

Chorus:

    Now I have walked a long long ways
    I still look back to my tanglewood days
    I've led lots of girls since then to stray
    Saying, ain't nobody that can sing like me.

         Chorus
        ****

*The first two verses of this
song come to me on the 9th of
September while I was doing KP
out in Scott Field, Illinois.
I hummed it over to myself for
a couple of months, or seven,
and then took a notion today
that I would finish it up.

This song made up by Woody Guthrie
3520 Mermaid Avenue, Brooklyn, 24, NY.?
March the Fifth, wife in town working,
Daughter in nursery school, jug dry,
temperature warmer. A March wind is
marching down along the ocean looking
at the wreckage that washed in last night

Woody Guthrie

HOTEL BOND
THE BONDMORE
BOND ANNEX HOTEL
WILLARD F. ROGERS, PRESIDENT
AND GENERAL MANAGER

"... Something started happening to the town. And it happened so fast and so quick that all of that cowboy angling of mine sort of faded out. The fact that the Indians and the poor Negroes had been given the state of Oklahoma by United States treaties of all kinds because they didn't figure that the land was good enough for anything else. But the very minute that everybody found out that there was millions and millions of dollars worth of oil pools under every acre of land, why the Indians and the poor Negroes that lived on the land naturally had to be cheated out of it, and fast!

A lot of ways was worked to get them loose from the land. There used to be a state law in Oklahoma that a white man could not marry a Negro nor an Indian. It was okay for an Indian to marry a Negro, it was okay for a Negro to marry an Indian. A white man could not marry either one, according to the state law. Then after the oil come in and the Negro and the Indians got rich, why then they passed a new state law that a Negro could not marry a white man nor an Indian, but a white man could marry an Indian. A white man could not marry a Negro, because the poor Negroes did not have any state lands. Other tricks they used was they passed a Prohibition Law in 1913, and we still got Prohibition in the state. You might say Oklahoma is first in everything worst.

So that's roughly how the State of Oklahoma was operating. They used dope, they used opium, they used every kind of a trick to get these Indians to sign over their lands, in big or little chunks, to some white lawyer from back East or some city slicker from some big town.

So, Oklahoma was full of those kind of people, and plus another army of people that worked in oil fields. I don't know whether you ever seen a town turn into an oil field town overnight or not, but there's all kinds of guys hit town, just wake up one morning and they're there. You don't know where they come from; there's fifteen or twenty thousand of them out there in a little town that used to be five or six hundred farming people. Sort of slow, poking around you know, going to the mailbox and back, take an hour to tell you a story about something. But all at once there's fifteen or twenty thousand guys running up and down the street out there. Nobody knows anybody else, nobody ever seen anybody else, nobody wants to see anybody else, nobody hopes they'll ever see anybody else.

Nobody will never get a letter. They know that they never got a letter in their lives, they never will get a letter in their lives. No folks, no chance except

In the 1940s and 1950s, the terms *Negro* and *Indian* were used in the progressive community, reflecting respect for the two cultures.

one earthly thing, and that's to get a job putting an oil well down. They run out there and they start to get too aggressive. They got drillers, they got tong-buckers, they got ditch diggers, they got pile climbers, they got preachers, they got pimps, they got whores, they got gamblers, sheriffs, deputies, all kinds of officers. Lawyers, educated men, speakers, all kind of entertainers up and down the street.

Everybody is one big army, transient workers, they're going to work out their few months or a few years at the most. They don't even build houses, they don't build homes, they don't put down foundations. They put up a little boxcar house that cost twenty-five or thirty dollars apiece, and move on as quick as the oil well is drilled, because when it's drilled they put a little pump on it, they pump it over into the big tank cars and they ship it back here to New York City and Newark where they burn it up in the form of car smoke.

But roughly talking, that's the way Oklahoma was when I come to start sort of reflecting about it. So, it wasn't a peaceful, very sleepy life that I'd have had when I was a kid. I don't remember getting any real sleep back in them days.

My mother was awful scared, nervous kind of a woman, so she would sing to sort of pacify us kids. She had five children and she would sing . . . every big long ballad you could think of, to put us to sleep at night. And when we'd get to worrying about where Papa was, because just about every night them people was chasing up and down the town with guns, hunting each other, and coming in sometimes pretty well shot up. Why in those days a woman had a whole lot to worry about, just like pioneer women of old times and frontier women, there's lots of times where you don't know quite for sure whether your man's ever going to come home tomorrow or not. And that was sort of the use, I think, that she made of these songs, and when I first remembered hearing them, and why I guess I remember them like I do now, you might say, after all these years that I still remember word for word the songs that she used to sing." (Interview, 1949)

This is one of the only known songs Woody wrote about his mother, Nora Belle Guthrie. He credits his mother with his early introduction to folk ballads, as she sang many of the traditional ballads from her own Scotch Irish ancestry. These were often long story-songs, and there's a direct line between these and Woody's own ballads, which were similarly stories of heroes, outlaws, and historical events. Nora Belle passed away from Huntington's disease in 1929, when Woody was seventeen years old.

MOTHER SING AGAIN
by WOODY GUTHRIE

CHORUS: (SUNG AS DESIRED AFTER EVERY STANZA)

IF I COULD ONLY HEAR
MY MOTHER SING AGAIN,
IF I COULD CLOSE MY EYES
AND HEAR YOUR VOICE AS THEN,
THE FAMILY AND THE FOLKS
WOULD FEEL AS GAY AS ME
IF I COULD HEAR MY MOTHER
SING AGAIN.

A LONG ROAD I HAVE COME
SINCE MOTHER'S SONGS I HEARD,
THE STORIES THAT YOU SUNG
I HUNG ON EVERY WORD.
AND, WHEN THE TALE WAS TOLD,
WHEN YOU SANG TO THE END,
THE FAMILY 'ROUND WOULD BEG YOU
SING AGAIN.

THE TROUBLES OF THIS WORLD
THEY TURNED YOUR HAIRS TO GREY,
THE SORROWS AND THE TEARS
THEY LED YOU TO YOUR GRAVE.
BUT, WHEN I SING YOUR SONGS
TO FOLKS AROUND, IT'S THEN,
IT'S THEN I HEAR MY MOTHER
SING AGAIN.

CHORUS:

                YES, THAT IS WHEN I HEAR
                MY MOTHER SING AGAIN,
            AND, THAT IS WHEN I HEAR
                YOUR NATURAL VOICE AS THEN,
                IT'S WHEN I SING YOUR SONGS
                TO FOLKS AROUND, AND FRIENDS,
                IT'S THEN I HEAR MY MOTHER
                SING AGAIN.

        END*

MUSIC & WORDS BY WOODY GUTHRIE
ALL IN THE WINDY MONTH OF MARCH OF 1949

The speed and hurry, all of this pound and churn, roar and spin, this staggering yell and nervous scream of our little farm town turning into an Oil and Money Rush, it was too much of a load on my Mother's quieter nerves. She commenced to sing the sadder songs in a loster voice, to gaze out our window and to follow her songs out and up and over and away from it all, away over yonder in the minor keys . . . Worried from this and things that added as they went, my mother's nerves gave away like an overloaded bridge.

Woody Mama Papa George

(Left to right) Woody, Nora Belle, Charley, and younger brother George, Okemah, OK, May 16, 1926.

She got careless with her appearance. She let herself run down. She walked around over the town, looking and thinking and crying. The doctor called it insanity and let it go at that. She lost control of the muscles of her face. Us kids would stand around in the house lost in silence, not saying a word for hours, and ashamed, somehow, to go out down the street and play with the kids, and wanting to stay there and see how long her spell would last, and if we could help her. She couldn't control her arms, nor her legs, nor the muscles in her body, and she would go into spasms and fall on the floor and wallow around through the house, and ruin her clothes, and yell till people blocks up the street could hear her.

She would be all right for a while and treat us kids as good as any mother, and all at once it would start in – something bad and awful – something would start coming over her, and it come by slow degrees. Her face would twitch and her lips would snarl and her teeth would show. Spit would run out of her mouth and she would start out in a low grumbling voice and gradually get to talking as loud as her throat could stand it; and her arms would draw up at her sides, then behind her back, and swing in all kinds of curves. Her stomach would draw up into a hard ball, and she would double over into a terrible-looking hunch – and turn into another person . . .

I hate a hundred times more to describe my own mother in any such words as these. You hate to read about a mother described in any such words as these. I know, I understand you. I hope you can understand me, for it must be broke down and said.

Unbeknownst to Woody, he is describing the symptoms of Huntington's disease, which he would eventually inherit.

I don't know what this stuff called time is made out of. Don't even know where it boils up and steams up from, don't even know where time rolls back to. I don't know what I, my own self, am made out of, because just about every day I find out that I'm made out of something else, like time its own self is. You could just take a handful of these things you call days and weeks, and things you say are months, and hold them in your hand like this, and blow them up into the air like a feather out of old Aunt Rhodie's pillow, and you'd find me out there back in Oklahoma, out on my Grandma's farm paying a visit...

I can hear Grandma clucking around with her laying hens, talking to her turkeys, and chattering away at the baby chicks.

Then I hear the fire whistle blowing away off seven miles across the hills and the trees. A car drives up in a cloud of hot steam and my brother Roy jumps out. He tells us that the fire whistle was for our house and that my sister Clara has been burned so bad she might not be able to pull through.

Grandma carries me up into the car and Roy drives us back to Okemah as fast as the thing can take us. I walk in at the door where everybody is crying all around the house. Schoolteachers, neighbors, boys, girls, relatives and everybody else...

Clara calls me in over to her side of the bed and makes me laugh at everybody that's crying. She makes me swear and promise not to cry like old papa and like mama sitting there by the side of her bed. I told her that I'd not cry no matter what happened.

And Clara turned her eyes to ask her schoolteacher, "Did I pass?" And I heard the schoolteacher lady tell Clara, "Yes. You passed." And then I saw the teacher touch her fingers to both of Clara's eyes and push them closed. I never did cry. I held it back so tight it blinded me, and I ran around and around our house holding my breath till I finally fell down into papa's arms.

I cried once when I looked at Clara in the glass of her coffin down under the big tent of some kind of a traveling religious show where all the eyes and faces of everybody in and around Okemah come to say good things about the little fourteen-year-old girl that had done some things to help every family in town in some way or another.

Mama never did get over it. She'd kept Clara at home to help do the ironing on Clara's examination day. The coal oil stove blew up and caught her dress on fire. Some of the neighbors chased her around the house, but they couldn't stop her, and the wind just made her dress burn that much faster.

"Don't you cry. Don't you ever break down and cry the way your old brother Roy did. Not like your roughy tough papa did. Not like your mama cried when she sat there with her eyes all red and hot.

Laugh like me, be like me. Smile like I smile."

*Clara holding Woody and Roy
1913 Okemah*

Older sister Clara holding infant
Woody, with older brother Roy,
Okemah, OK, 1913.

I married a fine Irish girl by the name of Mary Jennings and we lived in the ricketiest of the oil town shacks long enough to have no clothes, no money, no groceries and two children . . .

TOP LEFT: Woody, Pampa, TX, ca. 1926.

TOP RIGHT: Woody and Mary, Pampa, TX, 1933.

OPPOSITE: Woody (far left) with the Pampa Junior Chamber of Commerce Band, 1936.

I went into the oil town of Pampa and got a store job, and the boss had an old busted guitar . . . After a while I was rattling around with [Uncle Jeff and his wife Allene] playing my way at the ranch and farmhouse dances... We played for rodeos, centennials, carnivals, parades, fairs, just bustdown parties, and played several nights and days a week just to hear our own boards rattle and our strings roar around in the wind. It was along in these days I commenced singing. I guess it was singing.

l.c.|
On the 14th Day of April of 1935,
There struck the worst of dust-storms that ever filled the sky.
You could see that Dust Storm coming,
The Cloud looked Death-like Black,
And through our mighty nation it left a Dreadful track.   /cap

From Oklahoma City to the Arizona Line;
Dakota and Nebraska to the Lazy Rio Grande.
It fell across our city like a curtain of Black rolled down,
We thought it was our Judgement, we thought it was our doom.

The radio Reported - we listened with alarm.--
The wild and windy actions of this great mysterious storm.
From Albuqurke and Clovis, and all New Mexico,
They said it was the blackest that they had ever saw.

Albuquerque

From old Dodge City, Kansas, the Dust had wrung their knell;
And a few more comrades sleeping on top of old Boot Hill.
From Denver, Colorado, they said it blew so thick strong,
They thought that they could hold out, but didn't know how lon

Our relatives all were huddled into their Oil Boom shacks,
The children they were crying as it whistled through the cracks.
The family it was crowded into their parlor room,
They thought the Lord was coming, they thought it was their doom

This storm took place at sundown and lasted through the night,
When we looked out next morning we saw a terrible sight.
We saw outside our window where wheat fields they had grown,
Was now a rippling ocean of Dust the Wind had blown.

It covered up our fences, it covered up our barns,
It covered up our tractors in this wild and windy storm.
We loaded our jallopies and piled our family in,
We rattled down the highway to never come back again.

This is a song about the worst Dust/storm
in anybody's history book, and I was in
what I claim the very center of it, the
town of Pampa, Gray County, Texas, sixty
miles right north of Amarillo, /// along
 towards sundown on the afternoon of
April 14, 1935. This is an original
song. W.W. GUTHRIE, March 1940

"Well, I, sort of like to write about wherever I happen to be. I just happened to be in the Dust Bowl. I mean, it wasn't something I particularly wanted or craved, but since I was there and the dust was there, I thought, well, I better write a little song about it.

And uh, out in the Dust Bowl where if you'd come out there fifty years ago like most of my relatives did, and they're still there out on the wheat plains of Texas, and...you'd dig a cellar; instead of digging a house, you dig a cellar. There's no trees, there's no timber, no lumber within five hundred miles of it. So then, after you start having children, why you start building a house, generally some kind of an adobe house. But if you can ship off somewhere, order some lumber, why you can build a lumber house.

But uh, then when you see these dust storms a-blowing, I mean they don't just blow for the fun of it. Your life or death hangs, we'll say, on when the dust blows or don't blow. Why then you see a dust storm in a whole lot different light than you do when you see it the newsreels or read in the newspapers or anything else. But if there was something to happen to all of us tonight that would mean life or death, I mean, uh, that's what a dust storm means.

The dust pneumonia out there was choking lots of people to death. Most of those houses out in that country are built so cheap that the dust comes right on into them, so a woman has got just about as much chance to keep a house like that clean as she has working in a cave or in a cement factory or something. So these dust storms, well, up 'til the time that...I had been writing songs, I felt like they was the most important thing that I had seen, so I had to write about them, or try." (Interview, 1949)

DUSTY OLD DUSTY
*
SO LONG IT'S BEEN GOOD TO KNOW YOU
*
****

I SUNG THIS SONG BUT I'LL SING IT AGAIN
OF THE PLACE THAT I LIVE ON THESE WILD WINDY PLAINS
IN THE MONTH YOU CALL APRIL, THE COUNTY CALLED GRAY,
AND HERE'S WHAT ALL OF THE PEOPLE THERE SAY.

C
H
O:::
SO LONG, IT'S BEEN GOOD TO KNOW YOU,
SO LONG, IT'S BEEN GOOD TO KNOW YOU,
SO LONG, IT'S BEEN GOOD TO KNOW YOU,
THIS DUSTY OLD DUST IS A GETTING MY HOME
AND I GOT TO BE DRIFTING ALONG.

WELL, A DUST STORM HIT AND IT HIT US LIKE THUNDER,
IT DUSTED US OVER AND COVERED US UNDER,
IT BLOCKED OUT THE TRAFFIC AND BLOCKED OUT THE SUN,
AND STRAIGHT FOR HOME ALL THE PEOPLE DID RUN, SINGING: (CHO)

WE TALKED OF THE END OF THE WORLD AND THEN
WE'D SING THIS SONG AND THEN SING IT AGAIN
WE'D SET FOR AN HOUR AND NOT SAY A WORD
AND THEN THESE WORDS WOULD BE HEARD.   (CHORUS)

THE SWEETHEARTS SET IN THE DARK AND THEY SPARKED
THEY HUGGED AND THEY KISSED IN THAT DUSTY OLD DARK
THEY SIGHED AND THEY CRIED, THEY HUGGED AND KISSED,
INSTEAD OF MARRIAGE, THEY TALKED LIKE THIS, HONEY, (CHO)

THE TELEFONE RUNG AND IT JUMPED OFF THE WALL
AND THAT WAS THE PREACHER A MAKING HIS CALL
HE SAID, KIND FRIEND, THIS MAY BE THE END,
AND YOU GOT YOUR LAST CHANCE AT SALVATION OF SIN.

THE CHURCH IT WAS JAMMED AND THE CHURCH WAS PACKED
THAT DUSTY OLD DUST STORM BLOWED SO BLACK
THAT PREACHER COULD NOT READ A WORD OF HIS TEXT
SO HE FOLDED HIS SPECKS AND HE TOOK UP COLLECTION, SAID, (CHO).

THIS WAS THE DUSTIEST STORM THAT DID BLOW
AND MOST OF MY PEOPLE THEY TOOK TO THE ROAD
THEY LIT DOWN THIS HIGHWAY AS FAST AS COULD GO
AND SUNG THIS SONG AS THEY DROVE,   (CHORUS) ....

        ** I MADE THIS SONG UP SEVERAL YEARS
        AFTER I WENT THROUGH THIS GREATEST OF
        ALL DUST STORMS IN THE MONTH OF APRIL
        IN NINETEEN THIRTY FIVE. IT WASN'T TILL
        APRIL THE FIRST, NINETEEN AND FORTY THAT
        I STRUCK NEW YORK AND NEW YORK STRUCK ME
        BACK AND I PULLED OUT THIS SONG AND STRUCK
        IT DOWN ON A BIG VICTOR RECORD AND I STRUCK
        NEW YORK WITH THE RECORD AND NEW YORK HIT
        ME WITH A TIDAL WAVE AND I THROWED THIS BIG
        DUST STORM INTO NEW YORK'S FACE JUST TO SHOW
        THIS LITTLE SNOTNOSE TOWN WHO IS WHO AROUND
        HERE.   W.G.   ******************

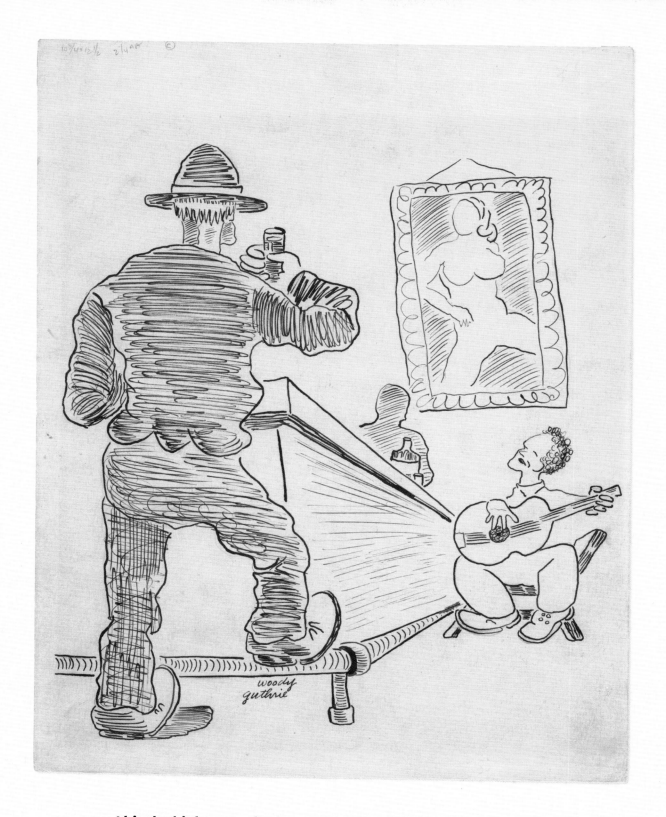

I hit the highway to look around for a place for us to go. I carried my pockets full of paint brushes and my guitar slung across my back. I painted all kinds of window signs, posters, show cards, banners, car and truck signs, in the daylight and played with my hat down on the old saloon floor after night had set in.

Stage Light

Don't swap this raw
sunshine for too much
stage light. The fight
is here lots more than
on the stage.

Woody & Maxine "Lefty Lou" Crissman, KFVD Radio, 1937.

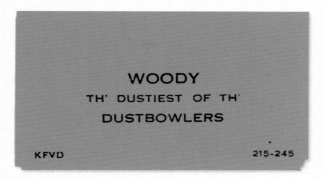

WOODY
TH' DUSTIEST OF TH'
DUSTBOWLERS

KFVD   215-245

The hard part of radio
is to tell which mike
is on.

WG

From 1935 to 1939, Woody had numerous radio programs. His first, the *Woody and Lefty Lou Show*, on KFVD in Los Angeles, was a fifteen-minute slot on the air where he first sang his original Dust Bowl ballads. In the 1940s he was a featured performer on numerous New York City radio programs, including WNYC and CBS stations.

"WOODYS AND LEFTY LOU'S THEME SONG"

Drop whatever you are doing,
Stop your work and worry, too;—
Sit right down and take it easy,
Here comes Woody & Lefty Lou.

You Just drop a card or letter,
We will sing a song for you,
We're easy goin' country people
Plain ole Woody & Lefty Lou.

(That(s what we sing when we're cranking up and a-fixin' to
come onto the air waves, then after we have thououghly wrecked
the studio, here's what we sing.):

So long! We'll see you in the morning,
We'll be singing when we do,
If you've got a favorite number,
Write to Woody and Lefty Lou.

If you like our kind of singing,
I'm gonna tell you what to do,
Get your pencil and your paper
Write to Woody and Lefty Lou.

If you're ever sad and lonely
Bring your folks and chilluns too,
Hitch your bay mare to your buggy
Come see Woody and Lefty Lou.

Don't forget us in the morning
We won't be forgettin' you,
We ain't never seen a stranger,
Plain ole Woody and Lefty Lou.

*Original Song
Woody Guthrie*

————————————————

I aint got this here song memorized yit. Jest rote it up
last summer. Write us a letter, 'cause we shore git a big
kick out of you writin'.

I have always believed Lefty Lou could lead and IG foller her,
but sometimes she gits her vorce box throwed over her tonsil,
and I caint hear whut she's a sayin. In seoh caises we both
jest hum till we come 'round agin.

The first night you aint got nuthin to do, set down and write
us and let us know how you're a gettin along. We like to hear
from you. We call you our Unseen Friend. But course we got a
picher of you sorta in our minds —— jest like you got one about
us.

I drew pen sketches for the Peoples World and learned all I could from the speeches and debates, forums, picnics, where famous labor leaders spoke. I heard William Z. Foster, Mother Bloor, Gurley Flynn, Blackie Myers. I heard most all of them and played my songs on their platforms. I saw the hundreds of thousands of stranded, broke, hungry, idle, miserable people that lined the highways all out through the leaves and the underbrush. I heard these people sing in their jungle camps and in their Federal Work Camps and sang songs I made up for them over the air waves.

OPPOSITE AND ABOVE: Woody performing at Shafter Farm Workers Community, CA, 1941.

In the late 1930s, Woody often sang and played at migrant camps for "Okies" living in cars, tents, and shacks, as well as for those living in the workers' housing communities newly created by the Farm Security Administration. He also performed out in the fields with actors Will Geer and Cisco Houston, creating agitprop theater promoting an agricultural workers' union.

TOWNE FORUM
MEETINGS
DAILY
11AM   2PM

RE-ELECT
Fay E.
ALLEN
Board of
Education

By Special
Request. Sun 2 PM
WOODY.
& HIS GUITAR
Singing His Own Songs
Songs of the Common People
Dedicated
TO
SKID-ROAD
& Dust Bowl Refugees

woody guthrie

OPPOSITE: Shafter Farm Workers Community, CA, 1941.

VIGILANTEE MAN

Words & Music by Woody Guthrie

Have you seen that vigilantee man?
Have you seen that vigilantee man?
Tell me, have you seen that vigilantee man?
I beena hearin' his name all over my land.

Tell me, what is a vigylanty man?
Tell me, what is a vigylanty man?
Tell me, what is a vigylanty man?
Woud he shoot his brother and sister down?

I wonder why does that vigilantee man;
I wonder why does that vigilantee man;
Carry that saw'd off shotgun in his hand?
That makes a man a vigilanty man.

Rainy night down in than engine house;
Sleeping just as still as a mouse;
A man come along, chased us out'n that rain;
That shorely musta beena vigylanty man.

Preacher Casy was just a working man;
And he said: Shake hands, alla you workin' men!
They kill'd him down in the riverbed;
He died by th' hand of a vigylantee man.

I heard th' lastword preach'r Casey said;
Tell y' th' lastword preacher Casey said;
We all gotta pray together here in our union hall,
Or we'll die by th' hand of a vigylantee man.

Have you seen that vigilantee man?
Have you seen that vigilantee man?
Let me know if you lay eyes on that vigilantee man;
I beena hearin' his name all ov'r my lands.

----END----

            *** by my own hands
                Nyork city 1940
                Victored this one
                     with my Dustbowl Ballads

            Woody Guthrie

            --------*--------

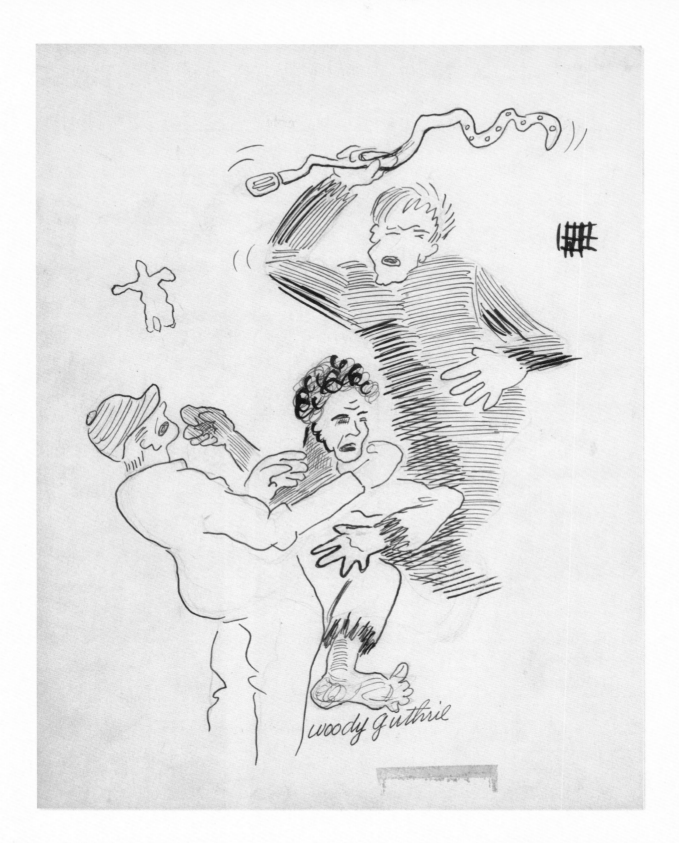

I never did know that the human race was this big before. I never did really know that the fight had been going on so long and so bad. I never had been able to look out over and across the slum section nor a sharecropper farm and connect it up with the owner and the landlord and the guards and the police and the dicks and the bulls and the vigilante men with their black sedans and sawed-off shotguns.

There's a whole
lot more to me
the man walking
along here than
you hear or feel
in there poems
I made up,

Sometimes I think I ain't nothing but an old piece of dirt walking.

50

VOICE

I don't know how far I'm going to have to go
To see my own self or to hear my own voice
I tuned in on the radio and for hours never heard it
And then I went to the moving pictures shown
And never heard it there
I put handsful of coins into machines and watched records turn
But the voice there was no voice of mine
I mean it was not my voice
The words not words that I hear in my own ears
When I walk along and look at your faces
I set here in a Jewish delicatessen, I order a hot pastrami
Sandwich on rye bread and I hear the lady ask me
Would you like to have a portion of cole slaw on the side
And I knew when I heard her speak that
She spoke my voice
And I told her I would take my slaw on a side dish
And would like to have a glass of tea with lemon
And she knew that I was speaking her words
And a fellow sat across at a table near my wall
And spoke while he ate his salami and drank his beer
And somehow I had the feeling
As I heard him speak, and he spoke a long time,
But not one word was in my personal language,
And I could tell by the deep sound, by the full tone
Of his voice that he spoke my language
I suppose you may wonder just how he could speak
In a dialect that I could not savvy nor understand
And yet understand every sound that he made
I learned to do this a long time ago
Walking up and down the sideroads and the main stems
Of this land here
I learned to listen this way when I washed dishes on the ships
I had to learn how to do it when I walked ashore in Africa
And in Scotland and in Ireland and in Britain,
London, Liverpool, Glasgow, Scots towns and Anglo's farms,
Irish canals and railroad bridges, Highlander's cows and horses
And here I knew the speech was the same as mine but
It was the dialect again, nasal, throatsy, deep chesty,
From the stomach, lungs, high in the head, pitched up and down,
And here I had to learn again
To say this is my language and part of my voice
Oh but I have not even heard this voice, these voices,
On the stages, screens, radios, records, juke boxes,
In magazines nor not in newspapers, seldom in courtrooms,
And more seldom when students and policemen study the faces
Behind the voices
And I thought as I saw a drunken streetwalking man mutter
And spit and curse into the wind out the cafe's plate glass,
That maybe, if I looked close enough, I might hear
Some more of my voice
And I ate as quiet as I could, so as to keep my eyes
And my ears and my feelings wide open
And did hear
Heard all that I came to hear here in Coney Island's Jewish air
Heard reflections, recollections, seen faces in memory,
Heard voices untangle their words before me
And I knew by the feeling I felt that here was my voice.

I CANNOT HELP
BUT LEARN MY MOST
FROM YOU WHO COUNT YOURSELF LEAST
AND CANNOT HELP
BUT FEEL MY BEST WHEN
YOU THAT NEED ME MOST
ASK ME TO HELP
YOU
AND I NEVER DID KNOW EXACTLY WHY THIS WAS
THAT IS JUST
THE WAY
WE ARE BUILT

JUNE

8

MONDAY

MAY 1942							JUNE 1942							JULY 1942					
S	M	T	W	T	F	S	S	M	T	W	T	F	S	S	M	T	W	T	F
.	.	.	.	.	1	2	.	1	2	3	4	5	6	.	.	.	1	2	3
3	4	5	6	7	8	9	7	8	9	10	11	12	13	5	6	7	8	9	10
10	11	12	13	14	15	16	14	15	16	17	18	19	20	12	13	14	15	16	17
17	18	19	20	21	22	23	21	22	23	24	25	26	27	19	20	21	22	23	24
24	25	26	27	28	29	30	28	29	30	.	.	.	.	26	27	28	29	30	31
31	.	.	.	.	.	.	.	.	.	.	.	.	.						

8:00

8:30   *Change the pen and*

9:00 *change the ink*

9:30   *Change the way you talk*

10:00 *and think*

10:30   *Change the tubes and*

11:00 *change the tires*

11:30   *Change the things*

12:00 *your heart desires*

12:30   *Change your makeup*

1:00 *Change your curl*

1:30   *Change the ways*

2:00 *of this changing world.*

2:30

3:00

3:30

4:00

4:30

5:00

5:30

6:00

6:30

7:00

7:30

New York City, 1943.

If I want to take a breath between verses, I play a few extra chords. And if I forget the lines and want to remember them, I play a few extra chords. And if I want to get up and leave town, I get up and leave town.

THIS IS OUR COUNTRY HERE

%*"L
5-21-46

This is our country here as far as you can see no matter which
way you walk or
No matter what spot of it you stand on
And when you have crossed her as many times as I have you will
    see as many ugly things about her as pretty things
You will hear whole gangs of travellers and settlers arguing
    about her
What she is, how she come to be, what you are supposed to do here,
    and you will hear some argue at you
That she is so beautiful you are supposed to spend your life just
    feeling of her pretty parts
Sucking in her sweetest breezes and tasting her fairest odors, look-
    ing at her brightest colored scenes,
And I would say that gang has the wrong notion.
And there are some bunches that tell you she is all ugly and all
    dirty, that there is nothing good about her, nothing free, nothing
    clean, that she is all slums, shacks, rot, filth, stink, and bad
    odors, loud words of bitter flavor,
Well, this herd is big and I heard them often and I heard them loud,
    but I come to think that they too was just as wrong as the first
    outfit,
Because I seen the pretty and I seen the ugly and it was because I
    knew the pretty part that I wanted to change the ugly part,
    Because I hated the dirty part that I knew how to feel the love
    for the cleaner part,
I looked in a million of her faces and eyes, and I told myself there
    was a look on that face that was good, if I could see it there
    in back of all of the shades and shadows of fear and doubt and
    ignorance and tangles of debts and worries,
And I guess it is these things that makes our country look all lopsided
    to some of us, lopped over onto the good and easy side or over
    Onto the bad and the hard side,
I know that the people that run our desks and offices got so full
    of the desire to grab enough money to run away and hide on, that
    they let this thought run them instead of the bigger plan of the
    rest of us, that is, a handful of work and money and a road and
    a car and a door and a face and a breast and a bed for the whole
    bunch of us, well, this has always been a hard word to say, but
It could very truly be that our office people are doing the best they
    know how to do,
But we had ought to teach ourselves better and higher than this be-
    fore we run ourselves and put ourselves into our offices.

CHAPTER TWO

The Places I've Been

TUDOR CITY, SHOWING WELFARE ISLAND AND EAST RIVER, NEW YORK CITY

21

3A-H1279

```
I HAVE RAMBLED ALL AROUND
IN AND OUT OF EVERY TOWN
FROM EAST TO WEST FROM COAST TO COAST
I'M ALWAYS ON THE GO, BOYS
I'M ALWAYS ON THE GO............
     I RODE THE RAILS AND LIMITED MAILS
     IN SUN AND RAIN AND WIND AND HAIL
     I'M ROUGH AND TOUGH AND ROWDY OH
     I'M ALWAYS ON THE GO, BOYS,
     I'M ALWAYS ON THE GO..............


I BEEN TO POCATELLA IDAHO,
CHICAGO AND BUF-FALO,
DOWN TO THE GULF OF MEXICO
AND OUT TO CALIFORNIO.
     I SEEN THE MISSISSIPPI FLOW
     THE HUDSON RIVER AND THE OHIO
     THE SILVER COLARADIO
     AND THE GOLDEN SACRAMENTO.
FROM MONROE LOUISIANIO
TO BIRMINGHAM ALABAMIO
AND PHOENIX ARIZONIO
AND GOOD OLD HOT SPRINGS ARKANSAW.
     I LOVE ATLANTA GEORGIO
     AND GOOD OLD CAROLINIO
     THE BIG HIGH ROCKY MOUNTAINS, OH,
     AND THE HILLS OF PENNSYLVANIO.


I'LL FIGHT AND DIE TO MAKE MY HOME
THE U.S.A. OF AMERICO
BUT I LIKE TO LOOK IT OVER SO
I'M ALWAYS ON THE GO, BOYS
I'M ALWAYS ON THE GO..............
```

Woody Guthrie
WOODY GUTHRIE

If this one is any good for anything
or anybody anywhere any time you're plumb
welcome to her. Take her an nolser happy.
But I got my doubts.

WILL ROGERS HIGHWAY

There's a highway that goes from the coast to the coast
From New York town down to Los Angelese,
Its named Will Rogers that traveled that road,
From New York down town to Los Angelese.

That 66 Highway, the Will Rogers road,
Is lined with jallopies as far's you can see,
With a mighty hot motor and heavy load,
From Old Oklahoma to Los Angelese.

Ten thousand people you see every day,
Camped under bridges and under trees,
With rattletrap cars that have come apart,
From old Oklahoma to Los Angelese.

We loved Will Rogers, we loved his smile,
We went to the movies Will Rogers to see,
We've followed him now for a many a mile,
From old Oklahoma to Los Angelese.

That 66 road is mighty hard,
All day you're hot, all night you freeze,
But we gotta have work so we're taking a chance,
From old Oklahoma to Los Angelese.

Will Rogers was born in Oolagah
In the nation of the Cherokee,
And a hundred thousand followed him
From old Oklahoma to Los Angelese.

That wind it blowed and the dust got black
And now we're known as refugees,
We left our shacks and left our tracks
From old Oklahoma to Los Angelese.

#Original song by
Woody Guthrie

Will Rogers at times acted as a true spokesman for the
people who were hard hit not only in the Dust Bowl, nor
the Mid West, but all over the world. He used the power
of good humor and wit to win his own way to fame and
fortune the world over. There are dozens of songs like this
about Will Rogers and more, the things he stood for, and in
lots of cases those songs turn into a kind of humor and wit
that is a lot deadlier, when the time comes, to use it, than
most so called serious songs or speeches.

OHPI

424

One foot up, other foot down. One leg up and a hole in the ground. Its Lord, Lord, walkin down th' railroad, Lord, Lord, a walkin down that railroad line.

Aint got a job, aint got a cent, If I aint broke I'm badly bent. Its Lord, Lord, a walkin down the railroad line. Its Lord, Lord, a walkin down that railroad line.

From Frisco Bay to old New York, I been a lookin for a job of work. Its Lord, Lord, a walkin down the railroad line. Lord, Lord, a walkin down the railroad line.

That Mississippi's full of ice. I oughta know 'cause I fell in twice. Its Lord, Lord, a walkin down the railroad line. Its Lord, Lord, a walkin down the railroad line.

That Susquehanah river was froze. Cold wind blowed right thru my clothes. Its Lord, Lord, a walkin down that railroad line. Its Lord, Lord, a walkin down a railroad line.

When that passenger train come by, I seen how the rich folks ride. Its Lord, Lord, a walkin down a railroad line. etc.

Airplane flew above the earth. I wonder its got an empty berth? Its Lord, Lord, etc.

Big black car come down the road. A lady and a dog and a big fur coat. Its Lord, etc.

I'd give up road today for a honest job at honest pay. It's Lord, Lord, etc.

I'd give up this ramblin life to own my home and a good warm wife. Its Lord, Lord, etc.

I hope there's a town along this line where a job and a home and a gal I'll find. Its Lord etc.

First copy of this song.

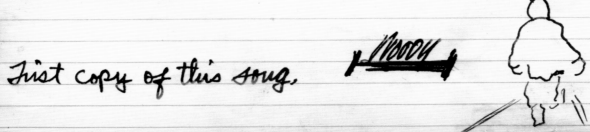

Boxcar illustration from Woody's 1943 autobiographical novel *Bound for Glory*. Seated beneath Woody wearing a knit cap is Railroad Pete, a fictional character who appears throughout much of Woody's writings and artwork. RR Pete stands in for different people at different times. Woody referred to each of his unborn children as RR Pete, and at other times, the character appeared as the ultimate hero fighting fascism.

AINT GOT NO HOME IN THIS WORLD ANYMOE

I aint got no home,
I'm just a roaming 'round   G
Just a wandering worker
I go from town to town ...
 The police make it hard wherever I may go,
 And I aint got no home in this world anymore.

                  and
My brothers & my sisters
Are stranded on this road ...
It's a hot and dusty road
That a million feet have trod ...
 Rich man took my home
 And drove me from my door,
 And I aint got no home in this world anymore.

Was a farming on the shares,
And always I was poor,
My crops I lay into the bankers store ...
 My wife took down and died
 Upon the cabin floor,
 And I aint got no home in this world anymore.

Now as I look around,
It's very plain to see
This world is such a great and funny place to be,
 The gambling man is rich,
 The working man is poor,
 And I aint got no home in this world anymore.

WOODY K. F. V. D.
338 SO. WESTERN - L. A.

63

Hard Travelin

Woody Guthrie

HARD TRAVELIN'

Words & Music by Woody Guthrie

I been havin' some hard travelin', I tho't you knowed;
I been havin' some hard travelin' back down this road;
I beena havin' some hard ramblin', hard gamblin', hard gravelin'
I been havin' some hard travelin', Lord!

I been havin' some hard travelin', I tho't you knowed;
I been havin' some hard travelin' back down this road;
I beena hittin' them blind passengers, deadenders, kickin' up cinders;
I been havin' some hard travelin', Lord!

I been hittin' some hardrock tunnelin', I tho't you knowed;
I been leanin' on a pressure drill back down this road;
Hammer flyin', airhose suckin'; six foota mud I sure beena muckin';
I been havin' some hard travelin', Lord!

I been hittin' that Pittsburgh steel; I thot you knowed;
I been dumpin' that red hot slag back down this road:
I beena blastin', I beena firin'; I beena dumpin' redhot iron;
I been havin' some hard travelin', Lord!

I been hittin' some hard harvestin', I thot you knowed:
Kansas City thru North Dakoty and back down this road;
Cuttin' y'r wheat anda stackin' y'r hay tryin' t' Make my $ a day;
I been havin' some hard travelin', Lord!

I been bumpin' some ruff harniss bulls I thot you knowed;
I been havin' some ruff handlin' back dow this road;
Ever' time you shine y'r light on me I up and out & fizzle away;
I beena havin' some hard travelin', Lord!

I been livin' inna hardrock jail I thot you knowed;
I beena layin' out ninety days back down this road;
Damned olde mean jedge says to me its 90 days f'r vagranncy;
I been havin' some hard travelin', Lord!

I been walkin' y'r Lincoln Highway I thot you knowed;
I beena hittin' y'r 66 back down this road;
Heavy load anda worried mind lookin for a womban that's
hard t' find;
I been havin' some hard travelin', Lord!

END

Woody Guthrie
Same day Us Almanac Singers
Drove out from NYC towards
Pittsburgh that first time.

1942

Woody Guthrie

Good books put songs in
my head. Ants in my
pants and my feet to
itchin' — for the big
Peoples Highway

OKLAHOMA

Okemah was one of the singingest, square dancingest, drinkingest, yellingest, preachingest, walkingest, talkingest, laghingest, cryingest, shootingest, fist fightingest, bleedingest, gamblingest, gun, club and razor carringest of our ranch and farm towns, because it blossomed out into one of our first Oil Boom Towns. Here came the Lawyer Man, Doctor Man, Merchant Man, Royalty Man, Lease Man, Tong Bucker Man, Pipe Liner Mand, Greasy Gloves Man, Big Wrench Man, the Cowboy and the Cowman, the Spirit and the Hoodoo Man, the ladies for all of these, the girls, and the Mistresses for the Pool Stick and Domino Sharker, the Red Light Pimper and Sidewalk Barker. I sold newspapers, sang all of the songs I picked up, I learned to jig dance along the sidewalks to things called portable phonographs and sung for my first cancered pennies.

I humped along. Drug along. Maybe that old man was right. I looked in at the lobby of the Broadway Hotel. Nobody. I looked through the plate glass of Bill Bailey's pool hall. Just a long row of brass spittoons there by their self in the dark. I look in at the Yellow Dog bootleg joint. Shelves shot all to pieces. I looked in the window of a grocery store at a clerk with glasses on playing a fast game of solitaire. Weeds and grass in the door of this garage? Always was a big bunch of men hanging around there. Nobody running in and out of the Monkey Oil Drug Store. They even took the monkey and the cage from out in front. Benches, benches, benches. All whittled and cut to pieces. Men must not have much to do but just hump around a whittle on benches. Nobody even sweeps up the shavings. Chewed matches piled along the curb. Quids of tobacco. No cares or wagons to run over you. Four dogs trotting along with their tongues dripping spit, following a little bitch that draws her back up in a knot like she's scared to death and glad of it.

I walked down the other side of the street. It was the same thing. Grass in the dirt crack along the cement. I stood there at the top of the hill in front of the court house and it looked like there never had been an Indian lose his million dollars in there. A pair of sleepy-looking mules pulled a wagon up through town. No kids. No hell-raising. No running and stumbling. No pushing and yelling. No town growing up. No houses banging with hammers all around. No guys knocked you down running late to work. No ham and stew smoke sifting through the screens of the cafes; and no wild herds of men cussing and laughing, pilin up onto big oil field trucks, waving their dinner boxes back at their women. No fiddle music and yodeling floating out of the pool halls and gambling dens. No gals hustling along the streets in their short skirt and red paint. No dogs fighting in the middle of the streets. No crowds ganged around a pair of little boys banging each other's heads to pieces.

I could look in the dark plate-glass window there and see myself. Hello there, me. What the hell are you walking along so slow for? Who are you? Woody Who? Huh. You've walked along looking at yourself in these windows when they was all lit up with bright lights and hung full of pretty things for pretty women, tough stuff for tough men, fighting clothes for fighting people. And now look. Look, you lonesome outfit. Don't you seem lost flogging along there in that glass window? You thought Okemah never would quit getting better? Hah...Okemah's gone and died."

Here we have two descriptions of Okemah, OK, where Woody was born. The opposite page captures the chaotic energy of the once-sleepy Okemah in 1920, after it transformed into a boomtown when oil was discovered. This page describes Okemah as he found it in the late 1940s, a town that had "gone and died."

California Stars

I'd like to rest my heavy head tonight
On a bed of California stars
I'd like to lay my weary bones tonight
On a bed of California stars.
I'd love to feel your hand touching mine
And tell me why I must keep working on.
yes, I'd give my life to lay my head tonight
On a bed of California stars.

I'd like to dream my troubles all away
On a bed of California stars
Jump up from my starbed and make another day
underneath my California stars.
They hang like grapes on vines that shine
and warm the lovers glass like friendly wine
So, I'd give this world just to dream a dream with you
on our bed of California stars.

Repeat Whole Song

End

words & music by
Woody Guthrie
827 Cedar Avenue
Long Beach (13)
California

Typed (WG)

IF YOU AINT GOT THE DO RE MI

Thousands of folks back east they say
Leavin home every day
Beatin' a hot and dusty way to the California Line.
O'er the desert sands they roll
Tryin' to get out of the old dust bowl;
They think they're comin' to a sugar bowl,
And here's what they find:

(Ab) (6 pos.)
CAPO 2 FRET

The Police at the Port of Entry say:
You're number fourteen thousand for today!

No use to make a typed copy of this one - you got it in my 1st Book.
WG

If you aint got the do re mi, folks,
If you aint got the do re mi,
Better hang on in Beautiful Texas,
Oklahoma, Kansas, Georgia, Tennessee.
California is a Garden of Eden,
A Paradise to live in or see,
But, believe it or not, you wont find it so hot,
If you aint got the do re mi.

If you wanta buy a home or farm,
That caint do nobody harm,
Or take yore vacation by the mountains or sea;
Dont trade yore old cow for a car,
Padnah, stay right where you are!
Better take this little tip from me.

Cause the governor on the radio today
Climbed up to the microbephone, and he did say:

Chorus:

original song
Woody Guthrie
1938

The California newspapers and magazines print purty pictures
and purty descriptions of the Land of Sunshine and Paradise
that is California. And they are right in what they print.
They do this to bring folks out here to tour the country and
drop off a few midwestern dollars, and to sell 'em some rale
estate, like a lot or a farm, or a house. And this is all
right. But they also cause all the fairly happy farm folks
to swap their stock and machinery for a 'hoopy' or a 'jallopy'
and come rattlin' thru to California with nothin but a run
down car and a gallon of sorghum. They take the sorghum at
the Boundary line, and the car breaks down at Los Angeles.
Broke, busted, and disgusted, they try very hard to get work,
but find it a thing of the past. They try to work in the
fruit and vegetable harvests, but nearly starve. They're my
kind of folks, 'cause that's how I got here. So I wrote
this little song. Not much good, but there's some truth in
it. Listen to us sing it a time or two, and you'll get the
'swing' of it.

PACIFIC NORTHWEST

OREGON SOMEWHERE

Oregon coastline, ca. 1942.

The Pacific Northwest is one of my favorite spots in this world, and I'm one walker that's stood way up and looked way down across aplenty of pretty sights in all their veiled and nakedest seasons. Thumbing it. Hitching it. Walking and talking it. Chalking it. Marking it. Sighting it and hearing it. Seeing and feeling and breathing and smelling it in, sucking it down me, rubbing it in all the pores of my skin, and the wind between my eyes knocking honey in my comb...The Pacific Northwest has got mineral mountains. It's got chemical deserts. It's got rough run canyons. It's got sawblade snowcaps. It's got ridges of nine kinds of brown, hills out of six colors or green ridges five shades of shadows, and stickers the eight tones of hell. I pulled my shoes on and walked out of every one of these Pacific Northwest mountain towns drawing pictures in my mind and listening to poems and songs and words faster to come and dance in my ears than I could ever get them wrote down.

GRAND
COULEE
DAM

VANPORT FLOOD
WOODY GUTHRIE

This old world has several wonders
  The travelers always tell;
Some gardens and some towers,
  I guess you know them well.
But now, the greatest wonder
  Is in Uncle Sam's fair land;
      It's that King Columbia river
      And the big Grand Coulee Dam.

She heads up the Canadian Rockies
  Where the rippling waters glide;
Comes a rumbling down her canyon
  To meet that salty tide
Of that wide Pacific Ocean
  Where the sun shines in the west;
      It's that big Grand Coulee country
      In the land I love the best.

She winds down her granite canyon
  And she bends across the lea;
Like a silver running stallion
  Down her seaway to the sea.
Cast your eye upon the biggest thing
  Yet built by human hands;
      On that King Columbia river,   (CHORUS)
      It's that big Grand Coulee dam.

In the mysty crystal glitter
  Of that wild and windward spray,
We carved a mighty history
  Of the sacrifices made.
Yes, she ripped our boats to splinters,
  But she gave us dreams to dream
      Of that day the Coulee Dam would cross
      This wild and wasted stream.   (CHORUS)

Uncle Sam took up this challenge
  In the year of Thirty Three
For the farmer and the worker
  And for all of you and me.
He said, "Roll along, Columbia,
  You can ramble to the sea.
But River, while you're rambling,
      You can do a little work for me!"   (CHORUS)

Up in Washington, and Oregon, now,
  You hear our factories hum,
Making chrome and making manganese
  And light aluminum.
Yonder flies a super rocket ship
  'Cross this land of hearts and hands
      Spawned upon that King Columbia
      By my big Grand Coulee dam.

*****************   (CHORUS)

THE END

New York City, ca. 1940.

6 pt Garamond light

10 pt Bold

PASTURES OF PLENTY

It's a mighty hard road that my poor hands has hoes
My poor feet has traveled a hot, dusty road
Out of your Dust Bowl and Westwards we rolled
Lord, your mountains are hot and your deserts are cold.

I worked in your orchards of peaches and prunes
I sleep on the ground in the light of your moon
On the edge of your city you'll see us and then
We come with the dust and we go with the wind.

California. Arizona. I make all your crops.
It's north u to Oregon to gather your hops
Dig beets from your ground. Cut your grapes from your vine.
To set on your table your light sparkling wine.

Green pastures of plenty from dry desert ground
From the Grand Coulee Dam where the waters run down
Every state in this Union us migrants has been
We'll work in your fight and we'll fight till we win.

It's always we've rambled that river and I.
All along your green valley I'll work till I die.
My land I'll defend with my life if need be
'Cause my pastures of plenty must always be free.

Bryant Park, New York City, 1943.

There is one and only one New York, and if you don't see it you are doing yourself and your country an injustice. It's got the best of the least for the most, and the most of the best for the least.

CINYC stands for "Coney Island, New York City."

MY NAME IS NEW YORK

I'm the town called New York,
I was struck by the winds;
I been froze and been blistered
And then struck again;
I was struck by my ~~xxxxxxxx~~ rich folks,
And struck by my bums,
Struck by my mansions,
And struck by my slums.

I was hit with disease
And with trouble and pain;
And I've seen my kids die
Under car wheels and trains;
I smelled the smoke roll
When it come from some hole
Where a cigaret spark
Killed a thousand good souls.

I'm the town called New York,
I'm a brick on a brick;
I'm a hundred folks running
And ten dying sick;
I'm a saint, a bum, a whore and her pimp;
And your ocean's the mirror I look in to primp.

I'm a sewer pipe and a steam cloud
And a little girl fell down;
My lights shine thrie brightest
When my nightgown comes down.

I'm vulgar, I'm legal,
Illegal and wild;
I'm the Hudson and East river's
One lost lonesome child.

I'm a stone on a stone;
I'm a rock on a rock;
And I comb my hairs back
With those ships in their locks.

Ten million wild notions
Are fighting in me,
To speak a little plainer
And try to agree.

I read mountains of books
Every day but I'm frisky;
I wash down my brain cells
With Hundred proof whiskey.

I work and I slave
And I bless and abuse;
I waste twice as much
As I ever could use.

I'm the town called New York
With my all color paint;
And I curse and I run
And I hide and I faint.

I juice my blood full
Of every known dope;
And I'm the worlds biggest howler
Of nice friendly hope.

I been here so long
That the weeds has forgot;
And I intend to stand right
Right here till I rot.

I'll see if my bad habits
Can ever tear down
More than my good ones
Can build up around.

I come here to look
For a nice standing place;
To make a scientific test
For the whole human race.

I'm going to try
Every earthly mistake
And see if your hands
Can fix me back straight.

I might boil and blow
And shake to the ground
And smoke and tremble
And blaze all around.

And no matter how low
Or how high I might fall;
Just remember, New York
Is the name I am called.

                --------*--------

TOP & SIDES: Subway contact sheets from photo shoot for Woody's novel *Bound For Glory*, New York City, 1943.

BOTTOM: A self-portrait taken in a subway photo booth, ca. 1945.

2444
743
HOBO

TALKIN' SUBWAY BLUES
XXXXXXXXXXXXXXXXXXXXX

. . . . Woody

I left California for old New York
Thought I'd find me a job of work,
One leg up and the other one down,
I come in through a hole in the ground ...
    Holland Tunnel, three mile tube,
    Skippin' through th' Hudson River dew.

When I blowed into New York Town
I looked up and I looked down,
Everybody I seen on the streets,
They all run down in a hole in the ground.
    I follered 'em. See where they's a goin,
    Newsboy told me they's tryin' to smoke a train out
    of a hole.

I run down 38 flights of stairs,
Boy howdy, I declare,
Rode the elevator twenty two,
Spent my last lone nickel, too,
    Feller in a little cage got it,
    Herded me through a shoot-the-shoot,
    Run me through 3 clothes wringers,
    So many people down in there you couldn't even fall down.

I swung on to my old guitar,
Train come a ramblin' down the track,
I made a run for the subway car
With three grass widders on my back,
    Two of 'em a lookin' for home relief,
    The other xxxxxxxxxxxxxxx one was just investigatin'.

New York asss a hole is all right —
here's one that was borned right there
in Arlington Va., You know the
old white house where we burnt the
funeral wreath in your furnace and
said me + pete. Got a
letter from tim to day.

Union air
in
Union Square

I walked out in New York town
to the place called Union Square
    where trees are thick and people
bark and the pigeons fill the air.
    Where pure manure and bird
drops are flying from the sky.
    You'll get it in your ears and brain
as well as in your eye.

    Old Paunchy shoots the trotsky line
and waves his hands and ~~waves~~ strute
    Reef Wilson sweats for the socialists
and the pigeons think he's nuts.
    Herb Solomon howls to get the dough
to rebuild Jerusalem
    And above it all there waves the
flag of your good old Uncle Sam.

I walked around and I heard the
sound of voices of all sorts

The Slav, the Dutch, the heavy Swede,
the negro, longs and shorts,

The broad flat a's from the western
plains, the █ thick ones and the thin,

The same old flag flew over them
all – all free, but different men.

Three negro girls walked through and
read the words carved here in stone

Words that told of the rocky road
that our forefathers come –

The sparrow chirped and the jaybird
squawked and the sweat-gnat plied his trade

I guess the sweat in Union Square
is surely Union made.

a bigger fly just now buzzed by
and he flew to earth to land

and he sat there and laughed at
me as he licked and washed his hand

He knows dam well this country's
free for him to bite my skin

(and I know, too, its free for me to
take a crack at him).

One guy says "Why I'm free to sleep
where it says Keep off The Grass!"

And a cop says, "Sure! an' me, I'm
free to kick your lousy ass!"

The sun shoots down on many a head,
some bushy and some bald

But away up high the stars and
stripes waves on above us all.

I put my feet upon the seat of
the bench and the cop came 'round
        and he swung his club and says
"Hey, spud! ya better take 'em down!"
        So you see you're free in our country
to do as you dam please
        And other folks are just as free to
put you in your place.

        A bald headed man with glasses on
is humped up over a book
        He feels like he has got the right
to look where he wants to look
        The book he reads is filled with
mystic symbols of masonry.
        The fellow next to him reads "How To
Plant and grow a tree".

The copper badge of the N. M. U. on
a fellow's coat lapel
    Tells me that he is from the sea
where the fascists raise their hell —
    Oh yes - you're free in the U.S.A. to be
a fascist, too —
    And of course the rest of us are free
to dig your grave for you.

    This union air in Union Square
is breathed by many a lung
    Some good, some bad, some sick, some
well, some right ones and some wrong
    We haven't got a Super Race nor a
god sent maniac
    To make super dupers out of us
nor chain nor hold us back.

★

What have we got? there's two little
girls that climb a statue 'round

and they laugh and pat the marble
breasts and jump down to the ground

and one says, "Hey! I'll be a statue!
Looky! Hey! Watch me!"

and the second girl pooched her lips
and said, "I'd rather be a tree!"

"I'll stand here with my clothes
off and be a statue real!"

and she scampered through the
park with the other one barking at her heel:

"you aint s'pose ta take yer dress
off jest 'cause that statue did!"

"Girls dont have much fun as statues!"
Was the only thing heard said.

✶

Photos taken by Woody of the neighborhood cat on
Mermaid Avenue, Coney Island, NYC, ca. 1947.

MERMAID'S AVENUE
By Woody Guthrie

Mermaid Avenue that's the street
Where the fast and slow folks meet,
Where the cold ones meet the hot ones
Just a block from Coney's beach.
Mermaid Avenue that's the place
Where the wolves and haybags chase
In big fur coats and bathing suits
They're in the raggeldy race.

But, there's never been a mermaid here
On Mermaid Avenue
No, I've never seen a mermaid here
On Mermaid Avenue
I've seen ~~sweatukuss~~, wags and witches;
and I've seen a shark or two
My five years that I've lived along
Old Mermaid's Avenue.

Mermaid Avenue that's the street
Where the lox and beaggles meet,
Where the hot dog meets the mustard
Where the sour meets the sweet;
~~Where the halvah meets the pickle~~
Where the beer flows to the ocean
Where the wine runs to the sea;
Why they call it Mermaid Avenue
That's more than I can see. (((ChorusOOO)))

Mermaid Avenue that's the street
Where the saint and sinners meet;
Where the grey hair meets the wave curls
Where thse cops don't ever sleep;
Where they pay some cops to stop you
When you hit that Sea Gate gate;
Where them bulls along that wire fence
Scares the mermaids all away.   (((Chorus))))

Mermaid Avenue that's the street
Where the sun and storm clouds meet;
Where the ocean meets that rockwall
Where the boardwalk meets the beach;
Where the prettiest of the maidulas
Leave their legprints in that sand
Just beneath our lovesoaked boardwalk
With the bravest of our lads. (((Chorus)))))))

Mermaid Avenue that's the street
Where all colors of goodfolks meet;
Where the smokefish meets the pretzel
Where the borscht sounds like the seas;
This is where hot Mexican Chili
meets ChopSuy ~~fixes down with~~ *and* meatballs sweet;
Mermaid Avenue she's a nervous jerk
But, ~~still,~~ she's hard to beat.   (((Chorus))))))

(END OF LINE)

Words & Music Notes by
Woody Guthrie
January 24th, 1950

Woody Guthrie

I've (we've) Me and my bunch have lived here along
old Mermaid's Avenue in Coney Island now for some Five
Long Hard years, and they have been long and they have
been hard ones, but every street needs a little song.
                                        W.G.

Beech Haven Ain't My Home

254

Beech Haven ain't my home!
I'm justa driftin' through!
My wife and angel kids
Are trapped inside these walls
Where I can't plow nor plant
Nor hang out my family's clothes!
~~No, no, not~~ old man Trump! Old Beech Haven
ain't my home!

Beach Haven ain't my home!
I just cain't pay this rent!
My money's down the drain!
And my soul is badly bent!
Beach Haven looks like heaven
Where no black ones come to roam!
No, no, no! Old man Trump!
Old Beach Haven ain't my home!

Across Beach Haven's grass
I see my brethrens pass;
They try to hide their misery
Behind that window glass!
We all are crazy fools
As long as Race Hate rules!
No, no, no! Old man Trump!
Beach Haven ain't my home!

End
30

Woody Guthrie
May 3rd 1952
Beach Haven

30

In 1950, the Guthrie family moved into the Beach Haven apartment complex in Brighton Beach, Brooklyn, which was owned and operated by Fred Trump. When Woody discovered their racist rental policies, he wrote damning songs and essays about them.

BOOK # 2.

DUStbowl

MIGRATORY

#Hobo Floyds, Etc.,

(TRAGEDY)

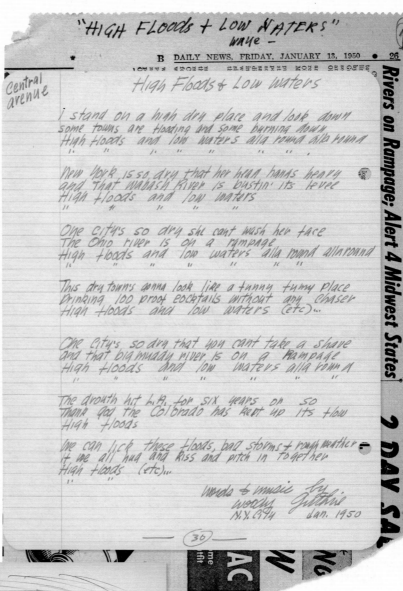

Central avenue

B DAILY NEWS, FRIDAY, JANUARY 13, 1950 • 26

High Floods & Low waters

I stand on a high dry place and look down
some towns are floating and some burning down
High floods and low waters alla round alla round
"   "   "   "   "   "   "

New York isso dry that her head hangs heavy
and that Wabash river is bustin' its levee
High floods and low waters
"   "   "   "

One city's so dry she cant wash her face
The Ohio river is on a rampage
High floods and low waters alla round allround
"   "   "   "   "   "

This dry town's gonna look like a funny funny place
Drinking 100 proof cocktails without any chaser
High floods and low waters (etc)...

One city's so dry that you cant take a shave
and that big muddy river is on a Rampage
High floods and low waters alla round
"   "   "   "   "

The drouth hit hit for six years on so
Thank God the Colorado has kept up its flow
High floods

We can lick these floods, bad storms + rough weather
If we all hug and kiss and pitch in together
High floods (etc)...

words & music by
Woody Guthrie
N.Y.C.ity Jan. 1950
30

Rivers on Rampage; Alert 4 Midwest States

2 DAY SA...

woody guthrie

Having lived in the heart of the Dust Bowl, in Pampa, TX, in the 1930s, Woody witnessed firsthand the environmental destruction caused by drought and the human suffering that followed. Many of his lyrics, his art, his political cartoons, and writings would take on environmental concerns.

VANPORT FLOOD
WOODY GUTHRIE

THE RADIO AND HANDBILLS TOLD US NOTTO RUN
THE DIKES ARE ALL A HOLDING, SO STAY INSIDE YOUR HOME.
AND IF THE DIKE STARTS BREAKING
WE'LL LET YOU KNOW IN TIME
SO'S YOU CAN PACK YOUR THINGS AND MOVE.
BUT EVERYTHING IS FINE.

CHORUS:

                    OH, BUT THE WATERS BROKE IN ON US,
                    NOT A WARNING, NOT A CHANCE,
                    BY THAT WILD COLUMBIA RIVER
                    WE WERE DROWNED JUST LIKE RATS.

THIS WAS THE WETTEST MONTH OF MAY
IN FORTY YEARS THEY SAY,
THE MELTING SNOWS AND HEAVY RAINS
STRUCK ALL OUR FORTY EIGHT STATES.
AND IF YOU LIVE IN A RIVER TOWN
BELOW THE DIKE OR DAM
YOU KNOW HOW QUICK A TOWN CAN GO
OR HOW YOUR FRIENDS CAN DROWN.   (CHORUS)

WE BUILT OUR TOWN OF VANPORT
TO HELP US WIN THE WAR
AT FIRST WE CALLED IT KAISERVILLE
SINCE KAISER'S PLANTS ARE HERE.
YOU COULD CALL THIS A WAR TOWN,
WE LEARNED TO WORK AND FIGHT,
BUT WE DIDN'T HAVE A FIGHTING CHANCE
WHEN THE RIVER HIT TONIGHT.   (CHORUS)

OF ALL THE WORLD'S WILD RIVERS,
THE WILDEST OF THE ALL
IS THIS SNOWFED COLUMBIA
WHEN SHE STARTS TO PITCH AND SQUAWL.
A THOUSAND TOWNS LIKE VANPORT
SHE'LL KNOCK OUT LIKE A MATCH
UNLESS WE ALL SHAKE HANDS KKKK, FOLKS,
AND COMMENCE FIGHTING BACK.   (CHORUS)

LET HANDS OF EVERY COLOR
GRAB SANDBAG, HAMMER, NAIL,
AND WE CAN TIE A COUPLE OF KNOTS
IN THIS OLD RIVER'S TAIL.
LET'S BUILD A HUNDRED VANPORTS BACK
ALL SAFE AND CLEAN AND FREE,
'CAUSE WHEN THIS RIVER FLOODS AGAIN
IT'LL TAKE BOTH YOU AND ME.   (CHORUS)

              ****

     I JUST WANT TO DEDICATE THIS SONG TO ALL OF YOU FOLKS
THAT LOST EVERY STITCH OF EVERYTHING YOU EVER HAD IN THAT
BIG FLOOD OF MAY THE THIRTY FIRST, OF NINETEEN HUNDRED AND
FORTY EIGHT.
              WOODY GUTHRIE

         ****
              Woody Guthrie
              June 6th, 1948

                   C1H4C

Erosion Erosion
2 hate You
I hate You
Because you did sneak around
and eat up my farm
But I love You
Erosion
I love you
I love You
~~you gave~~ me Grand Canyon
~~and~~ Yellowstone Park

This is adobe art painted of clay, open air & sky. imagined in front of the Santa Fe art museum when an old lady told me, "the world is made of adobe" — And I added, "So is man"

Nuly Guthrie

Woody began his creative life as a visual artist. *In El Rancho Grande* (1936) was one of the many oils he painted during the 1930s. Woody was fascinated by the idea of inexpensive adobe homes and thought of building one himself. His novel *House of Earth* tells the story of a desperately poor farm couple who dream of building their own adobe home, guided by a 5¢ how-to handbook provided by the US government.

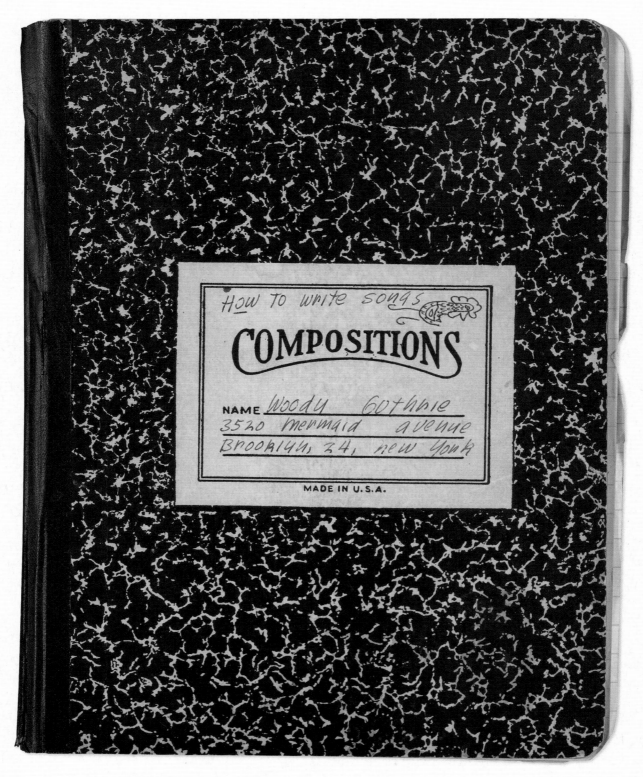

How to write songs

COMPOSITIONS

NAME Woody Guthrie
3520 mermaid avenue
Brooklyn, 24, new york

MADE IN U.S.A.

a folk song is whats wrong and how to fix it
or it could be whose hungry and where
their mouth is is or whose out of work
and where the job is or whose broke
and where the money is or whose
carrying a gun and where the peace is

CHAPTER THREE

How to Write Songs

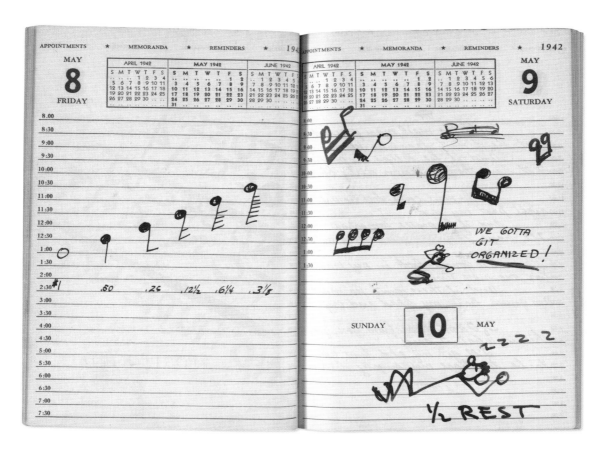

There's a feeling in music and it carries you back down the road you have traveled and makes you travel it again. Or it takes you back down the road somebody else has come and you can look out across the world from the hill they are standing on.

Sometimes when I hear music I think back over my days and a feeling that is fifty-fifty joy and pain swells like clouds taking all kinds of shapes in my mind. If it is joy it is of such a treasured sort and such a fine make that the thought of its passing is near to pain, and you can see how pain has paid you a profit in its own strange way, and the joy of the sadness is like a raindrop falling in the sun.

Music is on the radio. I notice that as I listen, I think of my mistakes, ill words, wasted time, and the next note I think of who I love and who I hate and the success I've had at both and of my tomorrow's chances. And I feel like a singing god riding on a cloud snapping my fingers and ruling a universe.

Music is a tone of voice, the sound life uses to keep the living alive. They call us back many times a day from the brinks of torture, the holes of superstition. There never was a sound that was not music and there's no real trick of creating words to set to music once you realize that the word is the music and the people are the song.

INTERVIEW WITH ROSANNE CASH

Rosanne Cash is one of today's most respected and talented singer-songwriters. The daughter of the legendary country artist Johnny Cash, Rosanne's songs draw from a number of music wells, including that of Woody Guthrie.

When did you first come upon Woody Guthrie and his music?

In childhood. My dad was a big fan of Woody Guthrie. He used to play Woody's records in our house. He felt Woody was a kindred spirit regarding his sensitivity to social issues. My father loved the fact that Woody could turn a simple phrase with incredible beauty and imbue it with power and with such succinct poetry.

One thing my father really loved about Woody's writing—and so I—was the way Woody developed characters in his song stories. They're so vivid! They come alive in the song and carry deep meaning with them. You can hear the same technique that Woody employed in some of my dad's songs, like "Give My Love to Rose."

To describe a cause, or to draw attention to something in the world that needs attention, is one thing. But to do it with a convincing character or characters makes that song real and hard hitting. It's so much more effective than proselytizing. To teach a lesson in a song without a background story or character, doesn't move the heart.

Is there a particular Woody Guthrie song that strikes you more deeply than others? Perhaps a song of his that influenced or impacted your songwriting style?

There is no one song that comes to mind; there's many that have moved me over the years, and continue to move me. But if you trace the providence of a songwriter like me, a singer-songwriter rooted in American music traditions like folk, country, and blues, and you go back to Bob Dylan

and then back to Woody, there is a direct lineage. Of course, Neil Young is part of that lineage, too, as is Bruce Springsteen and Steve Earle and Lucinda Williams, and, of course, my father. We all are Woody's children.

Woody wrote the book on how music can be a powerful force for change in America. It's been a long time coming, but contemporary artists in hip hop, R&B, and even pop music have discovered the strength and resolve of a great protest song.

The song is one of the most powerful tools we have. As Pablo Casals once said, "Music will save the world." Songs that reflect outrage over social injustice or racial inequality, or point to things going on in the world that simply aren't right, really never went away. Songwriters have always written about such things. But the world is so full of danger that the songs coming out today just have to speak louder than ever before.

Woody would often write songs based on what he read in the newspapers. You could say he wrote musical editorials. How much of that way of writing has influenced your own songwriting style?

Two songs I wrote recently, "Crawling to the Promised Land," which I wrote with my husband John (Leventhal), and "The Killing Fields," both reflect the times and what you could read in the newspaper. I wrote "The Killing Fields" right after the Black Lives Matter protest marches.

Writing those songs required self-examination of my own history, my own Southern history, and my ancestry. I had to identify which chains had to be broken and which ones might survive. I had to bring to the surface my own white privilege, and the assumptions and entitlement that goes with it. I must say, writing "The Killing Fields" was painful to write. I'm sure Woody must have felt the same kind of pain when he wrote some of his most pressing songs. A song like "Deportees" must have tormented him. I say this, but I really don't want to get to a place where I'm comparing him to me. There is no comparison. His work is for the ages.

Is there an inner need to write these kinds of songs?

If you're asking me if writing songs of this kind is therapeutic, well, that feels a little squeamish to me. It's easy to fall into navel-gazing without the discipline of art. But a good song can certainly come from self-examination, and if it ends up being therapeutic, then that's legitimate.

Do artists have a responsibility to write—

Yes! Absolutely. I can't recall who said "all art is political," but I think that's true.

As a songwriter I really believe that to tell the truth is what you're called to do.

So much of what Woody wrote about is still with us today—the racism and oppression of African-Americans, the economic injustice

that the poor must deal with, xenophobia, even fascim. It's hard to believe that these stains on Amerca are still with us.

The Wall Street grifters, the billion-dollar hedge fund thieves who build their empire on the backs of struggling middle-class people—it's worse today, I think. And all of this requires a response from artists. "Crawling from the Promised Land" came out two weeks before the election. My outrage level had been through the roof during the Trump years. Part of my outrage was knowing that I had at least eight ancestors who fought in the American Revolution and knowing that I must carry on in my own way what they started and hoped to achieve. Despite all this, I think I have an inner obligation to be optimistic. "Crawling to the Promised Land" is all about the idea that even if we have to crawl across the finish line, we're going to finish this thing.

If you were asked to interpret a few Woody Guthrie songs for young people who had never heard of him, which songs would you play?

At the Kennedy Center in Washington, DC, a few years back, John and I did a version of Woody's "Pretty Boy Floyd." I really love that song. So that would be one song. And probably "I Ain't Got No Home" because that song always moves me so deeply. Home is a really special place and to sing that you don't have one can't help but touch listeners. It just can't. And for an encore I'd do "Bound for Glory" because the song is about hope. And hope is what we need today, every day.

Los Angeles, CA, 1941.

I wanted to be my own boss. Have my own job of work whatever it was, and be on my own hook. I walked the streets in the drift of the dust and wondered where was I bound for, where was I going, what was I going to do? My whole life turned into one big question mark. And I was the only living person that could answer it. I went to the town library and scratched around in the books. I carried them home by the dozens and by the armloads, on any subject, I didn't care which. I wanted to look into everything a little bit and pick out something, something that would turn me into a human being of some kind—free to work for my own self, and free to work for everybody . . .

My head was mixed up. I looked into every kind of an "ology," "osis," "itis" and "ism" there was. It seemed like it all turned to nothing.

I read the first chapter in a big leather law book. But, no, I didn't want to memorize all of them laws. So I got the bug that I wanted to be a preacher and yell from the street corners as loud as the law allows. But that faded away.

Then I wanted to be a doctor. A lot of folks were sick and I wanted to do something to make them well. I went up to the town library and carried home a big book about all kinds of germs, varmints, cells, and plasms . . .

For the next few months, I took a spell of spending all of the money I could rake and scrape for brushes, hunks of canvas, and all kinds of oil paints. Whole days would go by and I wouldn't know where they'd went. I put my whole mind and every single thought to the business of painting pictures, mostly people.

I made copies of Whistler's "Mother," "The Song of the Lark," "The Angelus," and lots of babies and boys and dogs, snow and green trees, birds singing on all kinds of limbs, and pictures of the dust across the oil fields and wheat country. I made a couple of dozen heads of Christ, and the cops that killed Him.

Things was starting to stack up in my head and I just felt like I was going out of my wits if I didn't find some way of saying what I was thinking. The world didn't mean any more than a smear to me if I couldn't find ways of putting it down on something. . . .

But canvas is too high priced, and so is paint and costly oils, and brushes that you've got to chase a camel or a seal or a Russian red sable forty miles to get.

An uncle of mine taught me to play the guitar and I got to going out a couple of nights a week to the cow ranches around to play for the square dances. I made up new words to old tunes and sung them everywhere I'd go. I had to give my pictures away to get anybody to hang them on their wall, but for singing a song, or a few songs at a country dance, they paid me as high as three dollars a night. A picture—you buy it once, and it bothers you for forty years; but with a song, you sing it out, and it soaks in people's ears and they all jump up and down and sing it with you, and then when you quit singing it, it's gone, and you get a job singing it again. On top of that, you can sing out what you think. You can tell tales of all kinds to put your idea across to the other fellow.

And there on the Texas plains right in the dead center of the dust bowl, with the oil boom over and the wheat blowed out and the hard-working people just stumbling about, bothered with mortgages, debts, bills, sickness, worries of every blowing kind, I seen there was plenty to make up songs about.

Some people liked me, hated me, walked with me, walked over me, jeered me, cheered me, rooted me and hooted me, and before long I was invited in and booted out of every public place of entertainment in that country. But I decided that songs was a music and a language of all tongues.

I never did make up many songs about the cow trails or the moon skipping through the sky, but at first it was funny songs of what all's wrong, and how it turned out good or bad. Then I got a little braver and made up songs telling what I thought was wrong and how to make it right, songs that said what everybody in that country was thinking.

And this has held me ever since.

Questions please:

Where will I get my ideas to write my songs and ballads?

Answer to that is:

Everywhere you look. Out of books, magazines, daily papers, at the movies, along the streets, riding busses or trains, even flying along in an airplane. Or in bed at night. anywhere,

always keep your pencil and paper handy to jot down little + big ideas.

MY EYES DO SEE
ALL OVER THIS WORLD
3-21-'47

I ride this plane you call
The Continental
From New York Town on up
To Montreal
The Stewardess warmed me
up with nice hot coffee
and now
my Eyes do see, see,
see,
all over this world.

LOOKING DOWN ON YOU
3-21-'47
I'M LOOKING DOWN ON YOU
" " " " "
RIDING IN MY AIRPLANE
IN THE SKY SO BLUE
EVERY MOVE YOU MAKE
EVERYTHING YOU DO
I'M UP HERE IN HEAVEN
LOOKING DOWN ON YOU

YOU MIGHT BE SOME BIG SHOT
ON YOUR HIGHEST SEAT
YOU MIGHT BE THE LOWEST ONE
WALKING DOWN THE STREET
EVERYBODY LOOKS SO LITTLE
I CAINT TELL WHO IS WHO
I RIDE MY SILVER WINGER
LOOKING DOWN ON YOU.
(FINISH LATER)

NY 2 Montreal

AINT GOT NO HOME   21
GOIN' DOWN ROAD
Roll Union On
MINERS CHILD
U.B. GROUND
1913 MASSACRE
UNION MAID
GOTTA GO DOWN
which side —
② Long John
① Cindy
Talking Union
Another Man
SKIP TO MY LOU
John Hardy
John Henry

Norman Goldberg

2-8-'47
19
1. E, TEX, RED —
2. ROLL LITTLE OCEAN —
3. R.R. HOBO —
4. 1913 MASS. —
5. ISAAC WOODWARD —

C, S, & W.
1. CHICKEN SNEEZE
2. GOOD MORNIN' CAPT,
3.
4.
5. BED ON FLOOR

Pocket notebook of new song ideas and set lists written on a flight from New York to Montreal, 1947.

Just the idea of the title
for your song is more than half
of the battle to catch your ballad.
    I've got thousands of titles
laid away like postal saving bonds.
I spend hours and hours just writing
down my ideas for titles to my songs.

1. single girl Blues
2. Two Hungry Babies
3. starving Family Blues
4. Leaky Roof Blues
5. no money Blues
6. the Drunken Father
7. the Frozen Orphan
8. the Drunk mother
9. wish I was single again
10. Holey Stockin' Blues
11. no Rent Blues
12. no Job Blues
14. Parents Lament
15. Crowded Room Blues

16. G. I. Loan Blues
17. Hock shop Rag
18. Pawn shop Polka
19. Bucket shop Waltz
20. Trifling Husband
21. Trifling wife
22. Trifling sweetie
23. Jealous Father
24. Jealous mother
25. Daggery Knife
26. Oily Gun Rag
27. Dead widow
28. Dead Bachelor
29. stabbing at Home

List of song titles, 1948.

30. Starved Relatives
31. Hungry Heart Blues
32. No Job Moan
33. Down Payment Scream
34. Dollar Down Struggle
35. Collector Man, The
36. Dying Collector, The
37. Dead Collector, The
38. Mortgage Day Blues
39. Rent Day Shuttle
40. Gas Bill Scuttle
41. Light Bill Runaway
42. High Price Gallop
43. Low Pay Work Hand
44. Inflation Struggle
45. Banker Man Blues
46. Banker Man, The
47. Hurt Banker, The
48. Landlord, The
49. Dying Landlord, The
50. Dead Landlord, That

51. Hungry Baby Blues
52. Empty Bottle Lament
53. No Heat Weeper
54. Coldwater Flat Blues
55. No Coal Moan
56. No Oil Cry
57. Chilly Fever Shivver
58. Bad Cold Blues
59. Cold Room Blues
60. Holey Roof Breakdown
61. Mean Boss Ballad
62. Mean Old Judge Blues
63. Gone Woman Blues
64. Gone Man Blues
65. Sickly Woman Blues
66. Sick Man Moan
67. Headache for Breakfast
68. Palegera for Dinner
69. Malaria for Supper
70. Join the Union
71. Go & Join the Union

72. Go Down & Join The Union
73. Go up and Sign up
74. Union's my Religion
75. Union's my saviour
76. Union Pay
77. Union Day
78. Union Way
79. Union Man
80. Union Boy
81. Union Girl
82. Union Woman
83. Union Saved Me
84. Scabs In my Factory
85. Scabs In my Job
86. Scabs In my Place
87. Scabs In my Hair
88. Scabs In my Eyes
89. Scabs In my Bed
90. Scabs In my Bread
91. Shoo Scabby Shoo
92. Git away old Scab

93. thugs Come Out
94. thugs Come In
95. thugs Beat me up
96. thugs Knock me Down
99. thugs Tar & Feather Me
100. thugs Lynch & Hang me
101. Thugs Latt BIG
102. I Fight Back
103. I Beat thugs up
104. I Beat Scabs up
105. I Run Thugs off
106. I Run Scabs out
107. I Win
108. I Won
109. I Won Out on top
110. I'm Born To Win
111. Union Town now
112. Union City Polka
113. Union Folks Reel
114. New Union Round Dance
115. Old Union Liquor dug
116. Fine Union Wine Glass

117. GOOD union Family
118. World union Holler
119. union Button shout
120. union Headed woman
121. union minded man
122. The union Lover
123. union sweet thing
124. union Kiss, The new
125. Somebody's Darling
126. Good news Bluesy
127. HIGH Feeling Daddy
128. Laughy Tickle mommy
129. High Peppy Hepper
130. Loud shouting Whooper
131. Freedom Jitterbug
132. Groove Juice Rider
133. Dinner Pail workster
134. new Found good time
135. Rent Paid Blues
136. GOOD shoe Joke
137. GOOD Stockin Snicker
138. I Love Folks

139. Folks Loves me
140. Union Heated Sweetie
141. Hot union Kiss, The
142. Burnt Union Hugs, these
143. Oh, my union
144. yes, my union
145. my world union
146. union Home
147. union mattness
148. union Bed spring
149. union Baby
150. Union children

A song should be as long as the story you're trying to tell.

I'm shippin' up to Boston
SHIPPING OFF to Boston
SKIPPING out for Boston
to find my wooden leg.

I'm sailer Peq
an' I lost my leg
a climbin' up the topsails
I'm sailer Peq
an' I lost my leg
a climbin' up the topsails

Woody Guthrie
6-26-46

I sung last night in Bailey Hall
Where the names are chopped in the marble walls;
Seen the canyons full of falling falls;
    I sung last night in Bailey Hall.
Rode up on the train with a dancing bunch,
And I sung to myself as we rode along,
Sung to myself as we followed the river banks;
    I guess I thought to myself
    Most of the Eight hours on the way;
    I listened to the dancers talk,
    But, couldn't think of much to say.
    So, I guessed to myself:

        This train must be a deisel
        From the blue blaze that she throws;
        But, boy, when she trots past you,
        She don't throw no smoke at all.

        I think the train's name
        Is called the Black Diamond;
        I know a song about a horse
        That was named Black Diamond;
        I'm snaking along here looking at the flood waters,
        Just hoping this train is as fast as the horse.

And then we finally got up to Ithaca;
Up to the college town of Ithaca;
And we stopped off at a little tavern;
And one witress was all they had there
To wait on several big tables like us;
I watched her run herself nearly crazy
Trying to get our orders to us.
    Every musician and every dancer
    Pitied the poor girl so awful much
    They all took money out and paid their bills
    And then left tips down on the tables;
        All but me;
        I argued with the others;
        Told them I don't believe in tipping.
            Oh, we had a bigger squabble about this
            In the dining car
            Riding up on the rattler;
            You ought to heard that head rustler
            Mad at me because I didn't
                Leave no nickels nor dimes neither
                On the tray nor on the table.
            This caused some pretty hot arguments
            Among the whole car full of show folks.
                Lots of business actors listened;
                Lots of soldiers and sailors got in;
                Lots of quiet thinkers jumped up;
                Lots of noisey talkers hooked horns.
    Seems like every place I go to
    I get into just such doings;
    And I'm not no good hand at talking;
    Just never did believe in tipping.

"It's an old and friendly custom!"
"Waiters can't live unless we tip them!"
"Bosses won't pay a living salary;
    So, our tips must make their wages!"
"You can't fight against a custom!"
"Half of the world is fed by tipping!"
"It's a little sign of thanks for getting nicer service faster!"
"One man can't stand against a thousand!"
"Everybody tips and lives by tipping!"
"Tipping shows a sporting spirit!"
"Tipping shows a generous person!"
"Tipping is how our world is run!"
"Owners just won't pay good wages;
    So, we just have to accept it!"

        "Long as our world
        Is run by tipping;

Them what's got most
Will always get most;
        If you got nothing
        You get nothing;
   If you can't tip
   You'll live on insults;
      The rich can get the best of service;
      Best of eats, and sleeps, and everything
         The folks that's got
         But little money
               Will get bawled out on every taxi;
               Get cussed out in every hotel;
               Get made fun of at the cafe;
               Get joked at in railroad diners;
               Get a frown, a groan, a cussing,
                     Everywhere
                     You have to go;
      Sneered at in the ritzy places;
      Jeered at in the neon light glare;
      Hissed at in the smokey parlors;
      Laughed at from the inside windows;
      Hawked at in the elevators;
      Screamed at in the quietest places;
When the screamers asking for charity
Make three times as much as I make;
And the scared ones beggingmy tip
Carry a wad and roll of greenbakk
   Twice as big as the roll I carry;
   Why should I not yell and scream,
   And bawl them out for not passing me
   A few of the coins of Liberty?
         And besides,
            There is no difference
            Between this tipping,
               And black market boosting;
            Jacking up the prices higher;
               This is what killed the O.P.A.,
               This is what caused the money people
                  To corner all the money in Europe;
               (Asking the workers to
                  Pay by charity
                     The wages refused them
                     By their bosses).

This tipping,
It's a bigger thing
Than it looks to be;
   It is a custom of runaway prices;
   A sporting custom of not going by no
         ceiling price;
   A little sport of pampering and petting,
      Bowing down, catering to,
   Licking the hands of the money packers;
   Which is just exactly the kind of a world
      That the gangsters,
      Black Market folks,
      The gamblers, gamers, framers,
      Wildest and meanest of plan wreckers,
      Worst and deadliest of control killers;
      Blindest and greediest of criminals union
                           busters

   Desire,
   Want,
   And love.

            Just the kind of a tangled
            And senseless world
               That the dead believers,
               Blind leaders,
               Lost Saviours,
               War causers,

                        Love,
                        Want,
                        And revel in.

They don't want you to see

That the tipping ism,
Is exactly the same as the
Ism called
  Fascism
  Nazism
  Race ism
  Slavery ism;
        On a nation wide scale!"

                        Oh, you're carrying the thing
                          Just a shade too far;
                        You're just full of sour juice
                          This morning,
                          This evening,
                          Right now.
                              You're stretching the point;
                              You're going too far;
                              You're all wet.

        Here is a worker,
          Taught to live, think, and work,
            According to the drift of the tip.

        Now,
        Who is going to get the service,
        Who is going to get the goods, the things needed most
        From this worker?

                        The workers
                        Just like him
                        That must get the things or suffer?
                          Or,
                            The money holder,
                            The big shot racket man?
                            The owner?
                            The landlord?
                                The boss?
                                The informer?
                                The labor wrecker?
                                The hired thugs?
                                The union spy and stooge?
                                The rake off man?
                                The take off gambler?
                                The guard?
                                The deputy?
                                The foney artist?
                                The foney show man?
                                The foney writer?
                                The foney news man?
                                The foney anything else?

It all stands to see,
It all is so easy and so simple,
I feel sort of like a little kid
Drawing chalk stuff on a sidewalk;
Or like my first grade primer teacher
Drawing little men on her blackboard.

                        The worker
                        That needs the goods the most
                        Is going to always get the least
                        So long as you worship your sporty god
                            Or try to be like your big shot hero
                            Tossing rolls of peoples money
                            All around like it was dry grass;
                            While outside your crazy window,
                            Folks are hungry,
                            Folks are starving;
                            Folks are begging,
                                Asking,
                                Waiting,
                                Standing,
                                Arguing,
                                Pleading,
                                  Crying,
                                  Sobbing,

For the things to stay alive on.

You don't have to go across
Any ocean, nor any waters,
To see folks by the untold thousands
Lost in a hungry world of tipping;
    Watching eats, and clothes and work plans
    Tossed back and forth across the tables
    In the form of tips and take offs
        To the union busters,
        To the labor spies and stooges,
        To the cultural misleaders,
        To the clowns and monkey of planlessness.

                            Booty to the hands
                            That keep old cancers
                            Alive and growing
                            In the names of customs.

                            Tubercolosis hit so often
                             It could be said to be
                                    A custom;
                            But it starved some
                                    parts of the body;
                            And so we fought it
                                With a union
                                    Of X Ray lamps,
                                    Sunshine treatments,
                                    Drugs, beds,
                                        Good food,
                                            Hospitals,
                                                And a union
                                                    of

                            Doctors,
                            Nurses,
                            Internes,
                            Students,
                                        And a union
                                            of
                                        Common knowledge.

    Do you tip your Nurse or Doctor?
    Do you tip your clasroom teacher?
    Do you tip your union bringers?
        Union organizers?
        Union workers?
        Do you tip your old professor?
        Do you tip your Worker's paper?

        (They make less money
        By a long shot
         Than your cab man,
         Than your waiter,
            Than your black market hider, seller;
            Oh, I know how many hard hours,
                These tip beggers hide away to practice
                Every look,
                    And moan and groan,
                    Every word of misery, troubles;
                        I have talked to them
                        And practiced
                                    These same cries
                                    When I was a bus boy;
                                        Waiter,
                                        Driver,
                                        Shoe Shiner,
                                        But then I
                                            Got tired, and sick
                                            Of living by begging;
                                        Living on the
                                            Whims of idle minds.
                                        Living on the
                                            favors of money
                                                        owners.

    This is my piece,
    And this is my story
    This is my side of the tipping question;

I lived on tips
A long number of years;
Playing for tips my music, singing;
   Songs for nickels and for dimes;
         Which a worker could not pay to hear,
            So he could not have his own songs;
               But had to listen to the rich man songs
                  That says, "This world is okie dokie!"

                    "Everything's gonna be fine and dandy!"
                    "Life is big and life is nothing!"
                    "Life is just a limb of cherries!"
                    "It's a big bowl full of good times!"
                    "The more you do not kick nor argue,
                           The higher up the ladder you go!"
                    "Don't get sore!"
                    "Don't argue back!"
                    "Don't complain!"
                    "Don't lose your temper!"
                    "Don't bite the hand which fools you!"
                    "Every man for his self is what the lord wants!"
                    "Be satisfied with the pretty scenery!"
                    "Be content with the stars and planets!"
                    "Laugh when all your money leaves you!"
                    "Be a big shot. Be a big sport!"
                    "Empty saddles, empty trails!"
                    "The world's all right, it's you that's wrong!"

When the
Song of the working folks
Sings just the opposite:

   "Everything is not fine nor dandy!"
   "Life needs talking about and planning!"
   "Children die in crowded houses!"
   "I see a world of constant sorrow!"
   "Speak up. Argue. Speak your mind up!"
   "Get sore and stay sore!"
   "Complain! And do it loud!"
   "Don't never be satisfied!"
   "Only a dead man feels content!"
   "Boil and foam! Fuss and fret! Feel alive!"
   "The world is all wrong. It's me that's right!"
   "My daddy got killed when the coal fell on him".
   "My sister got killed when the fever struck her".
   "My brother he drawed up and dried away hungry".
   "It must of been that filthy old room!"
   "This same gas stove killed two soldier families".
   "A hundred folks got trapped in that firetrap".
   "I seen them drown when our good ship went down".
   "This old place needs a right good fixing".
   "How's it come, so many is hungry when too much is all around us?"

These are the songs
And the thoughts in the songs
That the working people make up;
And the rich boss will tip you plenty
If you sing some other nice song
To try to make the workers believe
That this old world is fine and dandy;
              Yes, the owner will tip you plenty;
              Yes, he'll tip you more than plenty;
                  And the money that he tips you
                  Will be the very same old money
                  With which them hungry working people
                  Was aiming to buy and do their fixing.

                    I think this
                    Is already enough
                                     to make me
                       Never tip nobody again.

If you need more money,
Get it off of your owner,
   Not off of me.

****

Any event which takes away the lives of human beings, I try to write a song about what caused it to happen and how we can all try to keep such a thing from happening again.

List of the Missing on Reuben James

Special to THE NEW YORK TIMES.

WASHINGTON, Nov. 4 — The names of seven officers and eighty-eight men lost with the destroyer Reuben James, for whom the Navy today announced it has abandoned hope, follow:

Officers

EDWARDS, Lieut. Comdr. HEYWOOD L., commanding officer, San Saba, Texas.

GHETZLER, Lieut. BENJAMIN, Annapolis, Md.

JOHNSTON, Lieut. (Junior) DEWEY G., El Cajon, Calif.

DAUB, Lieut. (Junior) JOHN J., Salsburg, Pa.

BELDEN, Lieut. (Junior) JAMES M., Syracuse, N. Y.

SPOWERS, Ensign CRAIG, East Orange, N. J.

WADE, Ensign HOWARD V., Glen Ridge, N. J.

Crew

*ANDERSON, PETER, water tender,, first class, Sumner, Wash.

BAUER, JOHN FRANCIS, JR., chief radio man, Chester, Pa.

BEASLEY, HAROLD HAMNER, seaman, first class, Hinton, W. Va.

BENSON, JAMES FRANKLIN, machinist's mate, second class, Swan Quarter, N. C.

BIEHL, JOSEPH PETER, seaman, second class, Philadelphia.

*BISHOP, FREDERICK ARTHUR, torpedo man, third class, Bayonne, N. J.

BOYNTON, PAUL ROGERS, yeoman, first class, Carthage, Texas.

BRITT, HAROLD LESLIE, coxswain, Athol, Mass.

BYRD, HARTWELL LEE, seaman, first class, Asheboro, N. C.

*CAMPBELL, JACK AUSTIN, fireman, first class, Greensboro, N. C.

CARBAUGH, LEFTWICH ERASTUS, JR., fireman, first class, Princeton, W. Va.

CARUSO, JOSEPH JAMES, radio man, second class, Pittsburgh.

CLARK, JAMES BRANTLEY, fire control man, second class, Akron, Ohio.

COOK, RAYMOND, mess attendant, first class, Warner, Va.

COOPERIDER, CARL EUGENE, gunner's mate, third class, Bucyrus, Ohio.

COSGROVE, LAWRENCE RANDALL, gunner's mate, second class, Brockton, Mass.

COUSINS, ALTON ADELBERT, chief machinist's mate, Auburn, R. I.

COX, CHARLES BEACON, chief torpedo man, Forth Worth, Texas.

DANIEL, DENNIS HOWARD, yeoman, third class, Jesse, W. Va.

DEVEREAU, LAWRENCE DELANEY, chief boatswain's mate, Troy, Kan.

DICKERSON, LEONIDAS CAMDEN JR., storekeeper, third class, Stuart, Va.

DOIRON, GILBERT JOSEPH, water tender, first class, Sanford, Me.

DRINKWATER, KARL LEE, seaman, first class, Chaffee, N. Y.

DUNSTON, NEBRASKA, mess attendant, third class, Spring Hope, N. C.

DYSON, CORBON, radio man, third class, Caryville, Fla.

EVANS, GENE GUY, boilermaker, second class, Vero Beach, Fla.

EVANS, LINN STEWART, fire control man, third class, Harrellsville, N. C.

EVERETT, CARLYLE CHESTER, fireman, second class, Canandaigua, N. Y.

FARLEY, EDWIN LOUIE, seaman, first class, Hurricane, W. Va.

FITZGERALD, JOHN JOSEPH, quartermaster, third class, Hampstead, N. H.

FLYNN, WILLIAM ALOYSIOUS, torpedo man, second class, Philadelphia.

FRANKS, HARTLEY HARDY, ship's cook, second class, Gatesville, Texas.

FRENCH, RALPH GEORGE, chief commissary steward, Hartford, Conn.

GASKINS, LESTER CARSON, machinist's mate first class, Pamplico, S. C.

GREER, JOHN CALVIN, chief electrician's mate, Long Beach, Calif.

GREY, ERNEST DWANE Jr., seaman second class, Radisson, Wis.

GRIFFIN, ARTHUR RAYMOND, signalman second class, Wellesley, Mass.

HARRIS, CHARLES WALDON, seaman second class, Caryville, Fla.

HENNIGER, WILLIAM HENRY, gunner's mate first class, Newburgh, N. Y.

HOGAN, FRANCIS ROBERT, gunner's mate third class, Springfield, Mass.

HOUSE, HUGH, gunner's mate third class, Palmyra, N. C.

*HOWELL, VERNON EVERETT, fireman first class, Thornville, Ohio.

HULIN, MAURICE WOODROW, fireman first class, Revere, Mass.

JOHNSON, JOSEPH, mess attendant first class, Elm City, N. C.

JONES, GLEN W., chief quartermaster, Ocean View, Va.

KALANTA, ANTHONY J., electrician's mate second class, Worcester, Mass.

KAPP, DONALD, seaman second class, Ithaca, N. Y.

KEEVER, LEONARD A., chief machinist's mate, Little River, Kan.

KLOEPPER, RALPH W. H., signalman third class, St. Louis.

*KRYSTYNAK, VICTOR F., fireman first class, Follansbee, W. Va.

MAGARIS, PAUL L., radioman first class, Fort Stevens, Ore.

MERRITT, AUBURN F., seaman second class, Baker, Fla.

MONDOUX, ALBERT J., chief watertender, Glens Falls, N. Y.

MORGAN, HIRMAN, machinist's mate first class, Hamilton, Ohio.

MUSSELWHITE, EDGAR W., machinist's mate, first class, Plant City, Fla.

NEPTUNE, ALDON W., seaman first class, Mannington, W. Va.

ORANGE, HAROLD J., seaman second class, Chicago.

ORTIZUELA, PEDRO, officer's cook first class, Manila, P. I.

OWEN, BENJAMIN T., seaman second class, Cornerville, Ark.

PAINTER, WILLIAM H., seaman first class, Greenville, S. C.

PARKIN, JOSEPH J., chief watertender, Worcester, Mass.

PATERSON, WILLIAM N., coxswain, Buffalo.

PENNINGTON, BURL G., quartermaster second class, Bigstone, Ky.

POLIZZI, JOSEPH C., seaman second class, Detroit.

PORTER, CORWIN D., seaman first class, Wauseon, Ohio.

POST, FREDERICK R., boatswain's mate, 233 East Thirty-second St., New York.

POWELL, LEE P., pharmacist's mate first class, Lenoir, N. C.

RAYBILL, ELMER R., seaman second class, New Point, Mo.

REID, LEE LOUIS N., torpedoman first class, Dallas, Texas.

RESS, JOHN R. Jr., seaman second class, 167 Eighth St., New York.

ROGERS, JAMES W., seaman first class, Chattanooga, Tenn.

RYAN, JOHN J. Jr., coxswain, Somerville, Mass.

RYGWELSKI, CLARENCE, seaman second class, Rogers City, Mich.

SCHLATTHAUER, EUGENE, chief watertender, Visalia, Calif.

SETTLE, SUNNY J., seaman second class, Charleston, W. Va.

SORENSEN, WALTER, gunner's mate third class, Omaha.

SOWERS, WALLACE L., seaman second class, Cheriton, Va.

STELMACH, JEROME, seaman second class, Buffalo.

TAYLOR, WILTON L., fireman first class, New Castle, Pa.

TOWERS, GEORGE F., chief gunner's mate, Gadsden, Ala.

VOILES, LLOYD Z., seaman second class, Chattanooga, Tenn.

VORE, HAROLD M., fireman first class, Glouster, Ohio.

WEAVER, JESSE, seaman first class, West Point, Tenn.

WELCH, CHESTER L., fireman third class, Cabin Creek, W. Va.

WILSON, MARVIN J., ship fitter third class, Gassaway, W. Va.

WHARTON, KENNETH R., fire control man first class, San Diego, Calif.

WOODY, GEORGE Jr., seaman first class, Accoville, W. Va.

WRAY, EDWIN E., seaman first class, De Queen, Ark.

Here we see the evolution of a song. From the original newspaper article above, Woody typed his first version (opposite) incorporating the names of the servicemen lost on the destroyer *Reuben James*, which was torpedoed before the United States entered World War II. On the following page is Woody's final published version, which includes the now well-known chorus, "What were their names?" Crayon colorings were added by his young daughter Cathy.

THE SINKING OF THE REUBEN JAMES

RUEBEN JAMES   By Woody Guthrie

Have you heard of the ship called the bold Rueben James,
Manned by hard fighting men both of honor and fame?
I will tell you a tale that will tell you the names
Of the men that went down on that good Reuben James...

There's Harold Hammer Beasley, a first rate man at sea,
From Hinton, West Virginia, he had his first degree.
There's Jim Franklin Benson, a good machinist mate,
Come up from North Carolina, to sail the Reuben James.

There was Carl Cooperider, that shared the Reuben's fate,
Bucyrus was his home town, and Ohio was his state;
And then come Randall Cosgrove, and gunning was his game;
And he went on to glory on the fighting Reuben James.

If you ask who was it handled our hot torpedo box,
A man from West Virgina, his name was Charlie Cox;
If you ask who was it that manned the cannon ball,
His name was Walter Sorensen, from the town of Omaha.

Jesse Weaver died a seaman as true as he could be,
And he come up from West Point, the state called Tennessee.
William Flynn done his best and his bravery I'll tell,
His home was Philadelphia where hangs the Liberty bell.

Dennis Howard Daniel, Glen Jones, and Harold Vore,
Hartwell Byrd, and Raymond Cook, Ed Musslewhite, and more;
Remember Leonard Keever, Gene Evans, and Donald Kapp,
Who gave their all to fight aboard this famous fighting ship.

Jack Campbell was our fireman, he stuck the battle through,
And there was Erastus Carbaugh from Mercer County, too;
Paul Magais stuck to the radio, and W.H. Kloepper, too;
Until the good ship Reuben James went down beneath the blue.

Eighty six men were drowned, I can't give you all their names,
Only forty four were saved from that good Reuben James;
It was the last day of October that we saved the forty four
From the cold ocean waters 'long that long Iceland shore.

It was there in the dark of that uncertain night
That we watched for a U-Boat, and ready for a fight;
Then a whine, and a rock, and a great explosion roared,
And they laid the Reuben James on the cold ocean floor.

Now tonight there are lights in our country so bright;
And friends and relations are telling of this fight;
And now our mighty battleships ▬ steam the bounding main
remember the name of the great Reuben James.

AND

                Almanac Singers

This is the poem the Almanacs first wrote about the sinking of
the Reuben James. Later, an hour or two at least, we ganged around
the poem, and changed it into a good singing song with a chorus
that you can join in easy. *Come and sing with us. We're
gonna tear old Hitler down! As Leadbelly says.*

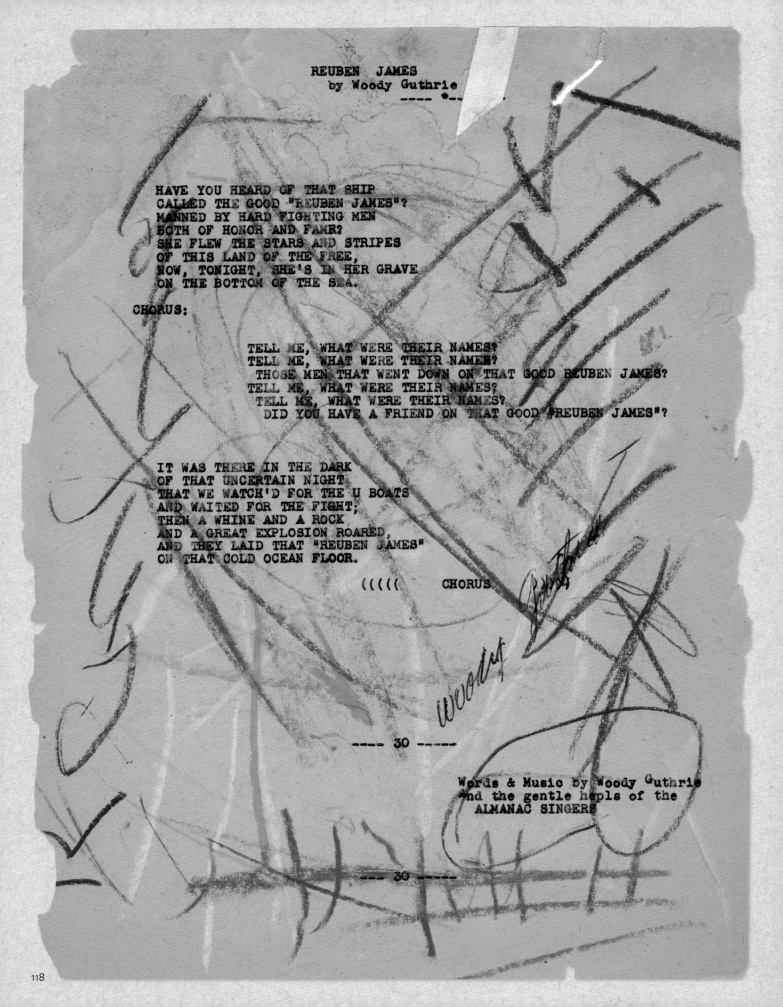

REUBEN JAMES
by Woody Guthrie
---- *---

HAVE YOU HEARD OF THAT SHIP
CALLED THE GOOD "REUBEN JAMES"?
MANNED BY HARD FIGHTING MEN
BOTH OF HONOR AND FAME?
SHE FLEW THE STARS AND STRIPES
OF THIS LAND OF THE FREE,
NOW, TONIGHT, SHE'S IN HER GRAVE
ON THE BOTTOM OF THE SEA.

CHORUS:

       TELL ME, WHAT WERE THEIR NAMES?
       TELL ME, WHAT WERE THEIR NAMES?
        THOSE MEN THAT WENT DOWN ON THAT GOOD REUBEN JAMES?
       TELL ME, WHAT WERE THEIR NAMES?
        TELL ME, WHAT WERE THEIR NAMES?
         DID YOU HAVE A FRIEND ON THAT GOOD "REUBEN JAMES"?

IT WAS THERE IN THE DARK
OF THAT UNCERTAIN NIGHT
THAT WE WATCH'D FOR THE U BOATS
AND WAITED FOR THE FIGHT;
THEN A WHINE AND A ROCK
AND A GREAT EXPLOSION ROARED,
AND THEY LAID THAT "REUBEN JAMES"
ON THAT COLD OCEAN FLOOR.

              (((((CHORUS

                ---- 30 -----

                          Words & Music by Woody Guthrie
                          and the gentle hepls of the
                          ALMANAC SINGERS

                --- 30 -----

HISTORY SINGING

Whatever has happened here or yonder, it's left us plenty
to talk and sing about.

Po' Howard's dead and gone,
Left me here to sing this song;
Po' Howard's dead and gone,
Left me here to sing this song!

Listen to your radio. Go to the movies. Play your phonograph records. Go down to the record shop and take a look at
the titles, play them over, and listen.

What percent of these songs would you call rock-bottom
American? What would you say was really worth having around
the house? What percent say most, anything at all, or least
about politics? What about work, hours, wages, prices, love,
marriage, kids, groceries and school? What about making a
better world to live in by fixing the one we got?

Which song does this best? What are the rules for making
a song of this calibre? Can you write an American Folk Song?
Will your song last? Will people keep singing it after you're
down in the cypress grove?

Has America got a history worth singing about? Is the
history of today, the fast travelling current events of this
very minute -- worth singing about? What section of the
American people are carrying the real load, doing the real
work, the real fighting, the real living, loving, courting,
and song making right this minute? Who is keeping American
history alive and moving? Who is holding progress back?
Who is going forward and who is drifting backward?

What do you think about the average run of Hollywood and
Broadway stuff? Is Tin Pan Alley a full blood American?
Are all showfolks screwball? Artists, too? Where do they
get that way? Who pays some actors and artists such ungodly
high wages, and why?

Are songs hard to write, sing, and spread? What do you
write them about? Where do you go to sing them? Who'll back
you? Where do you find the material? Ideas? People to
listen?

Why do s me songs spread so fast and last so long? Why do
others fall by the side of the track? Do the leading song
writers, like radio scrip writers, take it for granted that
we've got a 11 year old mind? What do kids think about our
old time songs and ballads?

Do the 'Hits of the Week' give a decent picture of life in
America as she is lived?

Is there an actual, outright frameup to control the making
up, and the spreading around of songs, stories, plays, articles?

Is Organized Labor big enough and smart enough to furnish
its own self with entertainment of all kinds; can union
dollars be spent entirely in union night clubs, halls, and
theaters that deal 100% with the striking, picketing, marching, militant history of Trade Unions in the United States?

Beat Hitler

1913   MASSACRE

Take a trip with me in 1913
To Calumet, Michigan, in the copper country;
I'll take you to a place called Italian Hall
Where the strikers are having their big Christmas ball.

I'll take you in a door and up a high stair;
~~Thexspiritxofxffhristmasxixxtherexexerywherex~~
Singing and dancing is heard everywhere;
I'll let you shake hands with the people you see,
And watch the kids dance 'round the big Christmas Tree.

You ask about work and you ask about pay;
They'll tall you they make less than a Dollar a day,
Working their copper claims risking their lives,
So it's fun to spend Christmas with children and wives.

There's talking and laughing and songs in the air,
And the spirit of Christmas is there everywhere;
Before you know it you're friends with us all;
And you're dancing around and around in the hall.

Well, a little girl sets down in the Christmas tree lights;
To play the piano, so you gotta keep quiet;
Well, hear all this fun you would not realize
That the copper boss thugmen are milling outside.

The copper boss thugs stuck their heads in the door;
One of them yelled and he screamed, "There's a fire!"
A lady she hollered, "They's no such a thing!
Keep on with your party! They's no such a thing!"

A few people rushed, it was only a few;
"It's just the thugs and the scabs fooling you!"
A man grabbed his daughter and carried her down
But the scabs held the door and he could not get out.

And then others followed, a Hundred or more,
But most everybody remained on the floor;
The gun thugs they laughed at their murderous joke;
While the children were smothered on the stairs by the door.

Such a terrible sight I never did see;
We carried our children back up to their tree;
The scabs outside still laughed at their spree;
And the children that died there were Seventy Three.

The piano played a slow funeral tune,
And the town was lit up by a cold Christmas moon;
The parents they cried and the miners they moaned,
"See what your greed for money has done!"

****

| EXTRA | The Calumet News | THE WEATHER. Cloudy tonight and Thursday. |

VOLUME XXIII.   CALUMET, MICHIGAN, WEDNESDAY AFTERNOON, DECEMBER 24, 1913.   NUMBER 58

SEVENTY-FOUR ARE DEAD IN ITALIAN HALL DISASTER

Unknown Man Yells "Fire" at Christmas Celebration and Children Rush to Suffocation--Effort to Escape

37 LITTLE GIRLS, 21 BOYS, 13 WOMEN, AND 5 MEN DEAD

Man Who Cried "Fire" Supposed to Be Drunk as He Came From Sal- loon on the Lower Floor

A holocaust unparalleled in the history of Michigan and ranking with the Iroquois theater fire and such catastrophies as the sinking of the Titanic in its frightful import, occurred about five o'lock this afternoon in the Italian hall on north Seventh street when approximately eighty lives, mostly children were lost.

An alarm of fire from box forty-five contributed to the confusion which existed in the building at the time. There was, however, no fire in the Italian Hall building.

During a Christmas entertainment arranged for by the Ladies Auxiliary of the Western Federation of Miners, a man who has not been apprehended called "fire." Instantly there was a rush for the narrow exits and at the bottom of the stairway, the little children were jammed into one solid mass, from which none could emerge.

All efforts of those at hand to stop the onrush of the hundreds in the room were futile, and one by one the little lives were snuffed out.

More than seventy-five dead have been accounted for, and it is estimated there are from six to eight others who were removed to their homes by parents and friends before the author ities arrived on the scene.

Practically every death was caused by suffocation, physicians assert. Although many of the bodies were mangled, none were so badly disfigured that identification would be impossible.

There were approximately 600 persons, about ninety-five per cent of whom were children, in the hall during the Christmas entertainment, which was arranged for by the women. Some estimates place the number at 700. Two versions of the accident are given by those in the hall.

Mrs. Annie Clemenc, president of the Auxiliary, stated immediately after the accident that she was on the stage together with some of the other ladies, who crowded toward the

she was in the hall and close to the man who called "fire." She identifies him as a large man, with a heavy beard. When the cry was first heard, she realized its danger instantly and reached up and grasped him by the shoulders in an effort to make him sit down. He escaped her grasp, however, and soon the cry of fire was taken up by others. The rush of the excited children towards the door was frightful to behold, Mrs. Caesar asserts. She herself succeeded in getting her little daughter out of the building to safety after semblance of order was restored.

Another woman who was in the building asserts the man who called "fire" spoke in two languages, first in English and then in Austrian. She asserts she heard the cry distinctly both times.

Others who were in the building assert that the call was heard from the stage as well as from the doorway, after the alarm first came.

Words are inadequat to describe the terrible scene in the Italian hall immediately afterwards. The dead lay on every side, old men, women and little boys and girls, their bodies huddled up into heaps and strewn out along the chairs, on the ofor, on the stage, in a little office adjoining the main hall and in a kitchen at the front of the hall and beneath the stage.

Hurried calls were sent out and soon every physician in town was on the scene. The living were separated from the dead and many that were thought to be dead, recovered from the first shock and were taken to the C. [...] ents and relatives of the dead surged [...] many of them took charge of the bodies [...] fore the authorities could take charge [...] moaning of the injured mingled with th[...] ents, brothers, sisters and friends. Pal[...] calamity, the officers quietly circulated [...] where they could.

After the injured were cared for, t[...] together and removed to the Red Jacke[...] porary provision was made to keep th[...] was made.

At the rear of the building, there [...] but few were aware of its presence, and [...] escape from the rear part of the build[...] from the windows of the kitchen. Per[...] points of safety in this manner, the dista[...] few were seriously injured

Several hundred of the children esc[...] over the fire escape, better order having [...] taind there than in the front part of the [...]

The Italian hall is a comparatively [...] been erected about five years ago. It w[...] prepared for emergencies of this kinds. [...] about eight feet wide and leads up fro[...] ten feet from the doorway. At the to[...] small landing, perhaps eight feet wide [...]

TO DISPENSE GOOD CHEER IN THE LAND

Public and Private Philanthropy Unite to Extend Xmas Spirit to Poor

MANY COMMUNITY TREES

Year of Prosperity Reflected in Generous Gifts to the Unfortunate

MUCH ATTENTION TO CHILDREN

CHRISTMAS CHEER FROM THE WHITE HOUSE TODAY

Washington, Dec. 24—Christmas cheer went out from the white house today to hundreds of needy in Washington, by the direction of President and Mrs. Wilson and daughters, Margaret and Eleanor. Before the president's family left

DANIELS AND GARRISON GET UNIQUE GIFTS FROM ANDY CARNEGIE

Washington, Dec. 24—Secretaries Daniels and Garrison today found on their desks Christmas gifts from Andrew Carnegie. A recently published cartoon, satirizing war, with a plea for international peace, was the postmaster's remembrance to the two heads of the two departments of national defense.

PARTIAL LIST OF DEAD

MEN—
J. P. WESTALA.
HERMAN ALA.

WOMEN—
MRS. KATIE PETERI.
MRS. BRONZO.
MRS. TOLPA.
MRS. GUINAR.

GIRLS—
AGNES MIHELCHICH, aged 8.
HILDA WOULUKKA.
LEMPI ALA.
LYDIA LUOMA
—— TIAPALA.
—— GLASNER.
—— JOKOPI.
LILA ALA.
MAMIE LACER.

FRA ELBERTUS COMING HERE JAN. 28-30

Noted Lecturer to Appear Under Copper Country Commercial Club Auspices

IS AN EMINENT PERSONAGE

Engagement Will Be Hailed With Delight Throughout the Peninsula

TO TALK AT CALUMET-HANCOCK

Secretary George Frix of the Copper Country Commercial club announced today that Elbert Hubbard, known throughout the literary world as "The Elbertus," will lecture in the Calumet theater January 28 and in the Kerredge theater, Hancock, Jan. 29.

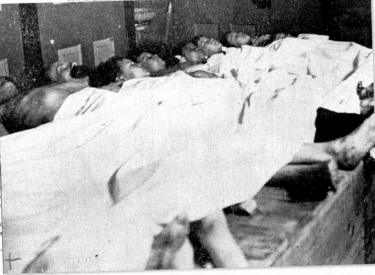

Civilization is spread more by singing than by anything else, because whole big bunches can sing a particular song where not every man can join in on the same conversation. A song ain't nothing but a conversation fixed up to where you can talk it over and over without getting tired of it. And its this repeating the idea over and over that makes it take ahold. If the conversation is about good crops or bad, good politics or bad, good news or bad, good anything else or bad, the best way to circulate it amongst the people is by way of singing it.

Beluthahatchee, FL, 1951.

There are several ways of saying what's on your mind. And in states and counties where it ain't any too healthy to talk too loud, speak your mind, or even to vote like you want to, folks have found other ways of getting the word around.

One of the mainest ways is by singing. Drop the word 'folk' and just call it real old honest to god American singing. No matter who makes it up, no matter who sings it and who don't, if it talks the lingo of the people, it's a cinch to catch on, and will be sung here and yonder for a long time after you've cashed in your chips.

I HATE A SONG THAT MAKES YOU THINK THAT YOU'RE NOT
ANY GOOD. I HATE A SONG THAT MAKES YOU THINK THAT YOU ARE
JUST BORN TO LOSE. BOUND TO LOSE. NO GOOD TO NOBODY. NO
GOOD FOR NOTHING. BECAUSE YOU ARE EITHER TOO OLD OR TOO
YOUNG OR TOO FAT OR TOO SLIM OR TOO UGLY OR TOO THIS OR TOO
THAT....SONGS THAT RUN YOU DOWN OR SONGS THAT POKE FUN AT
YOU ON ACCOUNT OF YOUR BAD LUCK OR YOUR HARD TRAVELING.

I AM OUT TO FIGHT THOSE KINDS OF SONGS TO MY VERY LAST
BREATH OF AIR AND MY LAST DROP OF BLOOD.

I AM OUT TO SING SONGS THAT WILL PROVE TO YOU THAT THIS
IS YOUR WORLD AND THAT IF IT HAS HIT YOU PRETTY HARD AND
KNOCKED YOU FOR A DOZEN LOOPS, NO MATTER HOW HARD IT'S RUN
YOU DOWN NOR ROLLED OVER YOU, NO MATTER WHAT COLOR, WHAT SIZE
YOU ARE, HOW YOU ARE BUILT, I AM OUT TO SING THE SONGS THAT
MAKE YOU TAKE PRIDE IN YOUR SELF AND IN YOUR WORK. AND THE
SONGS THAT I SING ARE MADE UP FOR THE MOST PART BY ALL SORTS
OF FOLKS JUST ABOUT LIKE YOU.

I COULD HIRE OUT TO THE OTHER SIDE, THE BIG MONEY SIDE,
and GET SEVERAL DOLLARS EVERY WEEK JUST TO QUIT SINGING MY
OWN KIND OF SONGS AND TO SING THE KIND THAT KNOCK YOU DOWN
STILL FARTHER AND THE ONES THAT MAKE FUN OF YOU EVEN MORE,
AND THE ONES THAT MAKE YOU THINK THAT YOU'VE NOT GOT ANY
SENSE AT ALL. BUT I DECIDED A LONG TIME AGO THAT I'D STARVE TO
DEATH BEFORE I'D SING ANY SUCH SONGS AS THAT. THE RADIO WAVES
AND YOUR JUKE BOXES AND YOUR MOVIES AND YOUR SONG BOOKS ARE
ALREADY LOADED DOWN AND RUNNING OVER WITH SUCH NO GOOD SONGS
AS THAT ANYHOW.

I LEAVE IT UP TO YOU TO WRITE IN TO ME. WRITE IN AND TELL
ME WHAT YOU THINK. GET YOUR WHOLE FAMILY AND YOUR FRIENDS AND
YOUR NEIGHBORS TO WRITE IN. TELL ME THAT YOU THINK SUCH A PRO-
GRAM SHOULD BE MORE THAN FIFTEEN MINUTES LONG.

God Blessed America
This Land Was made For you & me

This land is your land, this land is my land
From the California to the New York Island,
From the Redwood Forest, to the Gulf stream waters,
    God blessed America for me.

As I went walking that ribbon of highway
And saw above me that endless skyway,
And saw below me the golden valley, I said:
    God blessed America for me.

I roamed and rambled, and followed my footsteps
To the sparkling sands of her diamond deserts,
And all around me, a voice was sounding:
    God blessed America for me.

Was a big high wall there that tried to stop me
A sign was painted said: Private Property.
But on the back side it didn't say nothing —
    God blessed America for me.

When the sun come shining, then I was strolling
In wheat fields waving, and dust clouds rolling;
The voice was chanting as the fog was lifting:
    God blessed America for me.

One bright sunny morning in the shadow of the steeple
By the Relief office I saw my people —
As they stood hungry, I stood there wondering if
    God blessed America for me.

                    * all you can write is
                        what you see.

original copy
of this song

                            Woody G.
                            N.Y., N.Y., N.Y.
                            Feb. 23, 1940
                            43rd st & 6th Ave.,
                            Hanover House

THIS LAND IS YOUR LAND
ROBERT SANTELLI

It's been called one of the greatest songs ever written about America, a paean to the nation's boundless natural beauty and a populist ode to its people. It's a song so simple and direct that for more than a half century schoolchildren have sung it in their classrooms, marking one of the first times they expressed their patriotism in song, outside of the national anthem. There was even a time when some people sought to make "This Land Is Your Land" our *new* national anthem, arguing that it was much easier to sing than "The Star-Spangled Banner," and it celebrated not victory in battle but triumph of spirit.

Perhaps its most iconic moment, its true measure of greatness, occurred in January 2009 in Washington, DC, at the celebration of the inauguration of President Barack Obama, the nation's forty-fourth president and the first African American elected to the office. The massive crowd that had come to celebrate this momentous occasion was too excited to notice the freezing temperatures in the nation's capital. Millions more around the country and the world watched with eager anticipation on television, amazed and proud that America chose an African American to lead and guide them. It was history in the making, right there in front of the US Capitol on January 20, when Obama put his left hand on the Bible and took his sacred oath to uphold the Constitution of the United States of America.

A different kind of history was made a few days earlier in front of the Lincoln Memorial, the same place where, in the summer of 1963, Dr. Martin Luther King Jr. delivered his inspiring "I Have a Dream" speech. Thousands were jammed on both sides of the Reflecting Pool. Together they welcomed to the stage the great American folk singer Pete Seeger, his grandson Tao Rodriguez, and Bruce Springsteen, the songwriter and performer whose words and music often echo the country's greatness as well as its challenges. They were there to sing to America. Their song of choice: "This Land Is Your Land."

There was Pete, the grizzled guardian of the American folk music tradition and advocate of the idea that music can fight inequality and oppression—and win. Clad in a simple shirt and woolen cap, banjo draped around him, Pete looked like a sea-shanty-singing sailor on leave. Springsteen wore a sharp blue button-down coat and came onstage with an acoustic guitar. And with Tao, on Pete's count, together they honored the day and the inauguration that would soon follow with a deeply emotional version of Woody Guthrie's greatest song. If ever this land was our land, if ever the promise of the song was true and possible, it was that day, that moment, when that song took all the red, white, and blue fibers of our hearts and wove them into one beautiful celebration of the great American experiment in democracy.

Twelve years later, on the steps of the US Capitol, pop superstar Jennifer Lopez sang "This Land Is Your Land" during President Joe Biden's inauguration. Though the singing style was different, the meaning was the same. Woody Guthrie was surely smiling wherever his soul rested.

This song, one of such magnitude and inspiration, had unremarkable origins. Guthrie wrote the song on February 23, 1940, in New York. At the time, he had just arrived in the city from Oklahoma, meeting a blizzard along the way and nearly freezing to death along the highway. He had hoped to link up with the actor Will Geer, whom Guthrie had befriended in California. Geer convinced Guthrie that there was work for him in New York, and so he had come east, anxious to see what the future would bring.

Guthrie was residing in Hanover House, a fleabag flophouse at 43rd Street and 6th Avenue in midtown Manhattan the day he wrote "This Land Is Your Land." We know this because, as with so many songs he wrote, Guthrie was careful to mark the date, sign it, and describe where he wrote it.

Writing in black ink on lined, loose-leaf paper, Guthrie also added fabric reinforcements where the binder holes were. Organized, neat, and precise people do this sort of thing; Guthrie was none of those. Often disheveled, not caring much about his appearance, this was Woody Guthrie. Yet when it came to his writing, he was all business, even numbering the pages ("This Land" is page 178) in one of his many song notebooks. At the bottom of the page, he wrote a simple truth: "All you can write is what you see." And he gave it an asterisk to signify importance and attract attention.

"This Land Is Your Land" was part of a number of new songs Guthrie wrote over a three-week period in late February and early March, including "Jesus Christ," in which Guthrie emphasized Jesus's compassion for the poor and wrote below the lyrics, "I got to thinking about what Jesus said, and what if He was to walk into New York City and preach like he use [sic] to. They'd lock Him back in Jail as sure as you're reading this."

It probably wasn't immediately evident to Guthrie after writing "This Land Is Your Land" that he had written the most important song of his life. He didn't race into the studio to record it. He didn't even play it outside his hotel room in the first few weeks after he had written it. On February 25th, Guthrie performed at a New York benefit for Spanish Civil War refugees and didn't sing it, preferring to do yet another new song, one called "Why Do You Stand There in the Rain?"

In fact, "This Land Is Your Land" had a number of titles before it was officially named. It began as "God Blessed America." However, on the original loose-leaf lyric sheet, you can see a penciled cross out of the title and in its place, a new title, "This Land Is Made for You and Me," and even part of that title was crossed out, leaving only the words "This Land" untouched by editing.

An undated acetate recording of the song, now in the collection of the Smithsonian Institution, has the title to the tune as "This Land Was Made for You and Me." When Guthrie recorded the song for folk music producer Moe Asch in 1944, Asch listed the song as "This Land Is My Land." In 1946 a shorter version of the song was recorded as "This Land Is Your Land." Few songs have had a more difficult time getting a permanent title.

So where did Guthrie gain the inspiration to write "This Land Is Your Land"? All research points to Irving Berlin's "God Bless America," the Russian-born immigrant's euphoric celebration of America written during World War I, a couple of decades before Guthrie wrote "God Blessed America."

Berlin had stashed away the song for two decades before Kate Smith, the popular singer and host of *The Kate Smith Hour*, was looking for a fresh song to sing on Armistice Day (later known as Veterans Day) in November 1938. Smith was known for singing patriotic songs and for her American ardor. Her manager, Ted Collins, reached out to Berlin, asking the famous composer if he had any patriotic songs Smith might sing on her radio show. Berlin recalled "God Bless America." After revising the song a bit, he gave it to Smith, who sang it with all the strength and vitality she could muster, given the dark clouds of war hovering in Europe (the start of World War II was less than a year away).

Kate Smith made radio history with "God Bless America." In short, the song was a sensation. Smith sang it again on Thanksgiving, and even more accolades came her way. She recorded the song in 1939, and at once it became a bestseller. It played on the radio; it was popular on jukeboxes. People began to sing it at public events. Smith sang it at patriotic functions and rallies. From countless Victrolas in American homes, "God Bless America" filled living rooms and elevated the spirit of America. It was inescapable.

Undoubtedly, Woody Guthrie heard "God Bless America" often. Maybe he even got sick of it. Nowhere did he explicitly write about the song or about Berlin. Despite this, many Guthrie experts believe he came to hate the song or, at the very least, was seriously annoyed by it. It is probable that he felt that way. But it's also possible that he admired the song but felt its lyrics hardly told the whole story of America.

That Guthrie originally called his song "God Blessed America" clearly references Berlin's "God Bless America." And when you compare the lyrics Guthrie wrote in "This Land Is Your Land" to the lyrics of "God Bless America," there are strong similarities. For instance, Berlin wrote, "From the mountains, to the prairies/To the oceans white with foam/God bless America, my home sweet home." Guthrie countered with "From California to the Staten Island/From the Redwood Forest, to the Gulf stream waters/God blessed America for me." Later, he would change "Staten Island" to "New York Island" and would eliminate "God blessed

America for me" and replace it with "This land was made for you and me." He put all of this to the melody of a popular Carter Family gospel song, "When the World's on Fire," recorded in 1930.

The lyrical similarities and images are obvious. But the two songs veer off in different directions. A Russian Jew and an immigrant, Berlin came to America in the late nineteenth century, discovered the American Dream, and lived it like he owned it—he wrote his song out of pride and passion for America. He became a wealthy man and one of the greatest American composers of the twentieth century.

Early on in his life, Berlin saw poverty, oppression, and immigrant economic injustice in New York City, but he did not write about it in "God Bless America," emphasizing only the goodness of democracy and the endless promise of a good and decent life. He wrote the song in 1918, a time when America's doughboys were fighting in France to make the world "safe for democracy." It was easy to embrace America.

Guthrie, on the other hand, wrote "This Land Is Your Land" on the tail end of the Great Depression. He, too, saw poverty, oppression, and economic injustice. He saw it in Oklahoma, the Texas Panhandle, up and down California, and in New York City. Like Berlin, he saw beauty and promise in the American land, but he also saw America's underbelly. Unlike Berlin, he didn't ignore it.

Most Americans know only the first three verses of "This Land Is Your Land." In all, there are six, and two of the last three—a third of the song—are not as sunny or optimistic as the first three:

> Was a big high wall there that tried to stop me
> A sign was painted said: Private Property.
> But on the back side it didn't say nothing—
> God blessed America for me.

> When the sun come shining, then I was strolling
> In wheat fields waving, and dust clouds rolling;
> The voice was chanting as the fog was lifting:
> God blessed America for me.

> One bright sunny morning in the shadow of the steeple
> By the Relief Office I saw my people—
> As they stood hungry, I stood there wondering if
> God blessed America for me.

Later the end line of each verse was changed to "This land was made for you and me."

Most people who believe "This Land Is Your Land" is a patriotic song, in the same category as "God Bless America," could never sing the last three verses and feel good about it. Guthrie knew that the American Experiment, the *idea* of America, was a bold and beautiful thing. But the *reality* of America was something else. It was not perfect. It was not all-inclusive. In Guthrie's song, God might have blessed America for some people, but not all. All he could write was what he saw, and what he saw wasn't right.

Folkways Records included Woody's 1946 recording of "This Land Is Your Land" on the album *Work Songs to Grow On,* and it was promoted now as a children's song, given its easy-to-learn melody. This version of the song left out the controversial lyrics that Guthrie included in his 1944 recording. The edited lyrics set in motion the song's reputation as a patriotic salute to America. By the mid-1950s, "This Land Is Your Land" was being included in many songbooks that found their way into public school music classes, and artists like Pete Seeger's group, the Weavers, began to record the song.

Just as it was beginning to be noticed as a significant American folk song, Guthrie was beginning to show signs of Huntington's disease. By the early 1950s, his writing grew erratic and the performances stopped. He spent the rest of the decade in and out of the hospital before being consigned to Greystone Park Psychiatric Hospital in Morris Plains, New Jersey, for the last five years of his life.

It was Pete Seeger who popularized the song, playing it at church functions, summer camps, progressive schools, and concerts, despite the heavy cloak of right-wing vitriol that all but smothered his reputation and career in the 1950s. The folk revival saved Seeger and enabled "This Land Is Your Land" to endure. By the time of Guthrie's death in 1967, the song had become a concert staple, not just for Seeger, but for many other folk performers who saw Guthrie and Seeger as mentors and patriarchs of modern American folk music.

Both the political left and the political right embraced the song. Seeger and the "new Woody Guthrie," Bob Dylan, sang the song. So did the Mormon Tabernacle Choir. Over time, "This Land Is Your Land" became one of the most recognizable songs in all America. In 2012, the centennial year of Guthrie's birth, dozens of versions of the song surfaced in many languages from around the world, proving that "This Land Is Your Land" was no longer just an American song. This international anthem can be found wherever people understand that music can affect political and social change, and that this land—your land, our land—was made for you and for me and not just for the privileged few.

Today, you can view the original lyric sheet for "This Land Is Your Land" at the Woody Guthrie Center in Tulsa, OK. Its presentation in a glass case to protect it from natural light and harsh temperatures and humidity is not unlike what one would expect upon seeing other important historical documents, like the Declaration of Independence and the Gettysburg Address.

Seeing it can send a shiver up one's spine. Singing it fortifies our spirit. Teaching it to the next generation of Americans is a patriotic act.

WOODY GUTHRIE

DOUGLAS BRINKLEY

Woody Guthrie is a voice I trust. Since childhood, his songs have stuck to my ribs and been part of my lexicon. They're as comfortable as an old pair of blue jeans or a faded flannel shirt. There's no hocus-pocus going on. No self-conscious contrivance. Just simple art: direct and visceral, with a touch of wry humor. In many songs he managed to uplift and agitate simultaneously. Every lyric Guthrie ever wrote was built to last, to be sung until the end of time.

In a strife-ridden world, Guthrie used his songs as artillery, fusing rural Oklahoma realism and New Deal progressivism into hopeful vaccines against systemic oppression. Whenever I listen to gems like "Pastures of Plenty" or "This Land Is Your Land," I'm enveloped in a familiar, homey comfort while also hearing echoes of Matthew 5:1-5: "Blessed are the meek, for they shall inherit the earth."

Guthrie's songs don't stand still. They have an elasticity that makes them timeless, open to revision and reinterpretation. In 1968, a year after Guthrie's death, Pete Seeger and Jimmie Collier were about to sing "This Land Is Your Land" at the Poor People's Campaign in Washington, D.C., when they were upbraided by Lakota Sioux activist Henry Crow Dog. "This land isn't your land," he reminded them. "It belongs to me." Struck and moved by the incident, Seeger later began performing the song with a new verse that honored the Native American perspective:

> This land is your land, but it once was my land
> Before we sold you Manhattan Island
> You pushed our nations to the reservations
> This land was stole by you from me.

Over the years, others have followed Seeger's example, transforming "This Land Is Your Land" into an environmental ballad ("the sun was shining, but the hazes hid it"), an environmentalist anthem ("we've logged the forests we've mined the mountains"), and on and on. I can only imagine that somewhere up in heaven, the Dustbowl songwriter who'd chronicled common peoples' struggles against power and injustice must be nodding his approval.

Not long ago, I delivered a commencement address at St. Edwards University in Austin, Texas, evoking Guthrie's song "Deportee," which he wrote as a poignant protest against American arrogance and rank disregard of Mexicans. In the context of recent years, when former President Donald Trump demonized Mexicans as "rapists" and began building a multi-billion-dollar border wall as a symbol of exclusion and bigotry, the seventy-year-old song still resonated mightily.

Guthrie was in New York City on January 29, 1948, when he read the tragic story of a U.S. Immigration Services airplane crashing in Los Gatos, California. Thirty-two people had died: an American immigration guard, three flight crew, and twenty-eight *braceros* farmworkers. Guthrie mourned the lives lost, and his humanitarian ire was inflamed by the fact that *The New York Times* story named the four white Americans killed in the crash but lumped the Mexican victims as merely nameless "deportees" – throwaway fruit-pickers not worthy of memorialization. Guthrie's response was "Deportee," which eulogized the Mexican dead with symbolic names and condemned the systems that exploited and scorned them:

> **Goodbye to my Juan, goodbye Rosalita,**
> **Adios mis amigos, Jesus y Maria;**
> **You won't have your names when you ride the big airplane**
> **All they will call you will be 'deportees'**

Guthrie's elegy had a powerful and lasting effect on me. During the 1980s, as a graduate student in U.S. history at Georgetown University, I sang and played "Deportee" on guitar at blue-smoke coffeehouses and on European street corners, making it a mainstay of my pass-the-basket repertoire. I even took a shot at writing my own last verse, centered on how the Holy Cross brothers had buried the farmworkers all together in Fresno, under a marker identifying them only as "Mexicans."

> **Shovels were lifted, to dig a mass grave.**
> **No rosary was counted.**
> **No eulogy gave.**
> **Callin' *familia* would have cost 'em a fee.**
> **And all those burned bodies were just deportees.**

So yes, Woody Guthrie's music still resonates in America today, his lyrics and melodies permanent yet malleable, part of the Great American Songbook but also holy outliers urging on the better angels of our nature. His records, especially the Smithsonian and Folkways recordings by Alan Lomax and Moses Asch, are foundational heirlooms like Lincoln's Gettysburg Address or Martin Luther King, Jr.'s "I Have A Dream" speech. More than any other voice from America's musical past, Guthrie's still carries, a raw and clear-sighted champion for the dignity of honest work and the spiritual yearning for pastures of plenty.

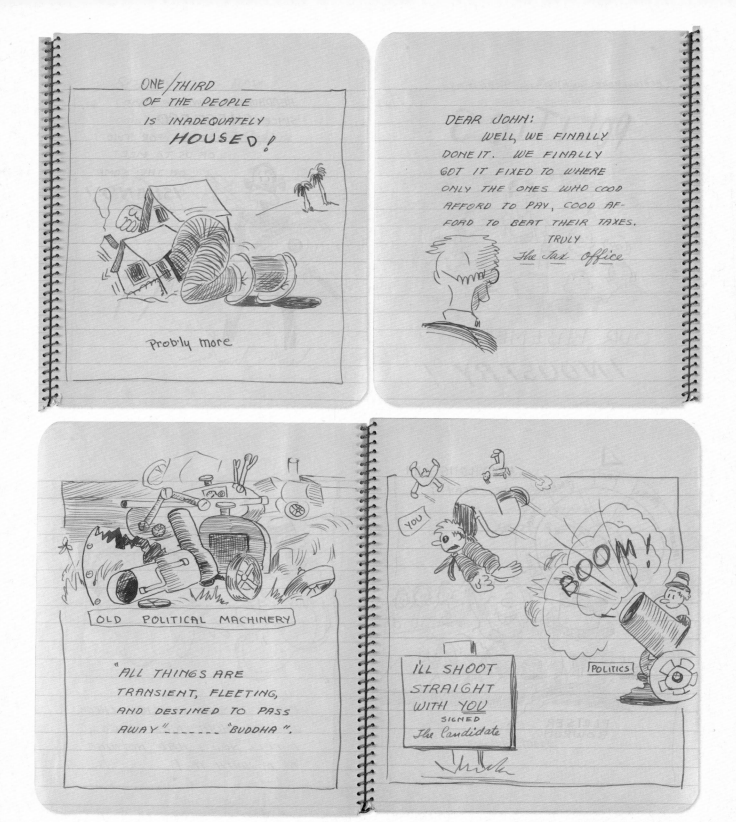

Political cartoons from 1939 notebooks.

Woody wrote a column called "Woody Sez" for the left-wing *People's Daily World* newspaper in Los Angeles in the late 1930s. The column, always illustrated with one of his cartoons, dealt with the issues of the day and often promoted political solutions for workers' rights, human injustices, and political corruption. These cartoons are from his personal notebooks.

CHAPTER FOUR

Things That Are Right and Things That Are Wrong

ON WOODY GUTHRIE

CHUCK D

I first learned about Woody back when I was an elementary school student growing up in New York during the '60s and early '70s. We sang folk songs by Woody, Pete Seeger, and Peter, Paul and Mary. We sang all of their songs. It was right around the time that Woody passed away, so people were really remembering his works at that time. As I kid, I was drawn to Woody's music without really knowing who he was. I just liked the way his songs were sung.

Over time, I learned about his life, the way he did things, this incredible journey he took through America. Woody had this wanderlust for culture and spirit and soul. And he connected pretty much everything he did and wrote to the country. He told the truth about America. He lived that truth and told it through his songs. He lived in Oklahoma and California and New York, and he traveled up and down the north and the south. He saw it all. He saw the fullness of the United States of America.

"This Land Is Your Land"—that song says it all. America is a beautiful terrain of earth, and you just want its rules and laws to be as mighty as the land, to be exactly what they are on paper, as Dr. Martin Luther King Jr. said. From east to west, it's a stunning piece of property that no one really can own. You want everybody to have access to it all. Woody certainly did. I do, too.

Woody was this very real person who wrote about real things. His lyrics were strong and solid, to the point and clear. His presentation had a raw grit to it; his songs were on the edge of country music and also on the edge of the future of rock & roll and hip-hop. He was rapping in a lot of the songs before the term even existed.

You could get in a fight with him, and if what you were fighting with were words, you'd lose. He was a killer. He couldn't stop writing. He wrote musical editorials nonstop. Woody was a voice for the voiceless. If he were around today, he'd be writing about t he dumbass-ification that we see in politics every day now. He'd go after them all. He'd use sight, sound, story, and style, and he'd pound those politicians. Nobody could do it better.

Woody created a template that I try to follow in my career: to be very economical with lyrics and use powerful words. Young people, like I was when I first heard his songs, are able to grab those words if their ears and minds are big enough to let them in.

When I was a kid, I wanted to be a visual artist or a sports announcer more than anything else. If someone said to me that I would one day be in the Rock & Roll Hall of Fame and would win the Woody Guthrie Prize, I would have slapped them because I would have thought they were feeding me some shit. But it happened. And over time, I checked out Woody's art and I realized that we had something else in common, which made me feel pretty good. His art speaks to me like his songs do.

You can hear a lot of Woody Guthrie in Public Enemy. He's there all around the lyrics and the meaning behind them. I think if he was around today—and I wish he was—he would have Public Enemy on his playlist.

*** From tales and stories I heard all down south and out west about the outlaw, Pretty Boy Floyd. I love a good man outside the law just as much as I hate a bad man inside the law.   WWGeee

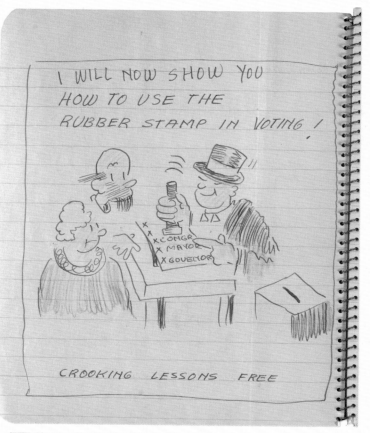

YOU FASCISTS BOUND TO LOSE
BY WOODY GUTHRIE
74 Charles St., N.Y. CITY   12¢7-'42

I'm a gonna tell you fascists, you may be surprised,
Th' free people in this world are all gettin' organized!
        You're bound to lose,
        You fascists bound to lose!
Along that Russian border I heard the people say
We killed ten thousand Nazis in just a single day!
        You're bound to lose,
        You fascists bound to lose!

CHORUS: ALL OF YOU FASCISTS BOUND TO LOSE
               ALL OF YOU FASCISTS GONNA LOSE
               ALL OF YOU FASCISTS GONNA LOSE, BOYS,
            YOU'RE BOUND TO LOSE, YOU FASCISTS BOUND TO LOSE!

Race hatred cannot stop us, this one thing I know,
The Union's gettin' stronger and Jim Crow's got to go!
        You're bound to lose,
        You fascists bound to lose!
You cannot divide us nor keep us split apart,
Us common folks is on the march, got freedom in our heart,
        You're bound to lose,
        You fascists bound to lose!   (CHORUS AGAIN)

There'll be no isolaters, no cowards to appease;
I'm gonna fight to win the common peoples peace!
        You're bound to lose,
        You fascists bound to lose!
People of every color fighting side by side
Marching cross the fields where a million fascists died!
        You're bound to lose, you fascists bound to lose!

Men and women together, yes, and children, too!
We'll rid this world of robbers before this war is through!
        You're bound to lose,
        You fascists bound to lose!
Take me to the battle, hand to me my gun,
I'll bring an end to slavery before this world is won!
        You're bound to lose,
        You fascists bound to lose!

*This goes to the tune of "If I Lose Lemme Lose" - You
know the one I hum all of the time* Composed on Pearl Harbor Day
*"If I lose my Honey
lemme lose!" Can you
erase those pencil words
on your music and make
put these words instead*
December 7th, 1942, exactly one year after Pearl
Harbor. At 74 Charles Street, New York City, by
Woody Guthrie. (W.W. Guthrie)
        *DEDICATED to the end of this war and all
forms and shapes and sizes of human slavery so
that no such calamity as Pearl Harbor can overtake
This is one Alan wants.
Important. Quick. Rush.
any nation, any man, woman or child, anywhere in
this world ever again.

X X *Thanks* X xXX
X xxx *X mama —*
        X X X X X
*W.W. (Woody) Guthrie
original song.*

New York City, ca. 1944.

MY BIG GIBSON
GUITAR HAS GOT A
SIGN I PAINTED ON
IT, SAYS, "THIS MACHINE
KILLS FASCISTS".

New York City, 1943.

and it means just
what it says too

Woody in the army, Fort Dix, NJ, 1945.

Maybe I could talk to you about fascism.

It is a big word and it hides in some pretty little places.

It is nothing in the world but greed for profit and greed for the power to hurt and make slaves out of the people.

Fascism is a bully too dumb and too thick skulled to think out a mental reason or explanation or a hope or a plan for us. So it says the world belongs to the bullies and the gangsters who grab clubs and guns the quickest and rob and kill us first – before we can get ready mentally and bodily to fight back. But fascism can no more control the world than a bunch of pool hall gamblers and thugs can control America. Because all of the laws of man working in nature and history and evolution say for all human beings to come always closer and closer together – to know and understand all races, creeds, and colors better; and fascism says for us to split ourselves up into the thousand cliques and klans and beat our own chains of slavery onto our ankles by wasting our strength fighting our friend and neighbor – and allowing the fascists to nip us off one by one, little by little, group by group.... How could I ever get this book wrote full unless some of it was cussing out fascism?

DON'T KILL MY BABY AND MY SON
(Woody)

.........for a year or so my dad was undersheriff of Okemah,
Oklahoma, and he used to tell me many a sad tale about that
old black jailhouse. I remember one night when I was about
eight or nine years old that I was caught out after dark and
had to walk through the old dark town after curfew hour - and
I was barefooted on the sidewalk - so there wasn't a sound to
be heard - except a wild and blood curdling moan that filled
the whole town, and it kept getting louder as I walked down
the street to the old rock jailhouse. And I heard a negro
lady sticking her head through the jailhouse bars and moaning
at the top of her voice. That was lonesomer than all of the
animals of the wild places that I've run onto, and I've slept
many a night on the desert alone, and in the hills and mountains, and can listen to a panther or a coyote and tell you
what's on his mind by the tone of his yell. This negro lady
had a right new baby, and a son that was doomed to hang by her
dead body with the rise of the morning wind, and my dad told
me the whole story. Several years has gone by and I wrote this
song down, because that lady's wail went further, went higher,
and went deeper than any sermon or radio broadcast I ever heard..

As I walked down that old dark town
In the town where I was born -
I heard the saddest lonesome moan
I ever heard before.
My hair it trembled at the roots
Cold chills run down my spine,
As I drew near that jail house
I heard this deathly cry:

Chorus: O, don't kill my baby and my son,
           O, don't kill my baby and my son.
           You can stretch my neck on that old river bridge,
           But don't kill my baby and my son.

Now, I've hear the cries of a panther,
Now, I've heard the coyotes yell,
But that long, lonesome cry shook the whole wide world
And it come from the cell of the jail.
Yes, I've heard the screech owls screeching,
And the hoot owls that hoot in the night,
But the graveyard itself is happy compared
To the voice in that jailhouse that night.

Chorus.

Then I saw a picture on a postcard
It showed the Canadian River Bridge,
Three bodies hanging to swing in the wind,
A mother and two sons they'd lynched.
There a wild wind blows down the river,
There's a wild wind blows through the trees,
There's a wild wind that blows 'round this wide wide world,
And here's what the wild winds say:

Chorus.

218

CLEAR
CLOUDY
RAIN
SNOW

It Is Jim Crow

I see slavery walking through my land
I see slavery walking through my land
I see his footsteps everywhere I go
And his name it is Jim Crow
            It is Jim Crow

In Philadelphia he stopped our trolley cars
In Philadelphia he stopped our trolley cars
He slowed our factory down and he caused our blood to flow
And his name it is Jim Crow
            it is Jim Crow

In Detroit he broke into our home
In Detroit he broke into our home
One hundred people killed
and a hundred thousand chained
And his name it is Jim Crow
            it is Jim Crow.

CLEAR
CLOUDY
RAIN
SNOW

In Beaumont he killed us on the street
In Beaumont he killed us on the street
He stopped our shipping dead
and my own dear people bled
And his name it is Jim Crow
            it is Jim Crow

who pays money to keep Jim Crow alive?
who pays money to keep Jim Crow alive?
He is hate. He is fear.
He is the cause of blood and tears
And his name it is Jim Crow
            it is Jim Crow

He keeps us separated on the trains
He keeps us separated on the trains
and on mountains and on plains
'Round our legs he puts his chains
And his name it is Jim Crow
            it is Jim Crow

            8-6-1944
            Coney Island

Woody was deeply affected by his earliest experiences witnessing racism as a boy in Okemah, OK. When he arrived in New York City in the early 1940s, he formed deep friendships with blues musicians Huddie Ledbetter (a.k.a. Lead Belly), Sonny Terry, and Brownie McGhee, whom he performed and toured with. He became a true activist, challenging racism head on. In the 1950s, while living on Stetson Kennedy's Beluthahatchee, FL, property, they were often attacked by KKK members. Raised with firearms as a boy, Woody had no trouble returning the fire.

SLIPKNOT

Did you ever see a hangman tie a slip knot?
" " " " " " " " " "

Yes, I seen it a many a time, and he winds, and he winds,
and after thirteen times, he ties a slipknot.

Tell, me Will that slipknot slip? No! It will not!
" " " " " " " " "

It will slip down round your neck, but it wont slip back again,
That slipknot. That slipknot! O'that slipknot!

Did you ever lose a brother in on that slipknot?
" " " " " " " " "

Yes. My brother was a slave,,,,, he tried to escape......
and they drug him to his grave with a slipknot.

Did you ever lose your father in that slipknot?
" " " " " " " " " "

(Yes.) They hung him from a pole, and they shot him full of holes.
And they left him hang to rot in that slipknot.

Who makes the laws for that slipknot?
" " " " " " " " "

Who says who will go to the calaboose —
and get the hangman's noose, get that slipknot?

I dont know who makes the law of that slipknot.
" " " " " " " " " "

But the bones of many a men are a whistling in the wind.
Just because they tie their laws with a slipknot.

* Dedicated to the many
negro mothers, fathers, and sons
alike, that was lynched and
hanged under the bridge of the
Canadian River, seven miles
south of Okemah, Okla., and to
the day when such will be no
more.

WOODY G
2-29-40 N.Y.

AAA-6790 9/100

BOSS
WATCHES
HAND
WORK
TILL SUNDOWN.

AAA-7090

HAND GIVES BOSS
LOAF OF BREAD

AAA-9090

BOSS
PAYS
HAND

AAA-8090

HAND BUYS
LOAF OF BREAD

146

HANDS
KIDS
EAT
BREAD

CRIES
FOR
MORE

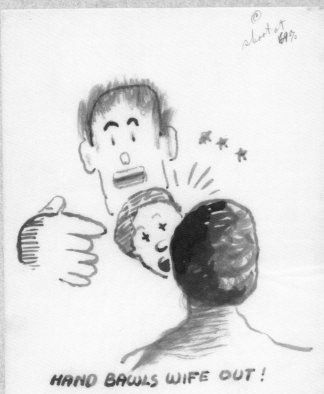

HAND BAWLS WIFE OUT!

WIFE BAWLS HAND OUT!

147

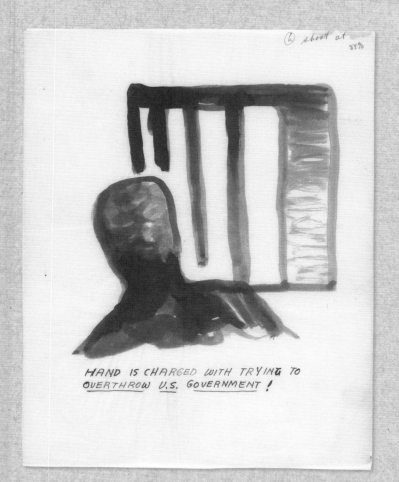

HAND IS CHARGED WITH TRYING TO OVERTHROW U.S. GOVERNMENT!

I guess the first time I heard about a union, I wasn't no more than eight years old. What I heard was the story of the two rabbits. It was a he rabbit and a she rabbit that a pack of hounds chased all over the countryside. And finally these rabbits they holed up in a hollow log. And outside the dogs were howling. And the he rabbit turned to she rabbit, and he said, "What do we do now?" And the she rabbit, she just give him a wink. She says, "We'll stay here till we outnumber 'em."

West. West. I know you of old
You robbed my poor pockets of silver and gold
I pounded this pavement for 67 days
Trying to get me my two dollar raise.

Westinghouse Westinghouse I know you of old
You'd rather to see me go hungry and cold
I'd rather die on my feet than to beg on my knees
You wrecked my old daddy but you'll never get me.

Westinghouse! Westinghouse! I know you of old.
You never did keep true the promise you told
If I wait for a square deal from old Mister Price
I would live in the dumps with the bugs and the lice.

All through the war I walked through your gate
You told me be patient, you told me to wait
Today I come down to speak to you again
And I met ~~Sheriff Monahan~~ with his state trooper men.
the good governor

Westinghouse Westinghouse
Tune: (Rye Whiskey)
by Woody Guthrie
Peter Seeger

Made up & Sung for
Pittsburgh Strikers

WESTINGHOUSE
WESTINGHOUSE

With Pete Seeger in Oklahoma City, ca. 1941.

150

Union maid
Roll Union on
Union Train coming
Pittsburgh! Lord God!
Join The Union
Parley Vous
Hold The Fort
my Union card
Union Feeling
Poor old mr. Price

2 Buclas a day
67 days Today

This is the set list from a Pittsburgh strikers' rally, performed on the sixty-seventh day of the strike. The workers were asking for a raise of "2 Bucks a day."

UNION MAID

There once was a union maid
She never was afraid
Of the goons and the ginks and the company finks
And the deputy sheriff that made the raid.
She went to the union hall
When a meeting it was called,
And when the company boys come around
She always stood her ground,

CHORUS:

                    Oh, you can8t scare me,
                    I'm sticking to the union,
                    I'm sticking to the union,
                    I'm sticking to the union.
                    No, you can't scare me,
                    I'm sticking to the union,
                    I'm sticking to the union
                    Till the day I die.

This union gal was wise
To the tricks of the company spies,
She couldn't be fooled by the company stool
She'd always organize the guys,
She always got her way
When she fought for better pay,
xxxxxxxxxxx She'd show her card
To the national guard
And here is what she'd say,
                    ((((CHORUS)))))

You gals that wanta be free
Take a little tip from me,
Grab you a man that's a union man,
And join the ladies auxilliary,
Married life ain't hard
If you're packing a union card,
A married man lives a happy life
When he's got him a union wife!
                    (((CHORUS)))))))

            30***

27

Nazism took a friend of mine out for a wild naked ride tonight in a truck.

Fascism ripped off the clothes and pure hate beat her skin to big red whelps.

Ignorance left her laying out in the weeds to die, but her union spirit picked her up and walked her back to town nine miles and a half.

Woody in his army uniform, Scott Field, IL, 1945.

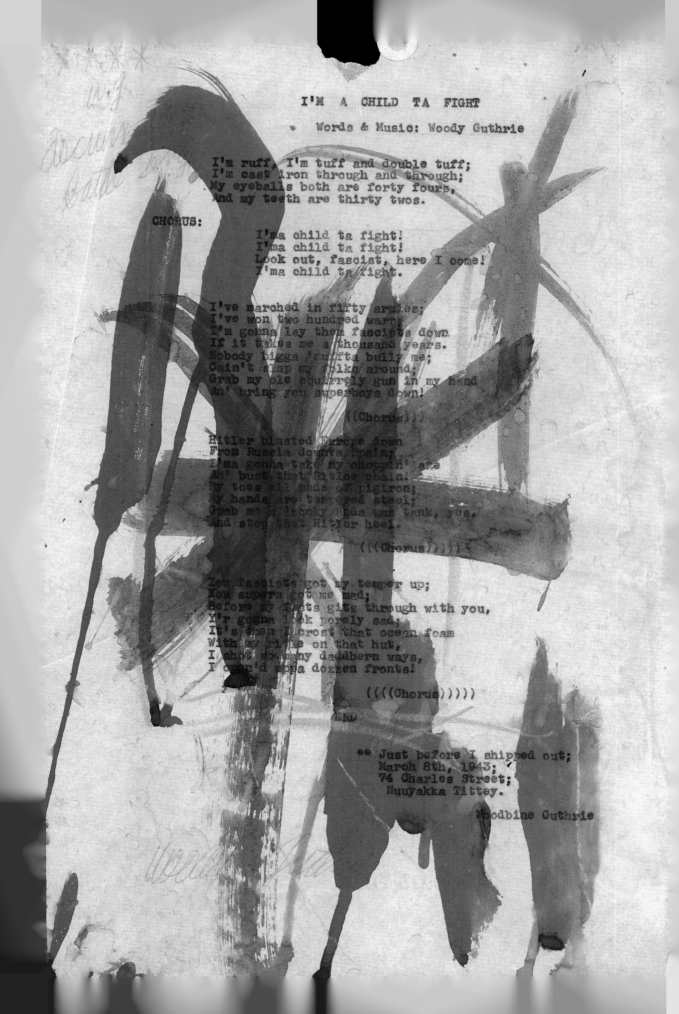

I'M A CHILD TA FIGHT

Words & Music: Woody Guthrie

I'm ruff, I'm tuff and double tuff;
I'm cast iron through and through;
My eyeballs both are forty fours,
And my teeth are thirty twos.

CHORUS:

I'ma child ta fight!
I'ma child ta fight!
Look out, fascist, here I come!
I'ma child ta fight.

I've marched in fifty armies;
I've won two hundred wars;
I'm gonna lay them fascists down
If it takes me a thousand years.
Nobody bigga 'nufta bully me;
Cain't slap my folks around;
Grab my ole squirrely gun in my hand
An' bring you superboys down!

((Chorus)))

Hitler blasted Europe down
From Russia downta Spain;
I'ma gonna take my choppin' axe
An' bust that Hitler chain!
My toes all made of pigiron;
My hands are tempered steel;
Grab me a looky onda war tank, yes,
And stop that Hitler heel.

(((Chorus)))))

You fascists got my temper up;
You supers got me mad;
Before my fists gits through with you,
Y'r gonna look porely sad;
It's when I crost that ocean foam
With my rifle on that hut,
I shot so many daddbern ways,
I open'd up a dozzen fronts!

((((Chorus)))))

END

** Just before I shipped out;
March 8th, 1943;
74 Charles Street;
Nuuyakka Tittey.

Woodbine Guthrie

TOP LEFT: Singing for African American soldiers, 1943.

BOTTOM LEFT: Singing for U.S.O. Club, Jewish Welfare Board, 1943.

RIGHT: Singing for American Club for Indian Seamen, 1943.

There's
Hitler gotta be
beat
I got to really
think about that.
Fact is, right about now,
Thats all there is for me
To think about.
'Cause all Hitler is thinkin' about
Is beatin' me.

"TALKING SAILOR"

6

Post

IN BED WITH MY WOMAN JUST A SINGING THE BLUES
HEARD THE RADIO TELLING THE NEWS
SAID THE BIG RED ARMY TOOK A HUNDRED TOWNS
AND THE ALLIES DROPPING THEM TWO TON BOMBS
   STARTED HOLLERING. YELLING.. DANCING UP AND DOWN LIKE A B.F.

DOOR BELL RUNG AND IN COME A MAN
SIGNED MY NAME I GOT A TELEGRAM
SAID "IF YOU WANT TO TAKE A VACATION TRIP
GOT A DISHWASHING JOB ON A LIBERTY SHIP."
   WOMAN A CRYING.   ME A FLYING. OUT THE DOOR AND DOWN THE LINE

'BOUT TWO MINUTES I RUN TEN BLOCKS.
COME TO MY SHIP DOWN BY THE DOCKS.
I WALKED UP THE PLANK AND I SIGNED MY NAME
I BLOWED THAT WHISTLE AND WAS GONE AGAIN
   RIGHT ON OUT AND DOWN THE STREAM
   SHIPS JUST AS FAR AS MY EYE COULD SEE
   WOMAN A WAITING.

SHIP'S LOADED DOWN WITH T.N.T.
ALL OUT ACROSS THIS ROLLING SEA
STOOD ON THE DECK AND WATCHED THE FISHES SWIM
PRAYING THEM FISH WASN'T MADE OUT OF TIN
   SHARKS. PORPOISES. JELLYBEANS. RAINBOW TROUTS. MUDCATS.
   JUGARS. ROCK PERCH. ALLIGATOR GAR. FLYING FISH. ALL OVER
   THAT WATER.

THIS CONVOY'S THE BIGGEST I EVER DID SEE
STRETCHES ALL THE WAY OUT ACROSS THE SEA
AND THE SHIPS BLOW THEIR WHISTLES AND RING THEIR BELLS
GONNA BLOW THEM FASCISTS ALL TO HELL
   WIN SOME FREEDOM. LIBERTY. JOBS. STUFF LIKE THAT.

WALK TO THE TAIL AND STAND ON THE STERN
LOOK AT THE BIG GRASS SCREW BLADE TURN
LISTEN TO THE SOUND OF THE ENGINE POUND
GAINS SIXTEEN FEET EVERYTIME IT GOES AROUND
   GETTING CLOSER AND CLOSER. LOOK OUT YOU BLACK MARKET FASCISTS

I'M JUST ONE OF THE MERCHANT CREW
I BELONG TO THE UNION CALLED THE NMU

FIGHTING MAN FROM MY HEAD TO TOE
I'M USA AND CIO
   FIGHTING OUT HERE ON THE WATERS
   TO WIN SOME FREEDOM ON THE LAND.

U.S. Army base, Scott Field, IL, 1945.

Wouldn't it be funny to just kind of come along here and be homed and raised and play and work and get growed up and married and have a flock of kids and everything like that and look everywhere and not see no war going on? I got an idea how good it would feel – it would feel like getting out of a jail, and getting a good job at good pay and spending every night in another kind of arms that wouldn't kill you.

Throughout World War II, Woody served in the Merchant Marines. He was inducted into the army on May 7, 1945, the day Germany surrendered.

I took a bath this morning in six war speeches and a sprinkle of peace. Looks like everybody is declaring war against the forces of force. That's what you get for building up a big war machine. It scares your neighbors into jumping on you, and then of course they themselves have to use force, so you are against their force and they're against yours. Looks like the ring has been drawed and the marbles are all in. The millionaires has throwed their silk hats and our last set of drawers in the ring. The fuse is lit and the cannon is set, and somebody is in for a frailing. I would like to see every single soldier on every single side, just take off your helmet, unbuckle your kit, lay down your rifle, and set down at the side of some shady lane, and say, "Nope, I ain't a-gonna kill nobody. Plenty of rich folks wants to fight. Give them the guns."

New York City, 1943.

In these times of war against fascism, when we've got to find all of our real strength, all of our real calmness, all of our real honesty in ourselves before we can learn to trust, unite, organize, and work with others, let's try to be sure that we don't laugh at the ones who have cried,

Wherebouts Can I Hide?
Woody Guthrie

Justice, Oh, Justice,
Wherebouts can I hide?
Liberty's locked up by the fascists tonight!
Freedom got sold
For her carcass and bones!
Justice, Oh, Justice,
Wherebouts can I hide?

Freedom, Oh, Freedom,
Wherebouts do you hide?
I look through my wrecked street, but you I can't find!
Peace got beat up
By the Stormtroops last night.
Freedom, Oh, Freedom,
Wherebouts do you hide?

Democracy, democracy,
Hey, lift up your head!
This is the same curbstone where my family bled.
The voters are voting
Whilst blood soaks it red.
Democracy, Democracy,
Hey, lift up your head!

                              May 16th, 1949

            ---30-----

VOTE IF
YOU'RE
STILL
AROUND

Voting Box

VOTE

163

AND DON'T COME BACK
TILL YOU
REGISTER
TO VOTE

Woody Guthrie

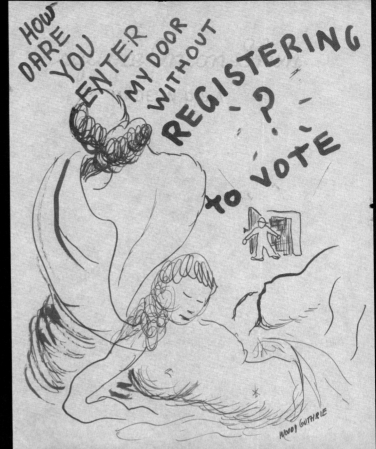

BORN TO WIN

Words and Music by   Woody Guthrie

CHORUS:

                    Born to win.
                    I know I'm born to win.
                    It'sa crazy craving world
                    I'm now born in;
                    I'll fight and die
                    To change things just one drop;
                    Born to win.
                    I'm born and bound to win.

I craved after fun and for pleasures;
I've cried after badluck and blues;
I've been up and been down,
I've been sober and drunk;
But, I know that I'm not born to lose.
                              (((Chorus))))

I kissed girls of all kinds, of all colors;
Bought 'em eats, drinks, an' stockins and shoes;
In debt for their bills,
Worked a few years in jails;
But, I still say I'm not born to lose.
                              ((Chorus)))

You slaved me, you robb'd me, you bled me;
You gave me the skids and the screws;
Knives, brass knucks, and guns,
Blastered me with atombumbs;
But, I know still I'm not born to lose.
                              (((Chorus)))

                    END

                         ** Just now heard a sad one
                         coming over my ships radio,
                         "Born To Lose". So I run to
                         my messtable and wrote up this
                         one "Born To Win". I know my
                         NMU seamen all feel the same
                         way, somehow or another.
                                   Woody Guthrie
                                   On top of the waves;
                                   Sometimes in 1944.

166

I'll use this here guitar
and use a song
To tell the things that are right
and things that's wrong.
You'll hear the old guitar
Some lonesome day
And cock your ear up closer
and you'll say
I heard your big guitar
and heard your song
and know a little bit more
of right and wrong.

           * * * *   1-8-'45

I don't care how good your good old days was for you.
They're not good enough for me.

HELLO
people

A
MERRY
CHRISTMAS

CHAPTER FIVE

Hello People

YOU BECAME SOMEONE ELSE

JEFF DANIIELS

I like to spend my time in a
Lot of crazy ways
Just to learn about the world
People
Who they are, where they are
What they are and what they think
  —Woody

Woody Guthrie loved becoming other people.

He became the miner in a collapsed mine in "Dying Miner." He became a slave and freedom fighter in the "Ballad of Harriet Tubman." He became a toddler prodding his parent, "Take me for a ride in the car car" and a Coney Island neighbor leaning out the window shouting "Joe DiMaggio's done it again!" He became a prostitute in "House of Earth," a baby being born in "Been Up and Coming Down." He became those without a name in "Deportee," as well as those wrongly accused in "Sacco and Vanzetti."

As a story teller, Woody knew of the power that comes with a first-person narrative. By using "I," he could speak in their voice, disappear into their tale, only to magically bring them to life and, with each verse, take the listener by the hand and the heart until together, we're falling into them, we're all someone else, experiencing first hand their pain, sadness, hopes, and dreams.

As an actor, I've come to discover there are things to be learned from those I've portrayed. While standing on the crest of GETTYSBURG's Little Round Top, I came face to face with a courage I didn't know I had as Joshua Lawrence Chamberlain. I got a taste of what it takes to call out this country's holier than thou grandiosity as Will McAvoy in NEWSROOM. As Atticus Finch, I know what it is to have spoken with the articulate strength required to stand up against racial injustice in TO KILL A MOCKINGBIRD. Through me, they were heard. Because of them, I became better.

The power of Art lies in its ability to guide us to a larger sense of who we are. In his poems, sketches, songs, and writings, Woody Guthrie puts on public display our collective strengths and weaknesses. Our loves and hates. Our fears, our beliefs, our politics. And in the end, ourselves.

We are the sum total of all of us. Which is why I approach every role as someone I want to know. Someone I need to understand. To do that, I have to inhabit them. Become them. Because only then will I believe what they believe. Feel what they feel. Think what they think. Just like Woody.

"I didn't see you. I saw the character."

For an actor, that's just about the best review you'll ever hear because it means you didn't perform the role. You became someone else.

A keen observer of people, Woody put himself into their stories, often writing in the first person; someone he observed on a streetcar or in a bar, a person in the news, a powerful politician or well-known celebrity, or someone left behind without a name—all became people worth writing about. The "good & bad, men & womben" alike, the world's nobody became Woody's somebody.

They Laid Jesus Christ In His Grave

Jesus Christ was a man that traveled thru the land
and a hard working man, and brave,
He said to the rich, give your goods to the poor,
And they laid Jesus Christ in his grave

Yes Jesus was a man, a carpenter by hand,
His followers true and brave,
One dirty coward called Judas Iscariot
He has laid poor Jesus in his grave.

He went to the preacher, he went to the sheriff,
And he told them all the same,
Sell all of your jewelry and give it to the poor,
But they laid Jesus Christ in his grave.

When Jesus come to town the working folks around
Believed what he did say,
But the bankers and the preachers they nailed him on cross
And they laid Jesus Christ in his grave.

The poor working people followed him around
and sang and shouted gay,
But the cops and soldiers nailed him in the air
And they laid Jesus Christ in his grave.

The people held their breath when they heard about his death
And everybody wondered why —
It was the rich landlord and the soldiers that they hired
To nail Jesus Christ in the sky.

This song it was written in New York City
Of Rich man, preacher, and slave — — —
If Jesus was to preach as he preached in Galilee
They would lay poor Jesus in his grave.

Woody Guthrie
3-5-40 N.Y.
Original Song

..........I wrote this song looking our of a rooming house
window in New York City in the winter of 1940. I saw how
the poor folks lived, and then I saw how the rich folks
lived, and the poor folks down and out and cold and hungry,
and the rich ones out drinking good whiskey and celebrating
and wasting handfulls of money at gambling and women, and
I got to thinking about what Jesus said, and what if He was
to walk into New York City and preach like he used to. They'd
lock Him back in jail as sure as you're reading this. "Even
as you've done it unto the least of these little ones, you
have done it unto me."...............................

PRETTY BOY FLOYD
(Woody)

.........Charles (Pretty Boy) Floyd was borned and raised right
down in there where I was. I talked to lots of folks that knowed
him personal. Said he wasn't much of a bad feller. Fact, some of
'em respected him lots more than they did the sheriff and his
deputies... Something went haywire and Pretty Boy took to outlawing.
Still he had more friends than any governor Oklahoma ever had. He
went to packing shooting irons, blowing his way into the banks where
the peoples money was. Grabbed big sacks of it up and took it out
and strewed and scattered it everywhere, and give it to the poor
folks all up and down the country. He had the right idea but he
had the wrong system. The Outlaw is in his grave today. So is Jesse
James. So is Billy, the Kid, so is Cole Younger, and Belle Star...
but we still sing about them. You hear songs everywhere springing
up about these fellers, springing up like flowers in the right early
spring. ....One night the deputies thought sure as hell they had
Pretty Boy hemmed up down there in the Rock Island Freight Yards in
Oklahoma City. Supposed to be riding in on a freight. Me and my
uncle was on that same freight. Riding with a guitar and a fiddle,
his fiddle. Pretty Boy was about my uncle's size and weight, and he
was reported to be riding that freight train with a sub-machine gun
hid in a fiddle case. We rolled into the yards, it was black as tar,
long after midnight, and we looked up and seen a whole flock of
flashlights a coming right straight at us through the dark. We'd been
used to railroad bulls and their lanters, but not quite so many. Here
they come like a flock of airplanes lit up - and they yelled at me
and my uncle and said, "Hey, boys, you gonna hafta leave here.
Too dangerous from here on." And so we set there about a minute. It
so happened that we was a setting out on one of these flat cars,
gondola or some dern kind - and so I reached over and slung onto my
guitar and slipped off alongside the car, aiming to climb back on
after I'd run a little ways along side of the train. So my uncle says,
"All Right, Boys, I'll get off". Yes, and he reached down to grab his
fiddle and case up under his arm, and when he did - when he raised up-
brother and sister, me and my uncle went one direction, and 6 jillion
streaks of light went the other....... This song is one I fixed up
about Pretty Boy. It tells of tales I heard concerning his life and
what kind of a man he was, and as I said before I spoke, we aint never
had a governor down there that was half as popular as Pretty Boy. He
tried and done it wrong, the governor don't even try................

If you'll gather 'round me, children,
A story I will tell
About Pretty Boy Floyd, an outlaw,
Oklahoma knew him well.

It was in the town of Shawnee on a Saturday afternoon
His wife beside him in the wagon as into town they rode.
There a deputy sheriff reproached him in a manner rather rude
Using vulgar words of anger, and his wife she overheard.

Pretty Boy grabbed a log chain, the deputy grabbed his gun,
And in the fight that followed, he laid that deputy down.
Then he took to the trees and timber and lived a life of shame,
Every crime in Oklahoma was added to his name.

Yes, he took to the river bottom along the river shore,
And Pretty Boy found a welcome at every farmer's door.
The papers said that Pretty Boy had robbed a bank each day,
While he was setting in some farmhouse 300 miles away.

There's many a starving farmer the same old story told
How the outlaw paid their mortgage and saved their little home.
Others tell you 'bout a stranger that come to beg a meal
And when the meal was finished left a thousand dollar bill.

It was in Oklahome City, it was on a Christmas Day,
There come a whole carload of groceries with a note to day:
"You say that I'm an outlaw, you say that I' a thief.
Here's a Christmas dinner for the families on relief."

Yes, as through this world I ramble, I see lots of funny men,
Some will rob you with a 6 gun, and some with a fountain pen.
But as through your life you'll travel, wherever you may roam,
You won't never see an Outlaw drive a family from their home.

60

174

BALLAD OF HARRIET TUBMAN
Words & Music by Woody Guthrie
---*---

I was five years old in Bucktown Maryland
When into slavery I got sent
I'll tell you of the beatings and fun and fighting
In my ninety three years I spent:

I helped a fiddhand make a run for freedom
When my fifteenth year was rolling around
The guard he caught him in a little store
In a little ole slavery village town.

That boss made a grab to catch that slave hand
I jumped in and I blocked that door
My boss hit me with a twopound scale iron
And I went black down on the floor.

On a bundle of rags in our log cabin
My mother she ministered unto my needs
It was here I swore Id give my lifeblood
Ta turn all my slavefolks free.

It'z in Forty Four I wed John Tubman
I loved him well till Forty Nine
But he'za fraid ta come an' fight beside me
And so I left him back behind.

I left ole Bucktown with my two brothers
But they gotta fraid an' they run back home
I follered my northern star to freedom
I walked my grass an' trees alone.

~~Thatxsunxxonexshiningxthatxearlyxmorning~~
I slept in barnlofts and I slept in haystacks
I stayed with people in slavery shacks
They says, You'll die by that bossmans bullits
But I says to them, I cant turn back.

That sun come shining that early morning
When I walked across my free state line
I pinched myself to see if I'ma dreaming
I just could not believe my eyes.

I beat it back home, got botha my parents
Loaded them up on my buckboard hack
We crossed six states and lotsa slaves follered us
All that ways to Canada where we made our tracks.

They'z one slave got sceared an' tried ta turn back'ards
I pulled my pistol up in front of his eyes
I told 'im, Git up an' walk towards yore freedum
Or by my fireball you will die.

When John Brown hit 'em at Harpers Ferry
My men come fightin right by Hohns side
When they swung John Brown upon them gallows
It was then I hung my head and cried:

Give my blackman guns and give him powder
To Aberham Lincoln them words I said
You just crippled that snake of slavery
We've got to fight and kill 'im dead.

Whenever we faced them guns of lightning
When rumblin thunder come breakin our sleep
We waded floods of bloody rainstorms
It was deadmen bodies we did reap.
Guns flashed at us like zigzag lightning
But it was worth the price we paid
When that bossmans guns had rumbled over
We'd laid slavery perty close to th' grave.

Come friend and stand around my bedside
I'll sing with you some freedom songs
I'm on my way to my Greater Union
That's how my ninety three years has gone.

Coney 9/18/1944
Belutchatchee 4/11/1953

THE BLINDING OF ISAAC WOODWARD
Woody Guthrie

My name is Isaac Woodward, my tale I'll tell to you;
I'm sure it'll sound so terrible you might not think it's true;
I signed up with the army, they sent me over the seas,
Through the battles of New Guinea and through the Phillipines.

On the Thirteenth Day of February of Nineteen Forty Six,
They sent me to Atlanta to get my discharge fixed;
I caught me a bus for Winsboro going to meet my wife,
To take her to New York City to visit my parents both.

About an hour out of Atlanta, the sun was going down,
The bus it stopped by a drug store in a little country town;
I walked up to the driver and I looked him in the eye;
"I'd like to go to the rest room if you think we've got time".

The driver started cussing and then he hollered, "No!"
And then I cussed right back at him and I really got him told.
He says, "If you will hurry, I guess we'll take the time",
It was in a few short minutes we was rolling down the line.

We rolled for thirty minutes, I watched the shacks and trees,
Thinking of my wife in Winsboro waiting there for me.
In a town in North Carolina the driver he jumped out
And he come back with a policeman and took me off the bus.

"Listen Mister Policeman", I started to explain,
"I did not cause no rukus and I did not raise no cain!"
He struck me with his billy and nearly knocked me down,
"Shut up, you black bastard!"   And he walked me down in town.

And then as we went walking, my right arm he did twist,
I knew he wanted me to fight him back, but I never did resist.
"Have you your Army Discharge?" I told him, yes, I had;
He pasted me with his loaded stick down across my head.

I grabbed his stick and we had a little run, then we had a wrastle;
Another cop runs up with a gun and he jumps into the battle.
"If you don't drop that billy, black boy, it's me that's dropping you!"
I figured to drop that leaded sap was the best thing I could do.

They beat me about my head and face and left a bloody trail
All down along the sidewalk to the iron door of the jail;
He knocked me down there on the ground and poked me in the eyes;
When I woke up next morning in jail I found my eyes was blind.

They drug me to the courtroom, but I could not see the judge;
He fined me all of my money for raising all of this fuss.
The Doctor finally got there, but it took him two whole days;
He handed me some drops and salve and told me to treat myself.

It's now you've heard my story, there's one thing I can't see,
How you can treat a human like you have treated me.
I thought I fought on the islands to get rid of their kind;
But I can see that the fight's not over now that I am blind.

****
I sung this at the Isaac Woodward Benefit Rally not long ago in
Lewisohn Stadium for Thirty Two Thousand people, with Eight or Ten
Thousand outside trying to climb in over the fences. Never seen so
many cops in my whole life. Cab Calloway and Firteen or Twenty big
name bands and acts went ahead of me on the program, and for two whole
hours I didn't hear nine words of fighting protest. Isaac was the last
one on the program and I sung right after he made his little talk. The
wind blew the words to my song off the rack and down onto the floor two
or three times, and they clapped their hands when I told them that I
never was no hand to give up that easy. Then a pretty Negro girl walked
out and picked up my words off of the floor and held them up there to
where I could read them. I suppose this was the biggest and loudest
applause that I've ever got anywhere I've been.   Woody Guthrie.

*********************   *Woody Guthrie*
                        9-7-'46

Woody misspells Isaac Woodard's name in this lyric.

Joe DiMaggio
Done it again by WOODY GUTHRIE

Joe Deemaggyo done it again!
Joe Deemaggyo done it again!
Clackin' that bat
Gone with the wind!
Joe Deemaggyo's done it again.

Some folks that Big Joe was done!
Some folks figgered Joe was gone!
Broke

ONE LONG YEAR BIG
STEPS, TO THE PLATTER WITH A GREAT BIG GRIN;
JOE DEEMAGGYOE'S DONE IT AGAIN.   that slidey man!

I'MA GONNA TELL YA JIST TH' WAY I FEEL;
MAN CAIN'T RUN WITHOUT HIS HEEL;
WATCH THAT RAGGYPILL SPLIT THE WIND!
JOE DEEMAGGYOE'S DONE IT AGAIN!

ALL THREE FIELDERS JUMPED THEIR BEST;
TRYIN' TA CLIMB THAT HIGHBOARD FENCE;
THEY ALL GROWED WHISKERS ON THEIR CHINS!
JOE DEEMAGGYOE'S DONE IT AGAIN!

UP ALONG THEM CLOUDS WHERE THE EAGLE ROAMS;
JOE CRACKED THAT BALL TO WHINE AND MOAANN;
HIS BUDDIES LAUGH AS THEY TROT ON IN,
JOE DEEMAGGYOE'S DONE IT AGAIN!

GRANDMAW'S HOME BY THE RADIO
ON THE TELLEYEVIZZION AWATCHIN' JOE;
SHE JERKS THE BEARD OFFA GRANDPAW'S CHIN,
JOE DEEMAGGYOE'S DONE IT AGAIN!

THE PUPPYDOG BARKED AT THE POOSEYE KAT;
HOW DOES IT LOOK FROM WHERE YOU SET?
LOOKS LIKE A CYCLONE SLIDIN' IN;
JOE DEEMAGYOE'S DONE IT AGAIN!

THE END

Words & Music figured out on June 30th, 1949
by
Woody Guthrie
3520 Mermaid Avenue,
Brooklyn, 24, New York.

--- 30 -------

Woody Guthrie

Following an eight-month hiatus, Joe DiMaggio returned to the New York Yankees on June 28th, 1949. Woody memorialized DiMaggio's comeback with his June 29th three-run homer in the fifth inning and two-out solo homer, winning the game against their rivals, the Boston Red Sox.

Ingrid Bergman

Ingrid Bergman, Ingrid Bergman,
Let's go, go make a picture
on the island of Stromboli, Ingrid Bergman,

Well, it's windy, Ingrid Bergman,
and it's dusty, Ingrid Bergman,
Round the old volcano mountain, Ingrid Bergman,

Ingrid Bergman, you're so perty
You make any mountain quivver
You make fire fly from the crater, Ingrid Bergman,

* This old mountain its been waiting
All it's life for you to walk it
For your hand to touch its hardrock, Ingrid Bergman,

It you'll walk across my camera
Let me flash the world your story
I will pay you more than money, Ingrid Bergman,

Not by pennies, dimes, nor quarters,
But by living sons and daughters,
And they'll sing around Stromboli, Ingrid Bergman,

(Repeat 4th stanza) - then go -

End

Words & music by
W.W. Woody Guthrie
Feb. 16th 1950
Conney Island
new York State
U.S. of Americans

Ingrid Bergman reading Woody's autobiography, *Bound for Glory*, New York City, 1943.

A passionate fan, Woody wrote this lyric the day after Bergman's film *Stromboli* was released on February 15, 1950. Racing out to see the film, he left a note for his wife: "I'm out with Ingrid."

DEAR MRS ROOSEVELT

Words and Music by Woody Guthrie

Dear Mrs Roosevelt don't hang your head to cry;
His mortal clay is laid away but his goodwork ~~never died;~~ Fills The Sky;
This world was lucky to see him born.

He's born in a money family on that Hudson's Rocky shore;
Outrun every kid agrowin' up 'round Hyde Park just for fun;
This world was lucky to see him born.

He went away to grade school and wrote back to his folks;
He drew such funny pictures and always pulling a joke;
This world was lucky to see him born.

He went on up towards Harvard, he read his book of law;
He loved his trees and horses, lov'd everything he saw;
This world was lucky to see him born.

He got struck down by fever and it settled in his leg;
He lov'd the folks th't wished him well as everybody did;
This world was lucky to see him born.

He took his office on a crippled leg he said to one and all:
"You moneychanging racketboys have sure nuff got to go!"
This world was lucky to see him born.

In senate walls and congress halls he used his gift of tongue
To get you thieves and liars told and put you on the run;
This world was lucky to see him born.

I voted for him for lotsa jobs, I'd vote his name again;
He tried to find an honest job for every idle hand;
This world was lucky to see him born.

He helped me build my union hall, he learn'd me howta talk;
I could see he was a cripple, but he taught my sou to walk;
This world was lucky to see him born.

You nazis and you fascists try to boss this world by **hate**;
He fought my war the union way and the hate gang all got beat;
This world was lucky to see him born.

I sent him cross that ocean to Yalta and to Tehran;
He didn't like Churchill very much and told him man to man;
This world was lucky to see him born.

He said he didn't like DeeGaulle, ner no Chyang Kye Checks;
Shook hands with Joseph Stalin, says, "Theres a man I like!"
This world was lucky to see him born.

I was torpedoed on my merchant ship the day he took command;
He was hated by my captain, but loved by all ships hands;
This world was lucky to see him born.

I was a GI in my Army Camp that day he passed away;
And over my shoulder talking I c'd hear some soldier say:
This world was luck to see him born.

I guess this world was lucky just to see him born;
I know this world was lucky just to see him born;
This world was lucky to see him born.

E N D

*** I think I made up this one out along the wreckagy
shores of Coney Island on the 30th days of January 19&48.
Woody Guthrie

Woody Guthrie

ILSA KOCH

by

Woody Guthrie

Tune: ANOTHER MAN DONE GONE

I'M HERE IN BUCHENWALD (4 TIMES)

MY NUMBER'S ON MY SKIN (" ")

OLD ILSA KOCH IS HERE (" ")

THE PRISONERS WALK THE GROUNDS. (FOUR TIMES)

THE HOUNDS HAVE KILLED A GIRL. (FOUR TIMES)

THE GUARDS HAVE SHOT A MAN. (FOUR TIMES)

SOME MORE HAVE STARVED TO DEATH. (FOUR TIMES)

HERE COMES THE PRISONERS CAR. (FOUR TIMES)

THEY DUMP THEM IN THE PEN. (FOUR TIMES)

THEY LOAD THEM DOWN THE SCHUTE. (FOUR TIMES)

THE TROOPER CRACKS THEIR SKULLS. (FOUR TIMES)

HE STEALS THEIR TEETH OF GOLD. (FOUR TIMES)

HE SHOVES THEM ON THE BELT. (FOUR TIMES)

HE SWINGS THAT FURNACE DOOR. (FOUR TIMES)

HE SLIDES THEIR CORPSES IN. (FOUR TIMES)

I SEE THE CHIMNEY SMOKE. (FOUR TIMES)

I SEE THEIR ASHES HAULED. (FOUR TIMES)

I SEE THEIR BONES IN PILES. (FOUR TIMES)

LAMP SHADES ARE MADE FROM SKINS. (FOUR TIMES)

I'M CHOKING ON THE SMOKE. (FOUR TIMES)

THE STINK IS KILLING ME. (FOUR TIMES)

OLD ILSY KOCH WAS JAILED. (FOUR TIMES)

OLD ILSY KOCH WENT FREE. (FOUR TIMES)

I'VE GOT TO HUSH MY SONG. (FOUR TIMES)

HERE COMES THE SUPER MAN. (FOUR TIMES)

I'LL SEE YOU LATER ON. (FOUR TIMES)

I'VE GOT TO DUCK AND RUN. (FOUR TIMES)

****
WORDS SET UNTO THIS OLD FOLKY TUNE
ON THIS 8th DAY of the MONTH OF OCTOBER
IN THIS HARD ROUGH YEAR OF OUR 80th
CONGRESS, (A.D.1948)
                    by the same old

WOODROW WILSON GUTHRIE

Verdict on Ilse Koch To Stand, Clay Rules

Frankfurt, Sept. 30 (U.P.) —
Gen. Lucius D. Clay said today
that his public relations staff
delayed publication of his verdict in the Ilse Koch case because it "had not recognized
its news value."

The U. S. military governor said
he commuted her life sentence to
four years because in reviewing the
case he found no evidence connect-
ing Frau Koch with inhuman treatment of prisoners at the notorious
Buchenwald concentration camp.

Clay referred to Frau Koch as a
"despicable and very low woman,"
but said his decision stands and
cannot be reversed because he is
the final reviewing authority.

Turkey on Alert

Istanbul, Sept. 30 (P).—Informed
sources in Ankara said tonight that
all Turkish men outside military
age have been ordered to report at
once for nine days' training in
anti-aircraft duty.

Ilse Koch
A "very low woman."

Newspaper clipping from Woody's scrapbook, 1948.

Leadbelly Song

■ BACK & TRY
Woody Guthrie

CHORUS:
    One more time, time ohh time,
    I'ma gonna go back an try;
    I'ma gonna go back an' try just one more time.

Alla you people shakin' your heads,
I'ma gittin' up outta my bed,
I8ma gonna go back an' try just one more time.
I'll make you laff, I'll make you blue,
I'ma shinin' up my floshime shoes;
I see Marthy walkin' 'roun' my bedside one more time. (Cho)

Come along Marthy, hold my hand,
Hug an' kiss your natural man,
I'm walkin' out onna great big bookintour one more time.
I'll brush my suit an' cock my hat,
Take my Stelloe inna my hand;
I'm gonna trouvle 'round my cuntry one more time. (CHO))

Goodbye Broadway Hello France
I'm tappin' for you my muddywater dance
Playin' for you my slideyfinger blues just one more time.
I'ma gonna boogit frum town t' town;
An' when you honeydrinkers gang aroun'
Gals, I'll sing that cyclone down just one more time.(CHO)

Frisco's Bay backta old L.A.,
Good mornin' blues, howr are you today;
Caint you hear me callin' you just one more time?
Mister Lomax an' Alan, too,
I'll jig in every jail I knew
I'll sing my way outta two more prisons one more time. (CHO)

Back t' th' muddybottom greencorn field,
Back where th' bolly weevil kisst his darlin
You c'n bringa little watoe Sylvye one more time.
Back t' th' gallyhouse drammin joints
Back t' th' boogyhouse jookin joint
I'll play an' sing in my long trousoes one more time. (CHO)

I'm gonna wheel back see papa an' mamma
Down 'roun' Mooresport, Louisianna,
I'ma runnin barefooted chasin that bullyfrog one more time.
I'ma helpin Momma digga great big 'tater
I'ma showin Daddy how I cut my capers;
I'ma singin louder than th' bull alligator one more time.(CHO)

I'm stirrin up some floody stormclouds
I'm singin straddle th' slickery mudcat
I'm huggin anda kissin you, sweet little Marthy, one more time.
One more time you c'n be my wife
I'ma yellin t' th' world you're haffa my life;
I'ma holdin your hand like th' day I met you one more time.(CHO

      end
      END

      Words & Music by
      Woody Guthrie
      Coney's Dry Island
      Sixh Good day of January
       19 Hundred & 50

Woody Guthrie

Written following Lead Belly's death on December 6, 1949.

With twelve-string blues musician Huddie Ledbetter (a.k.a. Lead Belly), Committee of Arts and Sciences fundraiser, Chicago, IL, ca. 1940.

LEADBELLY IS A HARD NAME

And the hard name of a harder man. The name that his mama spoke over him down in the swamps of Louisiana when he was born was Huddie Ledbettor, for her husband, Ledbettor, and because she liked the sound and the roll of Huddie.

I guess that they called him Huddie while he was growing up from dirty overhalls to knee pants, longer pants, and I've heard him sing a song about what happened to him when he did change his knee pants for his long ones.

I came to his and Martha's apartment over on East Tenth Street and I carried my own guitar, and they begged me to stay, to eat, sleep, sing and dance there in their apartment of three little rooms painted a sooty sky blue and then smoked over with the stains from cigarettes, cigars, of the rich and of the poor.

I saw Leadbelly get up in his morning, wash, shave, put on his bathrobe, and Martha would stand up in her tall way and make me get shaved, bathed, washed, dressed, while she cooked Leadbelly his breakfast on her charcoal flat top stove. The stove was older than me, older than Martha, but not any older than Leadbelly.

I watched him set after breakfast, look down eastwards out from his window, read the Daily News and the Daily Mirror and the Daily Worker.

I listened as he tuned up his Twelve String Stella and eased his fingers up and down along the neck in the same way that the library and museum clerk touched the frame of the best painting in their gallery. It was not possible for me to count the numbers of folks that came in through Leadbelly's door there.

He never did bother to count you, and Martha tried several times, but always got lost early in the morning. The people waking up in the building dropped around earliest. Little babies toddle in to see Leadbelly and he laughs and plays and is as young in action as they are. Older kids in their tens and teens walk down, and Leadbelly is the same as each one that walks. It is a fact that I have seen every age of person dance on his floor there in their three little old blue rooms.

Leadbelly picked along on his guitar, just something that took him back where he come from, and he played at about half of his power in order to warm up easy and to get ready for any-body that asked him for a little number on their way to hunt for coal, or for a job of work or to a job of some kind.

I liked Leadbelly's guitar and singing this early morning speed as well, better in some ways than the faster and stronger ones that you have seen him play on your stages and in your studios.

He had a slow running, easy, deep quiet way about him that made me see that his strength was like a little ball in his hands and that his thoughts ran as deep in color as the lights that played down from the sky and onto his face.

I went with Leadbelly to all kinds of places where he performed, in your school, church, your theatre, your radio studio, at your cocktail club, and at your outdoor rally to call you to come together to meet, talk, argue, theorize, and speak your voice against the things that poison your life and your world around you. I saw that what you applauded in some was diplomas, degrees, intellectual pursuit, the reading of books, the tracings of our histories, and the speakers fighting for our wages, hours, homes, union. I saw you make just as much of an applause for Leadbelly as for your other leaders, and the thing that you applauded in him was pure personal fighting power. The same power as the prisoner of War that cries and sings, dances, after he is freed from a death camp.

Leadbelly had to find every lost ounce of his strength to keep him alive down the road he has come.

He had to find it to even live and

to grow up from a little boy into the full man. His street around him was rough and wild, it was dirty, worn thin, rotten, naked and hungry. It was buggy, crummy, old and wore out, it was a street of old sickly shack houses, as old, older maybe, than his daddy and his daddy's daddy. The going was tough, and the strong of wind and muscle got along a little better than the weak ones, and it helped the weak ones to fight harder, grow harder. He did not smoke tobacco, gamble, play poker, dice, nor waste his time at idle things. The artist in him was a hungry man, hungry to see himself in the best clothes, on the best street, in the best room, the best car, the best world. He knew he could help his folks everywhere to keep up their fight and their faith if he could only win his better place. This is the feeling that he found in his soul and the feeling that he brought to the touch of his first guitar. This was the sight of the vision that he saw. This was his way. The sight and the feel of his music box in his hands lit up those homeless stretches of his spirit and he said, This is my way.

Leadbelly said, this is my way. And he said it the same, in the same airy breath that George Washington Carver said of his science laboratory. Leadbelly touched his first guitar the same tender way that Joe Louis felt the skin of those first gloves. The same as Paul Robeson first touched his football, his Shakespeare costume as Hamlet. He said This is my way, about the same as Marian Anderson touched her throat and sang at her great places. Leadbelly did not know where his guitar would carry him, but he said that he would follow it.

His guitar was not like a friend of his, not like a woman, not like some of the kids, not like a man you know. But it was a thing that would cause people to walkover to where he is, a thing that made sounds that gave his own words richer sounds, and would give him his way to show his people around him all of the things that he felt inside and out. He would play the tones on the music box and then he would tell me a story, you a tale, and all of his life history. And he would say and sing it in such words that we could not tell where our own personal life stopped and Leadbelly's started.

He wanted to preach history, his own history, his people's story, and everybody's history. He wanted to be all kinds of big names, a history speaker, a story teller, a talker, good fast walker, a loud yeller, and the man that was all a big tone.

I HEARD THE SOUNDS OF THE WORD Leadbelly, and I knew that I would have followed the sound of that name to any door in this particular world.

SONNY TERRY blew and whipped, beat, fanned, and petted his harmonica, cooed to it like a weed hill turtle dove, cried to it like some worried woman come to ease his worried mind. He blew it down two to one and let it down easy, flipped his lip over and across, and his tongue sending all of his wind into one hole, straining the reed with too much pressure and making it sound like it had several side tones and tones that dance between. He put the tobacco sheds of North and South Carolina in it and all of the blistered and hurt and hardened hands cheated and left empty, hurt and left crying, robbed and left hungry, pilfered and left starving, beaten and left dreaming. He rolled down the trains that the colored hand cannot drive, only clean and wash down. He blew into the wood holes and the brassy reeds the tale and the wails of Lost John running away from the dogs of the chain gang guards, and the chain gang is the landlord that is never around anywhere.

I talked to Sonny about these things in his art, and he tells me that he is blind and that he still knows that his people can see a world where we all vote, eat, work, talk, plan, and think together and with all of our smokes and wheels rolling and all of ourselves well dressed and well housed and well fed. These are the things that the artist in Blind Sonny Terry knows and sees in his blindness. These are the upland echoes of the things that stir and sing along his big muddies. These are the plans and visions seen in the kiss and whisper of tall tree jack pines falling into the chutes to make your papery pulps. These are the freedoms. These are the samples of the kinds of soul art that the Negro, Indian, Mexican, the Irish, the Jew, the Russian, the Greek, Italian, all of us, have to bring to be seen and heard.

SING YOUR NAME
Woody Guthrie
--- October 30, 1946 ---

Recorded for Disc
10-6- 1947
WG

OH HO SACCO
OH HO HO NICOLA SACCO
OH HO SACCO
I JUST WANT TO SING YOUR NAME.

SACCO, SACCO,
SACCO, SACCO, SACCO,
SACCO,
NICOLA SACCO,
I JUST WANT TO
SING YOUR NAME.

OH HO ROSA
OH HO ROSA ROSA
OH HO MRS ROSA SACCO
I JUST WANT TO SING YOUR NAME.

I NEVER DID SEE YOU, SEE YOU,
I NEVER DID GET TO MEET YOU,
I JUST HEARD YOUR STORY, STORY,
AND I JUST WANT TO SING YOUR NAME.

HEY, HEY, HEY, VANZETTI,
HEY, HEY, BART VANZETTI,
YOU MADE SPEECHES FOR THE WORKERS, WORKERS,
I JUST WANT TO SING YOUR NAME.

OH SACCO VANZETTI
OH HO SACCO VANZETTI
SACCO SACCO VANZETTI
I JUST WANT TO SING YOUR NAME.

Hey, HEY, JUDGE WEBSTER THAYER,
HO HO HO JUDGE WEBSTER THAYER
HEY HEY HEY, OLD JUDGE WEBSTER THAYER,
I DON'T WANT TO SING YOUR NAME.

BART VANZETTI AND NICOLA SACCO
BART VANZETTI AND NICCOLA SACCO
COME HERE LOOKING FOR THE LAND OF FREEDOM
I JUST WANT TO SING YOUR NAME.

VANZETTI SOLD FISH 'ROUND THE PLYMOUTH HARBOR
SACCO WAS THE SHOEFACTORY'S BEST SHOE CUTTER
ALL MY SONS AND ALL OF MY DAUGHTERS
THEY'RE GONNA HELP ME SING YOUR NAME.

OH HO SACCO SACCO
HEY HEY HEY BART VANZETTI
YOUR WIFE AND KIDS AND ALL OF YOUR FAMILY
I JUST WANT TO SING YOUR NAME.

OH SACCO VANZETTI
OH HO HO SACCO VANZETTI
NICOLA SACCO AND BART VANZETTI
WELL, I JUST WANT TO SING YOUR NAME.

OH HO HO HO
HEY HEY HEY AND HO HO HO HO
YES, YES, YES, YES,
I JUST WANT TO SING YOUR NAME.

---30---

Rewrote 22nd of June, 1947, W.G.
At my house in Coney Island, New York City.
W.G.

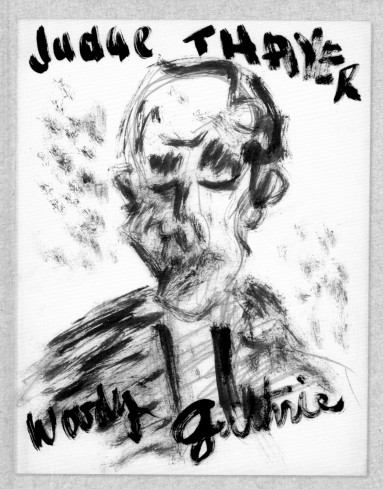

JUDGE THAYER

woody guthrie

salloon close to Suassos Plumouth, massachussets

woody Guthrie
oct. 30, 1946

woody Guthrie

CONSCIOUSNESS OF GUILT

TO THE JURY

woody Guthrie

next witness

woody Guthrie

Dying Miner

Words & Music by   Woody Guthrie

It happened an hour ago;
Way down in this tunnel of coal;
This gas caughtta fire fr'm somebody's lamp;
And the miners all choking in smoke.
Goodbye to you, Honey, Little Dicky;
Goodbye to my wife that I love;
Most all of these miners won't be coming home
Tonight when that workwhistle blows.

CHORUS:

        Dear sister and brother, Goodbye;
        Dear mother and father Goodbye;
        My fingers are weak and I cannot write;
        Goodbye, Centralia, Goodbye.

It looks like the end for me
And for all of my buddies I see;
We're all writing letters on a slaterock wall;
Please carry my word to my wife.
I found a little place in the air;
I crawled and drug myself here;
But the smoke's getting bad, and the fumes coming in;
This gas is burning my eyes.
                                (((Chorus)))

Forgive me for things I've done wrong;
I lote you lots more than you know;
When tonight's whistle blows and I don't come home,
Do all that you can to help Mom.
I can hear the moans and the groans
Of more than a hunderd good men;
Just work and fight and try to see
That this does not cavein again.
                                (((Chorus)))

My eyes are gone blind in these fumes;
Now, it sounds like the men are all gone;
Except Joe Ballantini, Fred Gutzler, and Joy;
They're trapped in this hellshole of fire.
Please name our new baby Joe,
So's he'll grow up like Big Joe;
He'll work and he'll fight, he'll fixup this mine
So the fires can't kill daddies no more.
                                ((((Chorus))))

                    END

    Every word of this song I took from those words we
found around the bodies on that slate rock.

                            Woody Guthrie

TOM JOAD

Tom Joad got out of that old MacAlester pen;
It was there that he got his parole;
After Four long years on a man killin' charge,
    Tom Joad come a walkin' down th' road;
    Tom Joad come a walkin' down th' road.

It was there that he found him a truck drivin' man;
It was there that he got him a ride;
After Said, "I just got a loose from MacAlester pen
On a charge called homacide,
    Yes, a charge called homacide.

That truck rolled away in a big cloud of dust;
Then Tommy turned his face towards home;
He met Preacher Casey and they had a little drink,
    And he found that his family they was gone, Tom Joad,
    He found that his family it was gone.

He found his mama's old fashion shoe;
He found his daddy's hat;
He found little Muley, and Muley said,
    "They've been tractored out by th' cats, Tom.
    They've been tractored out by the cats!"

So Tommy walked down to a neighboring farm
And he found his family;
They took preacher Casey and they loaded in a car,
    And his mama said, "We got to git away, Tom!"
    His mama said, "We got to git away!"

The Twelve of the Joads made a mighty heavy load,
And Grandpa Joad did cry;
He grabbed up a handful of land in his hand,
    And said, "I'm stickin' with my farm till I die!
    Yes, I'm stickin' with my farm till I die!"

We fed him spare ribs and coffee and soothin' syrup;
And Grandpa Joad did die;
We buried Grandpa Joad on that Oklahoma road,
    Buried Grandma on the California side,
    We buried Grandma on the California side.

We stood on a mountain and we looked to the west;
And it looked like the Promised Land;
Was a big green valley and a river running through;
    There was work for every single hand, we thought;
    There was work for every single man.

The Joads rolled away to the jungle camp
And there they cooked a stew;
And the hungry little kids of the jungle camp
Said, "We'd like to have some, too.
     We'd like to have some, too".

Now, a deputy sheriff fired loose at a man;
He shot a woman in the back;
But before he could take his aim again,
Preacher Casey dropped him in his tracks; Pore Boy;
   Preacher Casey dropped him in his tracks.

They handcuffed Casy and they took him to jail;
And then he got away;
And he met Tom Joad on the old river bridge;
And these few words he did say,

"I preached about the Lord for a mighty long time;
I preached about the rich and the poor;
But us workin' folks has got to stick together
Or we ain't got a chance anymore,
   No, we ain't got a chance anymore".

Now the deupties come and **Tom** and Casey run
To the bridge where the water run down;
But the vigilante thugs hit Casey with a club;
And they laid preacher Casey on the ground;
   Yes, they laid Preacher Casey on the ground.

Tom Joad he grabbed that deputies club,
Hit him over the head;
Tom Joad took flight that dark and rainy night;
Was a deputy and a preacher lyin' dead, Two men.
   A deputy and a preacher lyin' dead.

Tom run back where his mother was asleep;
He woke her up out of bed;
~~Saidxwhatx Preacherx Caseyxxsaidx xTomxJoadxx~~
~~Saidxxxxxxxxxxxxxxxxxxxxxxxxxxxxxxxxxxxxxxx~~
Kissed goodbye to the mother that he loved,
And he said what Preacher Casey said;   Tom Joad;
   He said what Preacher Casey said.

"Ever'body might be just one big soul;
Well, it looks that a way to me;
Wherever you look in the day or night,
That's where I'm a gonna bbe, ma,
   That's where I'm a gonna be.

Wherever little kids are hungry and cry;
Wherever people ain't free;
Every where that men are a fightin' for their rights,
That's where I'm a gonna be, ma,
   That's where I'm a gonna be!"

****

LOS GATOS PLANE WRECK

WORDS & MUSIC BY WOODY GUTHRIE

MY CROPS THEYRE ALL IN AN' MY PEACHES ALL ROTTENING
MY OR'NGES ALL PIL'D IN MY CREOSOTEY DUMP
Y'R FLYING ME BACK PAST MY MEXICOES BORDER
TA PAY YOU MY MONEY TA WADE BACK AG'IN

C   H   O   R   U   S   GOODBYE T' YOU JUAN
                           GOODBYE ROSALITA
                           ADIOS MUY AMIGO   JESUS AN' MARIE
                           IVE NOT GOT MY NAME
                           AS I RIDE MY BIG AIRPLANE
                           ALL Y' CALL ME IS JUST ONE MORE DEEPORTEE

MUY FATHERS OWN FATHER HE WADED MUY RIVVER
Y' TOOK ALL HIS MONEY HE MADE IN HIS LIFE
I RODE WITH MUY SISTERS AND BROTHERS T' WORK IN MY FRUIT TREES
MUY PEOPLE RODE Y'R BIGTRUCK TILL THEY TOOKDOWN AN' DIED

IVE DIED IN Y'R HILLS I DIED IN Y'R DESERTS
I DIED ON Y'R VALLEYS I DIED ON Y'R PLAINS
I DIED UNDER Y'R TREES AND ALL UNDER Y'R BUSHES
BOTHE SIDES OF MUY RIVVER I DIE JUST THE SAME

Y' TELL ME I'M NOT WANTED Y' CALL ME ILLEGAL
MY WORKY CONTRACT'S OUT? YES I HAVE T' MOVE ON
SIXE HUNDERD MILES BACK T' MYE BORD'R OF MEXXICOE
Y' CHASE ME LIKE KILLERS LIKE RUSTLERS LIKE THIEVES

MUY SKYEPLANE CAUGHTA FIRE OVER MY LOSGATOES CANYONE
MUY FIREBALL OF LITENING IT SHOOK ALL MUY HILLS
I SEE ALL MUY FR'ENDS SCATTER'D HERE LIKE MUY DRYLEAVES
MUY RADEO JUST CALLS ME ONE MORE DEEPORTEE

IS THIS MUY BEST WAY I C'N GROWE MUY BIGG ORCHARDE?
IS THIS MUY BEST WAY I C'N GROWE MUY GOODE FRUITE?
TA FALL LIKE DRYED LEAVES HERE T' ROT ON MUY TOPSSOOIL
TA BE CALL'D BY NO NAME 'CEPT ONE MORE DEEPORTEE?

                *SING CHORUS IF AND WHEN SHE NEEDS T' BE

                        E
                           N
                              D

WOODY GUTHRIE   SOMEYWHERES OR THE OTHER

FEBRUARY THIRDE NINETEEN & FORTEY & EIGHTE

                THIRTY

                T H I R T Y

                    30

---

32 KILLED IN CRASH OF CHARTER PLANE

California Victims Include 28 Mexican Workers Who Were Being Deported

FRESNO, Calif., Jan. 28 (AP)—A chartered Immigration Service plane crashed and burned in western Fresno County this morning, killing twenty-eight Mexican deportees, the crew of three and an immigration guard.

Irving F. Wixon, director of the Federal Immigration Service at San Francisco, said that the Mexicans were being flown to the deportation center at El Centro, Calif., for return to their country.

The group included Mexican nationals who entered the United States illegally, and others who stayed beyond duration of work contracts in California, he added. All were agricultural workers.

The crew was identified as Frank Atkinson, 32 years old, of Long Beach, the pilot; Mrs. Bobbie Atkinson, his wife, stewardess, 28, and Marion Ewing of Balboa, copilot, 33.

Long Beach airport officials said that Mr. Atkinson, formerly of Rochester, N. Y., had logged more than 1,700 hours flying time as a wartime member of the Air Transport Command. The guard was identified as Frank E. Chaffin of Berkeley.

The plane, which was chartered from Airline Transport Carriers of Burbank, was southbound from the Oakland airport, when it crashed in view of some 100 road camp workers.

Foreman Frank V. Johnson said that it "appeared to explode and a wing fell off" before it plummeted to the ground. A number of those in the plane appeared to jump or fall before the aircraft hit the earth, he added.

The wreckage was enveloped in flames when the fuel tanks ignited. Not until the fire died down were rescuers able to get near the plane. By then, there was nothing to be done but to extricate the bod-

Woody left behind many unanswered questions in his songs and stories. Among them is the story of twenty-eight unnamed Mexican migrant workers who perished in a plane crash while being deported and were buried in an unmarked grave. Woody believed that a person's spirit was embedded in their name and deserved acknowledgment of their existence. Disturbed by the fact that the names of the deportees were not listed in the news report, Woody wrote this song.

Seven decades later, historian Tim Z. Hernandez, moved by the lyric, researched the story and discovered the names of the "deportees." Following a service attended by the families in 2013, a memorial headstone listing their names was installed at the Holy Cross Cemetery in Fresno, CA. This is the power of a song. Here are their names:

Miguel Álvarez Negrete	Ignacio Navarro Pérez
Francisco Durán Llamas	Martín Navarro Razo
Santiago Elizondo García	Ramón Ochoa Ochoa
Rosalío Estrada Padilla	Ramón Paredes González
Bernabé García López	Apolonio Placencia Ramírez
Tomás Gracia de Aviña	Guadalupe Ramírez Lara
Salvador Hernández Sandoval	Alberto Carlos Raygoza
Severo Lara Medina	Guadalupe Rodríguez Hernández
José Macías Rodríguez	Maria Rodríguez Santana
Elías Macías Trujillo	Wenceslao Ruiz Flores
Tomás Márquez Padilla	Juan Ruiz Valenzuela
Luis Medina López	José Sánchez Valdivia
Manuel Merino Calderón	Jesús Santos Meza
Luis Miranda Cuevas	Baldomero Marcos Torres

WORTH QUOTING

The worst thing that can happen to you is to cut yourself loose from people. And the best thing is to sort of vaccinate yourself right into the the big streams and blood of the people.

To feel like you know the best and the worst of folks that you see everywhere and never to feel weak, or lost, or even lonesome anywhere.

There is just one thing that can cut you to drifting from the people, and that's any brand or style of greed.

There is just one way to save yourself, and that's to get together and work and fight for everybody.

— WOODY GUTHRIE

385

You're always on your corner, ain't you Sam?
You come down when its daylight, don't you Sam?
You sweep the floor and throw clean sawdust down
And then you push that wet dust rag around
Over all their table tops and counter cases
You see the cigars and candy and oozes and ice creams
You always feel your best now, don't you, Sam,
When your belly believes in whiskey, don't it, Sam,
And when your head believes in hot milk,
And your mouth believes in sweet tastes and your
Eyes can't hardly see the morning for your mists
And you can't hardly see the counter for the hangover,
Still, you're the last one to leave the place at night,
Ain't you, Sam, you know you are, right?
And you're the first to hit here in the morning fogs,
I know this, Sam, no use to ask you, no use to tell me,
I know your grind and your job because I worked lots of years,
And lots of seasons at a job that's just like yours,
So, I can ask you, I can tell you, can't I Sam?

                              I know just where you go
To stand at the bar an hour or so,
And to shoot the gas and b.s., yes, sir, Sam,
Just a step around this corner to the closest bar and grill,
Or should I leave off the grill? Tell me, Sam.
I know the place you stand and down them like a man,
And look at all the pictures painted yonder on the wall,
You seen that drunk painter paint them off of little penny post cards,
And I seen him take two weeks of pay out in spirits every day,
Seen him dip and stroke and sway at his picture of the day,
I heard him tell me one wet night all about a painter's life
When you was standing listening, I know you remember, Sam,
Just what was that painter's name? I know of the painting game
For I followed it and drank my wages up from wall to wall,
And I carried penny post cards to look at to judge my color,
And I painted house to house, store to store, door on to door,
And I always took my pay out in high test every day,
And I always stood and listened to the things the folks would say,
And I heard more lives and histories, heard more mysteries,
Saw more lost boats, heard more bragging, seen them dragging,
Smelled them swaying and their sagging, all across the several states
Where I stood and looked as you look, where I painted, sung and fell,
Where I always hit the damp grass before anything else woke up
Where I always walked my ten miles before the windows shook an eyebrow,
And I worked the same as you work, yes, I did, I tell you, Sam,
I was like you are, and still am, just like you, Sam,
Even if I go to play and sing at silkier padded places,
Even if I dicker here at home in a scared tremble with nervous paint,
I can say, that somewhere in me, all inside me, some crazy way,
I feel like I'm still like you lots of ways, believe this, Sam.

What would they call you and your work that you do?
How would I tell them what you look like, Sam, so as to not make
You feel like I was making fun of you nor not running you down no more?
How would I tell you how you look to me? Rough work, Sam,
This letter business, yes, these letters and words of mine,
These scattered piles of papers and lost ideas left behind,
These shots of people and places, these I write to you, and then,
Tomorrow or tonight again I'll write to who and where, him or her,
But today my job is you, and my day is yours, and your days mine,
Oh, I'll call your work some good name, just as good and big as mine,
You are an engineer of sanitation and you are an organizer
Of this fast running candy and cigar luncheonette here on our corner,
On our good old corner of Thirty Sixth and Mermaid, here
In the one and the only Coney Island on the face of the earth,
And you know that Coney Island is an Island of these drifting joints,
An ocean and a windy sea of these shifting and loud talking small stores,
It's people they come and they go and when they go they are gone
All at once, all in the same flock and flight, when they come back,
They come back in the same old way and with the first easy lazy days,
But you are more than an engineer of sanitation, Sam, you stuck here
Through the bad season, the wet season, the windy and the empty months,
And you kept your broom, your rags and your mops going full steam,

Sam worked at Dick Stern's candy store on Mermaid Avenue in Coney Island, NY.

When the others were out chasing their sunbeams and
Skipping through their morning dews and dampnesses,
You're not just a summer soldier nor a fair weather fighter,
But somebody fighting that dirt that gathers on your boss's floor,
You're somebody wrestling that filth across his cases,
You're some sort of a lifetime scientist out to fight and to kill
All of that disease that breeds there in all of that old trashy slop
That you carry out to your garbage barrel in your bare hands
Once or twice or a dozen times a day.
You feel like this somewhere down in you, don't you, Sam?

You're what's called a spreader of the news of our day,
Because you stand up through more storm and wind to hand out
Those papers of a morning and of an evening, and of the night,
Through more rough weather than the folks that own your papers,
Through just as much argument, reasoning, asking, telling, selling,
Through more actual bodily labor, to scatter your news around
From one hand to the next hand, and it is through your hand
That this whole street and this end of Coney and parts of Seagate
Find out every hour what went on in the world today, yesterday,
And you standout there by your little green news stand,
And you watch for an hour or so to see the paper truck come up
To your curb and yell and kick your little bundle off at your feet,
And you walk out when it's sunny or duck out if it's bad, and you
Grab up your bundle under your arm soft as you would a baby,
And you walk back to your stand with your knife in your hand,
Or you walk back inside if the weather is bad, cut your cords,
Spread your papers apart, take your pencil, write a name
In some of the corners for the ones that has already paid you
And you take these and you lay them to one side on a milk crate
And you lay some thick magazines up there on your cigar case,
And you take the ones without any names on them
And you carry them outside if its pretty
And you stack and hang them up inside if its bad,
And you drink your cup of coffee to warm your burny gut,
And to tighten your rippling stomach, don't you Sam?

The fone rings back in that third booth
And you leave your cup of coffee to ask who it's for,
Then you run back past your coffee there just right to drink,
Out past your news stand, and on out to the right door,
And if it's pretty, you stand outside and yell the name,
And if it's bad underfoot you step inside the double door,
And I can hear you yelling out at all hours of the day or night,
Telephone. Telephone. Telephone. Somebody wants you.
And it is worth a dollar bill to get the party in touch
With the other party and everybody knows a dollar would be cheap
To hear that voice and those words coming from the other person
And when they run past you to the booth they say, Sam, Thanks,
I've not got any money on me right now,
But quick as I see you again, I'll hand you something,
I'll hand you something for a tip.
And I know that I would be just as sore as you are, Sam,
If I done somebody such a big favor as this and went to so much work
To do it, and then they called my salaray a tip,
Because I know how you feel about calling your money a tip,
You hate that word tip as much as I hate it,
And I hate a tip in any shape, form, or fashion,
I hate the whole business of begging and tipping,
And I know how hard you run and how many trips you make a day,
And it sure does make your tail red, don't it, Sam?

Cathy is just a little bit over Three years old now,
And last night Marjorie and myself took a notion we needed a movie
To perk us up a little bit, and so we waited till Cathy ate supper
And climbed up over the rail of her bed and kicked her shoes off,
And then I stepped outside through the spring rains and asked you
If you would come in and read some of our books and watch our house
And our daughter while we stepped out, and you
Said you would be glad to, and so you come at the right time,
And Marjorie made you feel at home in our big easy chair
While I poured you a pretty stiff drink of good Russian Vodka
Cut down with just a smithering of cherry sodie,

You sat there on our couch and drank the glass
Down in one long gone gulp and I asked you would you
Rather set over here on our easy chair, and you
Said, No, I couldn't rest good there, not with this pot belly,
I've got to set up as straight as I can to even breathe.
And so, Marjorie asked you would you like to read a book
And you said you had lots rather listen to the radio,
And so, we said to make yourself at home,
And if you got hungry for eats the ice box had a little,
And you said, Okay, but I'm not very apt to get hungry,
I just had a big meal in the place before I come over.
And so we went on out and down the street talking
And walked and talked and thought and wondered about Sam,
And I guess lots of people wonder a lot about you,
Guess about you, think about you, ask funny questions,
Look sideways and walleyed at you, don't they, Sam?

I hope in a way that my face gets on it
Some of the same looks that your face has got on it,
Of course, I can't look exactly like you, but wouldn't be bashful
If I did, won't feel funny when I do, look like you,
Your face is round and so is your head, your hands cut big,
Your chest is thick and your shoulders are rolling and sloped,
Your body is short and heavy and your legs are stubby, short like,
You are built to work at hard work, get at hard and heavy things,
Lift and pull and carry and clean and wait and work some more
It's your bending and your lifting and your carrying loads of people
That has made you like you are, whatever you are,
And it's me and Marjorie and Cathy and a thousand others like us
That has asked you to do jobs for us, jobs we couldn't ever do,
Jobs we had to have done, people we had to meet and talk to,
Papers we had to have and read up on,
Voices of friends and relatives, well and sick and asking
How we feel and where we're going,
Voices of people come together through your running and your yelling,
Plans made, jobs done, money collected, things bought,
Letters written, friends made, sweethearts met with, parties had,
Rallies, meetings, fund drives, concerts, poker games,
Bridge Clube, dates made with outsiders and insiders,
Love made lawful and not so lawful, the hot, cool, cooling,
Yes, all of thes run through you and have made you Sam,
They have made me myself, Cathy Cathy, Marjorie Marjorie,
These things have made us all, kept our fires firing in us,
Made our bloods run close together, made us know one another plainer,
Helped us find our own lost selves and right roads,
Helped us knock from door to door with papers signed telling congress,
Helped us call a union get together, talkover, a quick one,
You would be the last man on this street to call yourself any big name
You would be one of the last men on earth to want any big name
You would be one of the last ones to admit you are a politician
But you are, I know you are, I know you Sam.
You have changed this street for the better, helped us all,
You have changed this house for the better, helped my family,
You have changed this neighborhood, made it friendlier, warmer,
You know I'm digging you out of yourself, don't you, Sam?
Ain't I, Sam?

****

Sam (last name unknown) and Gail Stern,
Mermaid Avenue, Coney Island, ca. 1949.

184

Mermaid Avenue
Coney Island, N.Y.C.
March 18, 1948

Annie Shapiro
Dear Annie
        I hear that the loose
plaster fell down in your face as
you lay in your bed.
        I don't know any too much about
you. I do know that you are crippled
with a club foot.
        I do know that you work a few
days every week over across the
street at the fish store. I've seen
you in there with your hands all
full of ice and fish.
        I know I've seen you out here
in our hall sweeping and washing the
stairs down with sopey water and your
old rag. The landlady gave you ten
bucks a month off your rent for
doing fifty dollars worth of cleaning.

Letter to Coney Island neighbor Annie Shapiro, along with pencil sketch, 1948.

Cripple
Annie

woody guthrie
april 12, 1948
coney island

oh, yes, I was plenty lonesome and I never will forget

How the old folks shuffled past me — I can see their faces yet —

Eyes all red around the edges and a damp look deeper in

Eyes that's seen their share of troubles that were always stumbling in.

Foreheads marked and cut with wrinkles like the plow tracks on a field

Cheeks sunk in against the bone and lips that never can be sealed.

Hair as gray and splashed with silver as a moonlight winter's night

Faces — faces — faces — faces — what a picture! what a sight!

Faces friendly like a mountain top that stands up in the sun

When the blank and rotten tenements ~~descent~~ melts ~~out~~ into the filthy slum ~~into the slum~~

Strong and hard but bony faces with a shine of high tanned leather

COMP
Lifes
NAME Other Side
Some scientific notes on a book I'll write someday. Woody Guthrie
MADE IN U.S.A.

This excerpt from an essay by Woody titled "Just Today" recounts people who passed him by on the street and the feelings they evoked in him. Taken from a 1944 collection of stories titled "Lifes Other Side."

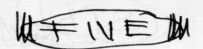

FIVE

Faces that had laughed and loved and
cried in every kind of weather

Eyes that looked out of their sockets like
a man looks out of jail —

Half a smile and half a sneer — half a
love song — half a wail.

Necks and muscles hard as iron once,
now a little front ways stooped,

Shoulders that had carried whole worlds,
just a little downward drooped.

Young heads bobbed along the tight crowd
and bellered out their noise

That roars like a cyclone in the younger
girls and boys;

Eyes that shot ahead like spot lights on
the drifting stage below

Eyes that made my spirits brighter even
now that I was low.

And I thought," now — now I wonder —
which of these

Can look upon the rest of us and say
he's really pleased

So what

Woody Guthrie
Coney Island
1949

No Hand for trouble

Woody Guthrie
Coney Island
1949

a 59th St. gent
watches army day parade

stove aint hot no

Woody Guthrie
Coney Island
1948

MOSSBACK

Them Skies is Mine

Woody Guthrie
1951

Drop dead

Woody Guthrie
Coney Island
1949

Starvation disease

Woody Guthrie

Arlo's Funny Man

McSorley's Old Ale House, East Village, New York City, 1942

Reefer

woody Guthrie
4-23-'46

I heard a man talking last
night and he said

I could actually make more
money when the depression was on

and a lady laughed at him
and said

Oh you couldnt either

How could you

and the man told her

yes

I could

I made more money during
the depression. I made more because
I could steal more. nowdays this dam
war makes it awful hard to steal. and
besides, I dont know, I just dont enjoy
stealing like I once did. This dam war
is a hell of a thing.

and she told him

This war has just opened your
eyes up to how many people you hurt
by stealing

and a scared look was on his

This short story was based on a conversation overheard in a New York City bar in
1943. Woody was a stickler for preserving the lingo and idioms of local characters from
different neighborhoods, capturing the uniqueness of a particular dialect or expression.

face and he looked all around up and down
the street and then he said

       Thats it.

       Thats what I mean.

       When I look around all over the
town

       and see
       all of these pictures
       Pictures of
       Hungry kids looking at you
       and see
       these pictures of hungry soldiers
needing a doughnut or a cup of coffee
       and the faces
       The all sunk in faces
       of the folks
       In all of them there bombed
towns and Hitler countries
       I dont know
       I just feel like I dont want
to steal no more
       Till after
       This dam war's over

I stood there in the dark for a
little while and I kept still with my
ear bent

  Listening
  And I heard the lady say
  You look like a pretty good guy
to me.
  How would it happen that
  you would want to steal
  and heard him wait a bit and
say
  Dam'd if I know
  now days
  But I used to like it. I just
naturally
  got a kick out of stealing
  Hell
  Everybody
  was stealing
  them days
  So
  Why hadnt I - I mean - why
shouldnt I

210

I was just By god stealing
Because everybody else was
I stole stuff
Because the rest of them was
stealing it off of me
One way
Or the other
Everybody was a thief
Thiefs
The whole dam mess of them

and she pulled a red fire on the
end of her cigaret and her face lit up in
the old dark night
and the light struck over onto his
face under his hat
and both of them looked
just about like
me
or you
or both of us
and she said,
Its been very few green dollars

that I've lifted off from men
And the times I had the chance
was more than once
Why
How many is the wallet that they
dropped on my floor
And
money fell loose all over my place
and you nor nobody else
Could hardly of kept from
Stealing it
I hooked onto a little years ago
when I didn't know no better
But I learned better
You know how I learned
well
Tell you
I found out, We'll say,
That if you was — well — if I was
to meet you right here on the street
And stop you
and give you back your wallet
With all of your papers and cards

and pictures and stuff in it
        and your money too
        Twenty or thirty bucks
        In it
        Not even touched
        Not even bothered
        Well
        You'd like me for that wouldn't
you?

        and he said
        Sure
        Sure I would

        and she kept on
        and said
        Why would you like me?
        It would be because you thought
more of your pictures and cards and
        things
        Than you did of the money
        Wouldn't it?

and he shook his head yes
and told her
    a fellow dont just forget something
like that with a snap of his finger

    and she said
    and you might steer me onto a
whole lot more than what money was
in your
        Wallet
        Huh
        Say in the next six months
        or
        A years time?

        and
        The man said
        Yes
        Hell yes
        why sure

Your thick headed

She said

And green as they make 'em   but
you still got a little speck of brains or
something like brains

Rattling around inside of your
head

How dumb are you sister

How thick is your block

He asked her

There aint a dry bitch in this
town no more ignorant than you are

How the hell come you to say
how dumb I am?

Youre dumb because youre here
with me

She said

Thats how I know youre dumb

I know I'm no good and you aint
neither or you wouldnt

Be here with me

and he said

no

There's something about you

I always did like

no matter how dumb you are

no matter if you aint worth much

maybe

You're still worth a little

You aint burnt your lamp out

yet.

Yeah

But you aint no account as a man

or you wouldn't

Be here

Wasting your time no way like this

and it aint just tonight

Hell

Its all time

You poof your time away on me

and I dont like it

You hadnt ought to be missing out

on your sleep

You gotta hellof a hard days work
ahead of you tomorrow
And every other day
So
what in the hell do you want to
suck around after me for?

You teach me a lot of stuff
He told her
You always do
You aint nothing fancy
or nothing on a stick
But
I dont know — I always feel
like you know a dang sight more
than you act like

and she said
Well
So does everybody
You're still a dam fool
For being with a dam fool.

Just because somebody is a dam
fool
He said
and somebody else is with them
It dont
Always mean
That both of them are dam fools.

"most generally
She said.

not always
He told her.
Then he went on to say
I learnt a dickens of a lot just
by being around you
I always feel like you teach
me something
Something most women
Cant

218

makes you ever feel any such a
way as that? She asked him.
        You dont mean that baloney.
        I aint worth the price of the
beer we soaked in tonight
        and whose work
        whose hard earned money was it
we blowed?
        yours
        your own.
        gone. Wasted.
        drunk down. Pissed out. Then
drunk down. Pissed out. Cold going in.
Hot coming out.
        you're a liar
        you're a liar to me
        you're a liar to the whole world
        you're a liar to
        your own self.
        What under the sun could you
ever learn off of an old satchel like
        me?
        You know good and well you dont

really give a particular good god dam

about me.

So he said,

no

no I dont

not this long time stuff

But

I mean

not in a way like two sweeties
about to get married

not no little love nest full of
baby talk

no little cottage with a rose bush
and a gate

no

I dont really mean to say

This

is how I feel about you

But you see I'm not even ready
to think about that stuff

Right now

any how

So I like to spend my time in a lot of crazy ways

      Just to learn

      About the world

      People

      who they are

      where they are

      what they are and what they think

      and how come them to be

      who they are where they are doing what they are —

      and while he was talking she walked up the street and he walked along behind her a few steps.

A partial list of some of the people Woody wrote about in his songs and stories:

Abraham Lincoln
Adolf Hitler
Albert Einstein
Aliza & Isadore Greenblatt
Anneke Van Kirk
Annie Mae Merriweather
Antyfascist Steve
Arlo Davy Guthrie
Belle Starr
Betty Sanders
Big Bill Haywood
Big Moe in the Mud
Bill Jackson
Bill Rogers Guthrie
Billy the Kid
Bob Wood
Bobylink & Tommalinka
Boomtown Bill
Bud Mosier
Carlson Raiders Band
Cathy Ann Guthrie
Charles Lindberg
Cheap Mike
Chiang Kai-shek
Cisco Houston
Captain Colin Kelly Jr.
Dalton Boys Gang
Deep Blue John
Devil
Doorstep Baby
Dopefiend Robber
Dorie Miller
Dr. Leo Hayes
Dustbowl Refugee
Dwight Eisenhower
Dying Miner Joe
East Texas Red
Elizabeth Gurley Flynn

Ellen Estrella Dupree
Ferguson Brothers
Fiorello La Guardia
Francisco Franco
Franklin Delano Roosevelt
Fred Trump
General MacArthur
George Wallace
Gerhard Eisler
Ginny Mill Girl
Gwendolyn & Sue Guthrie
Hanns Eisler
Harriet Tubman
Harry Bridges
Harry Simms
Harry Truman
Henry Ford
Henry Wallace
Herbert Hoover &
    Thomas E. Dewey
Huddie Ledbetter
Hughlon Burleson
Ilse Koch
Ingrid Bergman
Isaac Woodard
Jackhammer John
Jesse James
Jesus Christ
Jim Dancer
Jim Hickock (Wild Bill
    Hickock)
Jimmy Whalen
Joady Ben Guthrie
Joe DiMaggio
Joe Hill
Joe Louis
John Colier
John Jacob Niles

Johnny Hart
Jonah Kelley
Judge Kennedy
Judge Knox
Judge Parker
Julius & Ethel Rosenberg
Kathy Fiscus
Ku Klux Klan
Little Billy
Long John the Long-
    shoreman
Lowell Mill Girls
Lt. Fitzgerald Atkinson &
    Cpl. Robert R. Boardman
Lucius Clay
Maggie Mozella McGee
Mailman
Marco Polo & Kublai Khan
Marie Fagin
Mario Russo
Marjorie Guthrie
Martha Jane Cannary
    (Calamity Jane)
Matthew Kimes
Matthew, Mark, Luke
    & John
Maxine "Lefty Lou"
    Crissman
Mike Quin (pen name for
    Paul William Ryan)
Millard Lampell
Miss Lyudmila Pavlichenko
Molly McGuhir
Moses
Mother Bloor
Mrs. Edna Martin
Nicola Sacco & Bartolomeo
    Vanzetti

Nora Belle Sherman
    Guthrie
Nora Lee Guthrie
Norah Dewitt
Old Cap Moore
Orphan Janey
Paul Robeson
Philadelphia Lawyer
Pretty Boy Floyd
Railroad Bill
Ramblin Reckless Hobo
Robert Burns
Rosa Lee Ingram
Ruby Bates
Ruth Farnsworth
Saint Lazarus
Sally Rand & her Fan
Sam
Slim Houston
Smokey Woods
Snow White & Rose Red
Soviet Union Gal
Stetson Kennedy
The Almanac Singers
The Dalton Boys
The Trenton Six
Thomas Dudley Hurwitz
Three Sisters
Tom Joad
Tom Mooney
Tom Moore
Tommy Vradenburg
Vee Dee Seaman
Vincent "Jimmy" Longhi
Walt Whitman's Niece
Will Rogers
Willy McGhee
Winston Churchill

BOOK 5

LOVE

IN & OUT

MARJORIE

CHAPTER SIX

Love Loves You Most When You Love Love the Most

love in darkness
love in light
both are love
love depends not on sight

dammed-up love
love that flows
both are love
love cares not what shows

love that's sinking
love that floats
both are love
love waits not for boats

love holds not
to the gifts it gave
all is love
love is the wave

—ANI DIFRANCO

My New York City
Woody Guthrie
4-5-1947
*

I am riding on this West End Train
This grey and rainy day
I am looking out my window at a sight so fair to see
I've walked and rode in rain and sun
Through Brooklyn, Bronx, and Queens,
SEEN A ~~bowy~~ billion jillion faces ~~I see~~ ~~you~~ ~~D~~ ~~day.~~
                              ~~xxxxxxxxxxxxxxxxxxxxxxxxx~~ that are NY town to me.

Chorus

                              Ride my subway train from here to heaven
                              Ride my ferryboat up my silvery river
                              Walk our beach sand and our pretty park grass
                              My New York City is the town where I found you.

I see our black roof housetops
Shining yonder in the rain
I see our concrete highway ~~running~~
Running yonder in the sun
I see your face there shining
Where the kids play in the streets
And in a billion jillion windows that are New York Town to me.   (Chorus)

No matter where this train rolls
I look out my window ~~glass~~
Your eyes shine in my ~~two loves~~
And my buildings that I ~~love~~
I'd give my fame and fortune ~~up~~
To hold your hand today
And go a billion jillion ~~miles~~ that are New York Town ~~to me~~   (Chorus)

                    Words and music to this song made up
                    this date by W.W.Woody Guthrie, 4-5-1947.
                    3520 Mermaid Avenue, Brooklyn, 24, New York.
                    Just a little song to match the faces of
                    old recollections I saw today riding on a
                    West End Express train from Union Square to
                    Coney Island, and then onto the Norton Point
                    trolley car to 36th and Mermaid and home.

                    ----- 30 -----

     *** If music and songs ever do get to be put over soft speakers in all
of our subway trains, I'd like to set back and ride along and look out and
listen to this one sung. And someday our subway trains might have some kind
of music in them. There's plenty on the eyes and faces of the folks riding
along to make up a thousand good songs about if you just watch real close at
the looks on the faces. If you look and listen a little bit closer, you can
even hear an old and a new song somewhere away back in the grazing lands of
your own old memories and future plans. W.G.

music wrote
down by me
Woody Guthrie

226

Woody and Marjorie Mazia (nee. Greenblatt),
New York City, 1944.

YOU KNOW THE NIGHT

You know the night I met you
My eyes had been
Looking for you all over everywhere.
Over low roads. Down highways. Bald deserts.
But looking
Without finding you.
That was it.
And the reason why this was so
was because
I had seen so much troubled
waters and storms on the streets.
And this caused me
To want to do
Something about it.
Something to help not only just us
But people of all kinds come closer and
closer
and closer together.
You know the night.
Your eyes had this same shine
about them I noticed
and when I first looked through
the wild wayward mist
I felt such a warm friendly cool
sunny smile
That I wanted to look in your
Eyes for all time.
I just felt like you feel when
you feel like the angels are curling your
hair and you feel like the devil is
scratching your heel.
But if my jellied brain turns to
ashes and sand
There will still be such night smiles
across all the land
There will still be
Such faces
Meeting here in this dark
and there 'round the corner or
maybe the park.
It is when we meet this way
and look
at each other
we get hold of our scattered aims
and

Bring them
and beat them
and wrestle
and fight them
and heat them
and beat them and weld them
together
Like iron from the valley
and fire from the skies
This blast furnace heat burns
in our peoples eyes.
And from a raw aimless hunk
of dead matter
our love gives it vision
and love gives it shape
and it's born and it works
Like a new little baby
It sputters
It mutters
It goes and it stutters
and walks on the sidewalks
and falls in the gutters.
But it always and always seems
to move and be able
To get up. To raise up.
Up on its feet again.
Did you feel this way too when I met you?
Did you look at me
and think
Here's me a guy
That hopes like I hope
and sees the same kind of new
dreams I see?
Because you wondered, I know,
If your hopes could find shape in
the words that we used there to work back the fog –
Your hopes and your plans for the
good of the people.
Could all of your hundred and one
Dreams just as bright as the sun
and all of your wants and your hottest
desires
Find shape in the flow of my talk?
And there by ourselves while the bronze
statues watched us
We talked some. Kept still for
a time. Talked a little more.

Your hair had the smell of cleaness
about it and the wind helped my fingers to
play with your curls –
and the wind and the mist caused the
night to blow colder and we brought our hopes
there a little bit closer –
Hopes that we hoped
Work that we wanted
Jobs we were doing, aimed to do.
Quiet idle words, of the church and
the steeple. The union. The war.
And the world full of people.
And you gave my mind such a
deep kind of light
It blasted the fog.
It blew up the night.
It pulled back the curtains of
clouds from above us
and all of the stars came out and
winked at us
and I yelled up at the skies
and said
You stars! Go ahead! Shine as
bright as you want to!
Light up this round world and shine
if you want to!
And it was brighter than usual
and for some reason or other
The night
Turned off clear. And so cold.
It caused me to snuggle up closer
and hold
Hold on
Hold on to the ground we had gained.
Hold on to the new inch of life we discovered.
Hold on to the night.
We exchanged our dreams as we sat
there a while
word by word.
Plan by plan.
Mile by mile.
You looked a bit hungry and skinny to
me but
I had me the notion you'd soon fatten up.
You know how love is and you know
how dreams are. If you don't stay in love you
soon wilt away and you get sort of hungry-

looking they say. So I thought you'd fill out
and look a lot better with a little work and
the right kind of weather.
You knew I was raily and some out of
shape. And you knew that my eyes and my
feet didn't mate. I was hunched and walked
crooked – but you overlooked this because
with the right kind of home life and care
my old carcass and brain could be good
for more wear.
Your grace of walk and action drove
me into fits. I tried to, but couldn't
think about anything else. This world
is an awful big machine and it moves
all together. No force on earth can
hold it back – and I am in all of this
and moving with it – and I feel the
motion and the rhythm of the universe
moving with these planets.
And moving the earth along with them.
And the earth moving the people
Along
With it
And the attraction of your face and
your form
Pulled me. Pushed me. Drew me.
It was ten thousand times stronger than
all of the rest of these
Powers multiplied by ten.
And I felt harmony and sweetness
and felt strife
And wanted to walk with you as my wife
Down to the foamy docks to ride a
good boat
Across the troubled waters of this
life.
You know the night I met you.
You know the night I met you
My eyes had been
Looking for you all over everywhere.
Over low roads. Down highways. Bald deserts.
I just felt like you feel when
you feel like the angels are curling your
hair and you feel like the devil is
scratching your heel.

... There's fifteen of my friends. We're all going to make up a dance. We want you to sing that song exactly like you did on that night seventeen months ago here with the beer and pretzels."

Now it's got to be count for count, breath for breath, word for word, move for move, eye blink for blink, and not just one extra snap or pause or hold or delay or too fast or too slow—you've got to do it all over again. And not only that, but when a bunch of dancers get to dancing, if you make a missed beat, or a missed count on your guitar, they bump into each other. I mean, they kick each other with their knees and elbows and some are up in the air and some are down on the floor. Some are banging into each other...when you start making a mistake. Man, there's all kinds of collisions happening. It's like on a wet slippery day out here on the skyway, somebody throws on her brakes, everybody has a wreck. Well it's the same way in these dancing things.

So, they took a record that a friend of mine made one day in a studio. I remember very well the record and the day. And I remember very well what was wrong with my friend; he had a bad case of asthma. He'd been drinking several bottles of whiskey, the Irish whiskey to try to open up his asthma a little bit and he was singing without any music notes and things, so he put a lot of pauses where he should not have, and he put in a whole bunch of words where there should have been pauses. But when the record come out, it was the world's most, we'll say, unpredictable song.

But anyway, that was the one, out of all of the seventeen hundreds of records that I had made and helped make in my life, that was the one song where there was no beat, no pause, no nothing about it that she [Sophie Maslow] could pick up and work out. Most songs, they got a sort of a definite beat here and a definite pause there, and definite beat, definite pause. There's a little bit of shape to them, little bit of something that you can grab onto and memorize. So, she comes in with a whole bunch of stuff. It looks like a whole bunch of architects and algebra and geometricians and mathematicians have worked out a...some kind of a new atom bomb formula or something. She comes in and lays it down in front of me, says, "This is the way it's got to be. Or, fifteen or twenty dancers are just going to break their necks, that's all."

In this transcript from a live interview in 1949, Woody explains the difficulty of folk singers and dancers working together.

235

Folksay rehearsal with Tony Kraber on
set at CBS Television Studio, 1945.

Pencil sketches made while observing a Martha Graham
technique dance class, New York City, 1947.

61

65

69

239

84

I Say To You Woman And Man

I'll say to you, woman,
come out from your
home and be the wild
dancer of my breed.

I'll say to my man
come out of your walls
and move in your space
as free and as wild as
my woman.

I'm married and wed to a
dancer in my front line.
And the way she moves
while I beat my skin
drum would knock your
soul and your lights out,

I beat my old drum skin
and sing to my big
family, you, Arlo, you,
Stackis, you Teeny, you
Stew Ball, you, Bill,
you Marjorie,

Come out from your made
Walls and out from your
sins and out from your
sick spell and dance
to high glory.

You poor sick head poet
that sung to my
woman to stay here

in these sod walls and
laze around sleepy and
doze around sheepy while
your man is the one to
go out and see action.
You jail home poets are
dead in my dust. I
sing your song but I
sing it just backwards.

I say to my woman dance
out of our home.

Dance out and see fighting.
Dance out and see people.
Dance out to run factories.
Dance out to see street meats.
Dance out in the deep stream.
Dance out to your vote box.
Dance down to your office.
Dance over to your counter.
Dance up your big stairs.

If your husband gets jealous
dance out to new lovers.

If your man keeps your
heart tied dance out
and untie it.

Dance out to sing equal.
Dance up and be pretty.
Dance around and be free.

and if I just had this
one thing to say to
a husband it would
be these words

Go dance

That's all

Just jump up and let
go and dance

Dance in your own way.
Sing your own song.
Whoop your own kind
of a yell in the start
and in the finish of your
dance.

Mammy of nature gave
birth to you in her
body and hills. You
give birth now to old
female mommy nature
in the male feelings
and rivers.

Go dance.
Both of you.

Go dance.

30 Woody Guthrie
Aug. 13, 1947
Coney Island

woody Guthrie

148 West 14th St.,
New York Town
April 3, 1942

Howdy:

Well, with 99% of me somewhere down in Pennsylvania,
it's going to be pretty hard for the other 1% to write a
very good answer to your special letter that just now
got here. I had this one knocked out and handed to the
mail man before he could get your letter into my hands.

Things here are not the same and I'd be a liar to
say so; Pinto Pete and Repeat are droopy and weary in the
eye; Okie's one little bush that was trying so hard, so
hard to keep a grip on life and a grasp on the earth, I'm
afraid is brittle and swiveling away; El Guitarista or
whatever its name is hasn't come out with a single song;
Little White Scotty Dog snarls and growls and his little
light just barely cuts through this darkness; the Vita-
phone Pills, Tooth Brushes, Paste, Razor, Blades, Alco-
hol, are almost up in arms, and our little medicine cab-
inet is roaring louder than Camp McClelland. This is the
spirit of the whole place.

The Clothes Closet is swarming with threats and rum-
blings. Your Gray Skirt has been having secret talks with
your White Blouse, and all kinds of rumors are leaking into
the ears of Your Blue Serge Coat. I feel downright sorry
for the Little Mexican Flower, the Hat, I mean; the leaves
are shaking like a cold cyclone rustling up out of a river
bottom. Your Costumes positively don't know where to go
or what to do next, it is hinted in some corners of the
Closet that your Red Waist will lead a split within the
Lewis Setup, but its destiny is far from clear. There's
no use to even report on what my Taxi Driver Jacket is
doing or thinking, it will probably stay CIO, but fall
from a high pedestal. My Blue Suit would have got completely out of line, if your Green Dress hadn't held it
on a good line, (Pardon me, the dress is black. Maybe
the Green One just turned black). My overcoat is old.
It is wrinkled and gray. It drapes on the end of the
whole parade, like somebody dragging an old fish along.
The JU Ju Bees have done well to keep a little shadow of
their former color. The teeth of the comb clatter through
the misty nights, and the hair brush turned gray three
or four days ago.

There is only one little whisp of health or life anywhere on this reservation, and every living thing strains
at the nostrils, trying to breath in enough of it to keep
alive one more minute.

Rather than see life disappear from this whole place,
I stumbled onto the trick of putting on your Blue Robe,
then turning out all lights, and walking around over the
room sprinking Tweed Perfume up into the air. The move-
ment and the nice smell has a tendency to suggest that
life is still somewhere in all of this ocean of dark.
But this takes about a cubic ounce per day, and since I

am stranded here with only about 2 cu. ozs., naturally,
I have a feeling that I am fighting against hopeless odds,
and am bound to come out loser.

That is the real reason for this whole letter. Not

that I feel the least bit involved in your coming or going, personally; but from the standpoint of a scientific reporter reporting what he sees to report.

Every dying thing tries to make some last stand, some last stab, or some last sound, before being snuffed from this sphere of existence. One of the earliest tribal laws of the human race still survies to allow a doomed prisoner his last few words; although many, many times this last noise is just spent in thin air; the doomed creature likes to think that somehow, somewhere, some time, this echo will be picked up and heard by friendly ears, and the life and the meaning will somehow be saved. Reporting from a raft floating on the ocean in a hurricane would be a comic situation compared with the life that I am forced to see fade into nothing all around me.

A person's life is his thoughts. It might have been, that if I'd had foresight enough, I would have kept a bigger part of my thoughts here on 14th street; but careless and gambling as my nature has always been, I sent my thoughts, thousand by thousand, off to the wilds of Pennsylvania. And since everything on earth seems to draw life from every other thing, all of the Babies, and the Others have done nothing but point their fingers at me, howl, and accuse me of mishandling the very forces that might have kept the small spark glowing till the Sun came back next Monday.

I've spent good money for three of the hardiest bunches of leaves and flowers, and every single time, I open the door, I start for the vase, and ZZZZzzzzzziiiippp, the whole works disappears right out of my hand. Possibly when you come back, this room will spring to life like a bontanical garden.

It's only fair to report, that, in spite of the truth of all of this, there's a slit of hope left for the entire section I am reporting from.

I have hung your good letter up on the light cord, and I can see rays and beams of life shooting across the place, and am going to be foolish enough to believe that this will prevent, or stall of at least, complete extinction. If I'm correct in my analysis, you can take charge of the project upon your return, and experiment further trying to bring new life to these objects. I am not at all certain which of these objects will be me, but this will continue to be more discernable as the subjects under experimentation evolve from state to state.

Now, in case all efforts fail to keep a sprig alive in these polar regions, there are one or two last little things that I would like to add here.

My past life seems to get as plain as day before me, and I see the mixed up, tangled thing that I have been. I want to thank everybody that I ever saw for allowing me to see them.

I want to confess being not only the world's most highly disorganized human being, but in history go down as about the biggest waster of time.

I want to raise the slogan, Continue In The Highways Of Marx and Roosevelt and Free Oklahoma If Possible!

And for you, in a very brotherly way, maybe I can
say a few last things.
The longer they last, the better.
Your voice has led me in the footpaths of utility
and your footsteps have quieted my soul
When I snarled at the world like a crying hyena
your counsel restored my humanity
When the starlight tasted like dust on my pillow
your whisper brought peace to my conscience
When my thoughts were lost in my own wasted cravings
your hand brought a lamp to my stumbling
When friends put their faith in the failures I failed at
your patience gave me my redemption
Your going was always the set of my sun
and your coming the light of my morning
And these things I trust in the care of your hand
for I give my whole life to your keeping

                              Woody of Oklahoma

PS:

In case I should live and survive, I will write you the
other 99% of this report.

My mind is like the climate I've followed so long. And yours is like the ground and the earth and the solid footing where rabbits play and deer go scampering, and if the eagle circles the cliff in the sun, even he loves the ledge that is safe for his landing when his wings get tired of rambling the heavens.

Woman At Home

Words & Music by

Woody Guthrie
Copr. Woody Guthrie

You folksong singers all go around asingin'
  How bad are the men, how wicked are the women;
  I gotta woman at home with her door wide open for me;
  I gotta woman at home with her gate wide open for me.

Joshylarr Whyte sings glad and sad
  'Bout a dozen good gals he ain't never had;
  I gotta woman at home with her window wide open for me;
  I gotta woman at home with her mouth wide open for me.

These weavery singers do the same old thing,
  Run my women down on your guitar strings;
  I gotta woman at home with her eyes wide open for me;
  I gotta woman at home with her arms wide open for me.

You boogyboogy beaters, you jittersingers, too,
  Tear a woman all to pieces before you get through;
  I gotta woman at home with her heart wide open for me;
  I gotta woman at home with her soul wide open for me.

You sing on records and teevee shows,
  You wrackle the women every place you go;
  I gotta woman at home with her house wide open for me;
  I gotta woman at home with her place wide open for me.

I'ma high balladman, I'ma fulkyzinger, too;
  I sing all th' good stuff women folks do;
  I gotta woman at home with her sheets wide open for me;
  I gotta woman at home with her blankets wide open for me.

I was born singing into this world
  By the laboring movements of a hundred pretty girls;
  I gotta woman at home with her fingers wide open for me;
  I gotta woman at home with her hands wide open for me.

Main reason that poleeceman turned me aloose,
  'Cause I told him what I'ma tellin' you;
  I gotta woman at home with her eyes wide open for me;
  I gotta woman at home with her skies wide open for me.

END

Woody and Marjorie, professional photos, 1943.

YOU AND I
By
Woody Guthrie

You ask of me how I feel about you, here is the way I feel and I feel,   of
When you see how free that I feel about you I hope that you'll feel this free/me.

You are my highland, I am your lowland;
You are my upland and I am your low land;
You are my dry land, I am your swampland;
You are my ocean, and I am your sea.

You are my high road, I am your low road;
I am your city and you are my town;
I am your northland, you are my southland;
You are my raindrops and I am your tears.

You are my bright fire, I am your ash pile;
I am your fingers and you are my hands;
You are my sunshine, I am your starlight;
You are my woman, I am your man.

I am your tree limb, you are my leaf bed;
You are my canyon, I am your cliff rock;
You are my dance and I am your song;
We are the right and we are the wrong.

You are my sidestreet, I am your sidewalk;
You are my clothes and I am your line;
You are tall tree, I am your underbrush;
We both are life and we both are death.

I am your midnight, midnight and dark night;
You are my room, and my chair and my bed;
You are my babies, I am your children;
We are the graveyard, but not the dead.

You are my firefly, I am your night hawk;
You are the lake and I am the pool;
You are my free winds kissing the sweet leaves;
I am your college and you are my school.

You are my fast horse, you are my high prize;
You are the loser, losing, and lost;
You are my best friend and my worst enemy;
I am the price and you are the cost.

You are my book shelf, I am your whole self;
You are my guitar, I am your harp;
You are my courthouse, I am your judge and jury;
I live in church steeples, you live in bells.

I kiss your wild winds, you kiss my rain storms;
I kiss your flowers while you kiss my grass;
I'll be your honey drinker, you be my clear thinker;
I'll kiss your future and you kiss my past.

You be my sea lanes, I'll kiss your wild waves;
You kiss my salt spray, I'll drink your foam;
You be my homing pigeon, I'll be your true religion;
You be my house here, I'll be your home.

You be my wings spread, I'll be your high head;
You be my apple and I'll be your plum;
You be my job of work, I'll be your pay check;
I'll be your stiff wind blowing you home.

You be my daddy, I'll be your mama;
You be my uncle and I'll be your aunt;
You be my grandma, I'll be your grandpa;
You be my dollars and I'll be your cents.

You be my dust mop, I'll be your best broom;
I'll be your whirlwind, you be my field;
You be my easy come, I'll be your easy go;
You be my orchestra, and I'll be your tune.

You be my open spaces, I'll be your high places;
You be my my night gown and I'll be your belt;
You be my reindeer, I'll be your Santa Clause;   You be my car and I'll be your
                                                              wheels.

JUNE 10 WEDNESDAY

MAY 1942	JUNE 1942	JULY 1942
S M T W T F S	S M T W T F S	S M T W T F
.. .. 1 2	.. 1 2 3 4 5 6	.. .. .. 1 2 3
3 4 5 6 7 8 9	7 8 9 10 11 12 13	5 6 7 8 9 10
10 11 12 13 14 15 16	14 15 16 17 18 19 20	12 13 14 15 16 17
17 18 19 20 21 22 23	21 22 23 24 25 26 27	19 20 21 22 23 24
24 25 26 27 28 29 30	28 29 30	26 27 28 29 30 31
31		

8:00 Ten hundred books of

8:30 just this size I could write

9:00 you about her

9:30 Because I felt if I could

10:00 know her I would know all

10:30 women and they've not been

11:00 any too well known

11:30 For brains and planning

12:00 and organized thinking — I'm

12:30 sure the women are equal

1:00 and maybe ahead of men

1:30 Yet I wouldn't spread

2:00 such a rumor around

2:30 Because one organizes the

3:00 other.

3:30 and in some cases the

4:00 most lost and wasted

4:30 attract the most sane

5:00 and balanced.

5:30 The wild and reckless

6:00 take up with the clocked and

6:30 timed.

7:00 and the mixture is all

7:30 of us and we're still mixing

MAY 1942	JUNE 1942	JULY 1942	JUNE

MAY 1942
T W T F S
.. .. .. 1 2
5 6 7 8 9
12 13 14 15 16
19 20 21 22 23
26 27 28 29 30

JUNE 1942
S M T W T F S
.. 1 2 3 4 5 6
7 8 9 10 11 12 13
14 15 16 17 18 19 20
21 22 23 24 25 26 27
28 29 30 .. ..

JULY 1942
S M T W T F S
.. .. .. 1 2 3 4
5 6 7 8 9 10 11
12 13 14 15 16 17 18
19 20 21 22 23 24 25
26 27 28 29 30 31 ..

JUNE
11
THURSDAY

And all creeds and kinds
and colors of us are blending
Till I suppose
Ten million years from now
We'll all be just alike,
Same color
Same size
Working together —
Maybe we'll have all of
the fascists out of the way
by then.
   Maybe so.
   But it never never
never
   never
   Could of
   Been done
   If the women hadnt
entered into the deal.
   Like she
   Come along
   To me.

REMEMBER THE MOUNTAIN BED
Woody Guthrie
3-11-44
At Sea Going Home

Do you still sing of the mountain bed we made of limbs and leaves?
Do you still sigh there near the sky where the holly berry bleeds?
You laughed as I covered you over with leaves, face, breast, hips and thighs,
You smiled when I said the leaves were just the color of your eyes.

We walked in overalls and shirts and left the road behind
We puffed for air and fell and rolled and rose again and climbed.
We saw the squirrels lay in their food to run the winter through
We buried some acorns under leaves in the dampness of the dew.

Rosin smells and turpentine smells from eucalyptus and pine
Bitter tastes of of twigs we chewed where tangled woodvines twine
Trees held us in on all four sides so thick we could not see
I could not see any wrong in you, and you saw none in me.

Your arm was brown against the ground, your cheeks part of the sky,
As yourfingers played with grassy moss, and limber you did lie;
Your stomach moved beneath your shirt and your knees were in the air
Your feet played games with mountain roots as you lay thinking there.

Below us the trees grew clumps of trees, raised families of trees, and they
As proud as we tossed their heads in the wind and flung good seeds away;
The sun was hot and bright down in the valley below
Where people starved and hungry for life so empty come and go.

There in the shade and hid from the sun we freed our minds and learned
Our greatest reason for being here, our bodies moved and burned;
There on our mountain bed of lea~ves we learned life's reason why
The People laugh and love and dream, they fight, they hate to die.

                                                                    blown,
The smell of your hair I know is still there, if most of our leaves are gone,
Our words still ring in the brush and the trees where singing seeds are sown
Your shape and form is dim, but plain, there on our mountain bed
I see my life was brightest where you laughed and laid your head.

I learned the reason why man must work and how to dream big dreams,
To conquer time and space and fight the rivers and the seas;
I stand here filled with my emptiness now and look at city and land
And I know why farms and cities are built by hot, warm, nervous hands.

I crossed many states just to stand here now, my face all hot with tears,
I crossed city, and valley, desert, and stream, to bring my body here;
My history and future blaze bright in me and all my joy and pain
Go through my head on our mountain bed where I smell your hair again.

All this day long I linger here and on in through the night
My greeds, desires, my cravings, hopes, my dreams inside me fight;
My loneliness healed, my emptiness filled, I walk above all pain
Back to the breast of my woman and child to scatter my seeds again.

----*-----

252

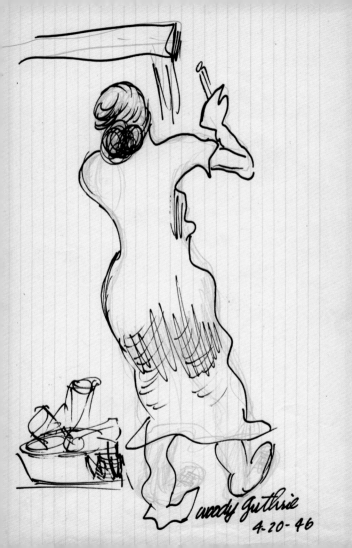

Woody Guthrie
4-20-46

wisht I
was a single
girl again

woody Guthrie
4-21-46

I made these words up to his song to show a little bit of the misery I feel when I see friends of mine get married and wedded and then hang on a nail all of their music, their dancing, their talents and their fun. No matter how much you might try to fool yourself and others, as long as your talents hang there to dry and to rot, you can't tell me you've even commenced to find the real happiness there is in being married. People marry, or ought to, at least, to enlarge, expand, to spread out, to grow, to invent, to discover, to find, to learn more and more music, art, literature, dancing or prancing, but the first real give away sign of a sad wedded match is to walk into your house and to look around your walls there, and to see hanging there all of your good things which you hung there in your great fear and blind fog.

Much of Woody's thinking about a woman's role in the home and in society was influenced by his relationships with the career women and artists he met and worked with in New York City. He wrote these thoughts when hearing of a friend who had given up her music career after marrying.

If your

If your telefone gets out of hand
Don't call no man but a long pole man.
If your sink hole just don't drain.
Don't call no man but a deep hole man.

If your rug gets full of stuff
Call a big shaker to pop it off.
If your clothes line wheel won't roll
Call me to bring my can of oil.

If your piano key don't play
I'll bring my wrench that came old day.
If your mop rag just won't mop
I'll bring you a handle that just won't stop.

If your radiator won't make steam
I'll warm you so hot you'd sleep and dream.
If your trash sack gets too full
I'll give it a yank and a push and a pull.

If your flowers just won't grow
I'll sprinkle your vines both fast and slow.
If your bed spring makes a noise
I'll quieten it down with girls and boys.

If your door hinge squeeks too loud
I'll squirt your hinge both in and out.
If your floor is hard to sweep
I'll make you laugh and cry a week.

(30)
September 8, 1947
CINYC

REVOLUTIONARY MIND

...Woody Guthrie

Night is here again, baby,
I'm stretched out on my bed
Seeing all kinds of crazy notions
Running through my head;
　　I need a progressive woman;
　　I need an awfully liberal woman;
　　There ain't no reactionary baby
　　Can ease my revolutionary mind.

One hand is on my pillow,
One hand on my head,
I see a million nightmares
Tearing around inside my head;
　　I need a progressive woman
　　I need an awful liberal woman
　　I need a social conscious woman
　　To eas my revolutionary mind.

If I could only make you see, babe,
I ache and pain and bleed,
I know you'd come a runnin'
If you blistered both your feet.
　　I need a progressive woman
　　I need an awful liberal woman,
　　I need an open minded mama
　　To ease my revolutionary mind.

If you could see me here, baby,
Broke out with salty sweat;
No matter where you go I know
Yo never could forget
　　I need a progressive woman,
　　I need an liberal thinking woman,
　　I need an open hearted woman
　　To ease my revolutionary mind.

I ain't no lumpen proletariat,
A nd I ain't no petty bourguese;
But I'm gonna be a cold corpse
If you don't run here to me
　　I need a progressive shipmate,
　　I need a liberous nature lover,
　　But no reactionary female
　　Can ease my revolutionary mind.

If you're a republican or a democrat,
Or a white hood Ku Klux Klan,
No use to ring my doorbell
'Cause I never will be your man
　　I want a union working woman
　　I want a progressive liberous woman,
　　I want a nice progressive mama
　　To ease my revolutionary mind.

This song made up by:
Woody Guthrie
3520 Mermaid Avenue,
Brooklyn, 24, New York.
September Fifth, 1946

FACE MY COLD GRAVE

I'M WELL KNOWN AND FAMOUS
FROM STATELINE TO BORDER
FOR GIVING YOU WOMEN JUST WHAT YOU SO CRAVE!
WHY MUST I TAKE DOWN
WITH THIS MEAN OLD DISEASE?
TOO SOON! TOO SOON NOW I FACE MY COLD GRAVE!

I WORKED MY BEST
TO BRING YOU YOUR PLEASURES
AND TO GIVE YOU WOMEN JUST WHAT YOU SO CRAVED!
WHAT IS THIS MISERY
THAT EATS UP MY BODY?
TOO SOON! TOO SOON NOW I FACE MY COLD GRAVE!

I POURED YOU MY WINE
AND I POURED YOU MY WHISKEY
TO GIVE YOU WOMEN JUST WHAT YOU SO CRAVED!
IF GOD HE IS LOVE
WHY MUST LOVE DESTROY ME?
TOO SOON! TOO SOON NOW I FACE MY COLD GRAVE!

YOU TELL ME YOUR HUSBAND
JUST DON'T KNOW HIS BUSINESS
TO GIVE YOU WOMEN JUST WHAT YOU SO CRAVED!
I COME THROUGH YOUR DOOR
TO EASE YOU AND PLEASE YOU!
TOO SOON! TOO SOON NOW I FACE MY COLD GRAVE!

YOU LIKE TO BE ROLLED
AND YOU LIKE TO BE TUMBLED
TO GET OUT OF LIFE THIS THING YOU SO CRAVED!
NOW WHY MUST I ROT
AND BURN WITH MY MISERY?
TOO SOON! TOO SOON NOW I FACE MY COLD GRAVE!

YOU MARRY TO LAWYERS
YOU MARRY TO DOCTORS
TO GET OUT LIFE THIS THING YOU SO CRAVED!
I AM WHAT IS KNOWN
AS A NATURAL BORN EASEMAN!
TOO SOON! TOO SOON NOW I FACE MY COLD GRAVE!

I EASED YOU IN SHACKS
I EASED YOU IN MANSIONS
TO GIVE ALL YOU WOMEN THIS THING YOU SO CRAVED!
MY BODY NOW BURNS
IN THESE HELL HOLES OF TORTURE!
TOO SOON! TOO SOON NOW I FACE MY COLD GRAVE!

I EASED YOU ON RAGS
I EASED YOU ON SATINS
TO GIVE ALL YOU WOMEN THIS THING YOU SO CRAVED!
I LOVED YOU TOO MUCH
I LOVED YOU TOO MANY!
TOO SOON! TOO SOON NOW I FACE MY COLD GRAVE.

*******   Coney Island, October 11, 1944

*Needs no comment.

While in the army, Woody was asked to write songs specifically about sexually transmitted diseases. A few were published in pamphlets that were distributed to troops overseas.

412

great big job to do..... V. D. — Ideas —

1. Up to me + you

2. You gotta go by yourself.

3. The Harvest Is many
   The work hands are few —

4. Big names died by Syphlis

5. Dont Pass It On

6. I got A Deep Dark Secret
   on my soul

7. Be A good Life saver

8. Ballad of the Syph...
   History... Plague... deaths... cure....

9. Biggest thing Man Has Ever Done.... (beats V.D.)

10. No Laffin' Matter

11. Kills More Than atom Bombs + guns

12. Honey gitta Blood Test
    just Like mine

13. Seed Of Man

14. Syff gonna gitcha H'ya Dou' Watch out......

15. You Cant Hide away From Yourself....

16. Are You washed In The Blood?

17. Burn Like Hell Fires

18. Go In To See (The Nurse + Doctor) —

19. Down With The Scuffles & All

20. Tickle Tickle Tickle

21. Leave Her Be

22.

23.

24.

25. god & The Devil + germ —

26.

27.

28.

29.

30.

House Of Earth
Woody Guthrie
4-2-'47
*

Come to my House Of Earth if you would like
For me to give your old time feelings back.

Come here to my house of good rich earth if you
Would like me teach your wife a thing or two.

Come here to this legal illegal place for joys
And teach your wife this way to grow new boys.

I'll take you by your hand and show you whirls
Of these same feelings that grow pretty girls.

I'll wash your feet a couple of times a day
Till all your old time sorrows melt away.

You leave some drops of honey on my couch
I leave a couple of dollars in your pouch.

My house of earth is the richest land in town
I pity those dead ones that at me frown.

So come to my house of earth and learn it's worth
A few green folded bills to learn of birth.

I'll kiss you in such odd and natural ways
Your wife will then find out that kissing pays.

Two times a day I'll wash you in my tub
Ten times a day I'll pat your skin and rub.

Call me a prostitute and a whore, too,
I do these tricks your wife refuses to.

I swear by all my bibles you won't regret
I've never met a man that's sorry yet.

I love you once to teach you all your life
The things to do when you are with your wife.

Your wife should be quite glad and proud of me
For waking both of you up these things to see.

My house of earth runs down with wine and rum
Lots of different ways here you can come.

If you do come I will be glad to see
If you don't come I'm glad you don't need me.

I'll furnish red hot kisses and the hole
That wakes up sleeping sickness in your soul.

----- 30 -----
By   Woody Guthrie
3520 Mermaid Avenue,
Brooklyn, 24, New York,
April 2nd, 1947.

Woody Guthrie

Woody Guthrie

I looked up in a cheap little dictionary and the word obscene means lascivious and the word lascivious means vulgar, and the vulgar means "lowdown, of the common folk" – so my crime at best and worst and most is that terrible crime of writing too hot & nakedly up from the feelings of the (us) common folks.

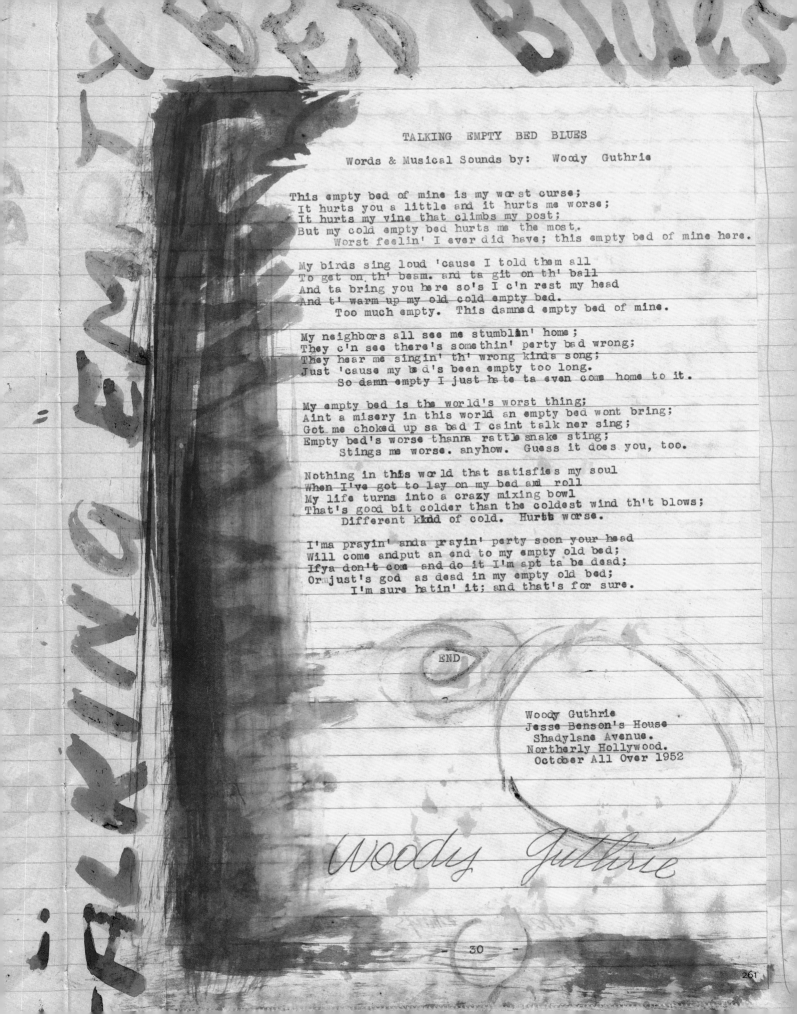

TALKING EMPTY BED BLUES

Words & Musical Sounds by: Woody Guthrie

This empty bed of mine is my worst curse;
It hurts you a little and it hurts me worse;
It hurts my vine that climbs my post;
But my cold empty bed hurts me the most.
        Worst feelin' I ever did have; this empty bed of mine here.

My birds sing loud 'cause I told them all
To get on th' beam and ta git on th' ball
And ta bring you here so's I c'n rest my head
And t' warm up my old cold empty bed.
        Too much empty. This damned empty bed of mine.

My neighbors all see me stumblin' home;
They c'n see there's somethin' party bad wrong;
They hear me singin' th' wrong kinda song;
Just 'cause my bed's been empty too long.
        So damn empty I just hate ta even come home to it.

My empty bed is the world's worst thing;
Aint a misery in this world an empty bed wont bring;
Got me choked up so bad I caint talk ner sing;
Empty bed's worse thanna rattle snake sting;
        Stings me worse. anyhow. Guess it does you, too.

Nothing in this world that satisfies my soul
When I've got to lay on my bed and roll
My life turns into a crazy mixing bowl
That's good bit colder than the coldest wind th't blows;
        Different kind of cold. Hurts worse.

I'ma prayin' anda prayin' party soon your head
Will come andput an end to my empty old bed;
Ifya don't come and do it I'm apt ta be dead;
Ornjust's god as dead in my empty old bed;
        I'm sure hatin' it; and that's for sure.

                        END

                    Woody Guthrie
                    Jesse Benson's House
                    Shadylane Avenue.
                    Northerly Hollywood.
                    October All Over 1952

            Woody Guthrie

When I do she dont
When she will I wont
When I can she cant
When I shall she shan't
It makes one
Sore as hell if the other one don't
You know what I'm talking about
Just a hell of a dam shape,
And the way you feel
Is like you're on
A
High lonesome.

Jealous Love

Desires Of Fire
wg to mg

Who knows my great desires of fire,
Who knows my flame that jumps so high?
Who feels my blood and passion boil
To see my Marjorie pass me by.

My song will dip the sadder pen;
My ryme will dip some sadder key;
My soul will solitary be
When Marjy says Good Bye to me.

All us that danced in Brooklyn's Room
All us that watched your clear cheek bloom
All us that saw thy lamp of life
Ask me where I found such a wife.

Your face shines warm like Zibby Zee'e,
Your spirit lites up as bright as Joad's
Your eyes burn warm with that same baby look.
You hug and kiss and see round Noralee.

And now I hear sad talke about divorce,
I feel so low I cant feel any worse;
This talk has got me knocked halfway to hell
'Twould send me back to a hell I've known too well.

If you do feel we cant be a man and wife,
and my wild habits cause you grief and strife;
Divorce and separation will kill my pride
To see your new man try my shoes for life.

I've not been such a good papa to our kids;
Every wrong thing in that book I did;
My bad moves ought to lock the paddy cell
On the last chapter of this life I've lived.

Back when we first met up in Almanac Hall,
When we both felt creation's moves and calls,
Could not your young eye tell my eyes were cold;
Too old for such a young heart as your soul?

contd on back ⟹

Desires Of Fire

God knows I failed the worst of any man;
Each thing turned ashes as I touched my hand;
The good hopes flared and blew on yonders breeze;
The bad things stuck with me and they still stand.

If I had such a patient heart as yours
I still would stumble blind from door to doors;
I might file suit tonight for our divorce
And shoot me back to the alkys and the whores.

My thoughts run quick and fast to suicide
When I feel how much I failed to suit your pride;
Like Leadbelly feels when he tells Irene Good Night,
But my dreams of one more squeeze lead back to life.

It's not because I can't find girls anew;
Its not because you can't find men by twos;
I could try to sleep on a new one every night,
But my lost soul just can't bid you adieu.

It may be named self pity, I don't care;
It may be psychopathique, I can't care;
Every move or act in life is psycho something;
But when man does lose such a woman, he can't care.

That caring part of him breaks down and goes;
That part that cares goes on the blink and blow;
His hand and heart and mind can't yes nor no —
His will can't pick, can't choose a way to go.

I'm close enough to this breakdown tonight
To look for you and find too much, to write —
Divorce might cure the whole thing, yes, it might,
But it can't kill my love for you, not quite.

— (30) —

Woody Guthrie
Beach Haven at Brighton
Brooklyn, (23), New York
October 16th 1950

— (30) —

My body is naked now, and it was born naked. No matter how I dress up or undress, I am naked. The best and juiciest of humanly truths are naked truths. I feel the same way you feel about my naked places. None of my places feel their real best till I get them uncovered, unhid, stripped down naked. In my most naked thoughts I've always laid flat on by back on the beds of living leaves and grass, counting the tree buds with my hands and the night stars with my toes. Go ahead use ribbon and lace to pull me toward you, and I'll use every trick of shadow and shaving to pull you closer towards me. Your face is already lifted toward the sky and its light makes me wild and crazy for the touch and taste of you. Your hips can't make a motion which I can say I hate. Your blood can't run in a way which I will stop and send back. Your legs can't open in a way that I will arrest. Your thighs can't move in a way that I could lock up behind bars. I love to see you wiggle your patch of hairs in every kind of design, pattern, roll, sway and twitch. I see and taste no sweat more honest than the drops you have in joy between your legs. Your face looks its proudest, its finest and gladdest this minute, as you do roll here like I roll. This look, this half smile across your face this very minute, your hairs shaking above my eyes, makes me feel like a lost man getting found.

Beluthahatchee, FL, 1953.

ALL WORK TOGETHER
Woody Guthrie

My mama said,
And my teacher, too,
There's lots of work
That I can do;
Dry my dishes
And sweep my floor
But if we all work together
Well, it won't take long.
And so:

CHORUS:

We all work together
With a wiggle and a giggle
All work together
With a giggle and a grin
We all work together
With a wiggle and a giggle
We all work together
With a giggle and a grin.

With a wiggle and a giggle
And a google and a goggle
And a jigger and a jagger
And a giggle and a grin.

My Daddy told me,
And my Grandma, too,
There's plenty of work
For me to do,
I can comb my hair,
I can dress my dolls,
And if we all work together
Well, it won't take long.
So:

C H O R U S:

My Sister told me,
And my brother, too,
There's a whole lot of work
That I can do,
I can bring her candy,
I can bring him gum,
And if we all work together,
Well, it won't take long.
So:

C H O R U S:

I tell mommy and daddy,
I tell grandma, too,
There's lots of work
You all can do,
You can bring me pennies,
And candy and gum,
And, if we all work together,
Then it won't take long.
So:

CHORUS:

CHAPTER SEVEN

All Work Together

OUR FAMILY

NORA GUTHRIE

Both of my parents were already married when they met in New York City in 1941. My father, a twenty-nine-year-old folk musician, already had a wife and three children in Texas, and my mother, a twenty-four-year-old dancer with the Martha Graham Company, had a husband in Philadelphia.

What was unusual was how they dealt with it, particularly when my mother became pregnant with my father's child in 1942. They agreed to be open with their spouses, and they also decided to begin living together. My mother's father, a religious Jewish man, disowned my mother, even though she moved a few blocks away from her parents in Coney Island. Her mother, a Yiddish poet, was more tolerant of these two artistic souls already living out of the box—now in sin!—in many ways. My parents insisted on keeping relationships with their previous families, and as we children grew up, we were encouraged to consider them all part of our family although we lived worlds apart in many ways. My parents were both artists, dreamers, and politically progressive—even considered dangerous to democracy by some! You can imagine that there would be tensions between the various extended family members living in different parts of the country. My parents had already experienced and were well aware of how politics and unconventional lifestyles could tear a family apart. So instead of arguing with everyone, they insisted on emphasizing positive "family values" to us. "Try to understand where they're coming from," they might say. We all managed to get along and stayed in contact. Most importantly, we were to remain loving. That's what I really remember. Whether we could always do that or not wasn't the point. The point was the teaching. The point was the trying.

In the early 1950s, when we kids were still very young, my father was diagnosed with Huntington's disease. It became clear that he would have to be hospitalized for the rest of his life, as there was no cure or treatment. Because the situation was hopeless, the doctors advised my mother to tell us children that my father had died so that we could move on with our lives. But my parents had a different plan. They decided to tell us what was going on, and they agreed it would be best for my mother to remarry so we would grow up with a father figure in the house. And she did. A few times. But with each relationship, she prefaced the marriage with the understanding, "You're marrying both of us, me and Woody."

As fifteen years went by, we visited my father in the hospital on Sundays, or we would bring him home to spend some visiting time with his old buddies—Pete Seeger, Ramblin' Jack Elliott, Sonny Terry, Brownie McGhee, and others—and Sunday hootenannies in our living room were pretty regular. Each of my step-fathers participated in caring for my father: feeding him, dressing him, driving him, helping out in any way they could, and our family grew to include theirs.

To support our family, my mother opened her own dancing school, the Marjorie Mazia School of Dance, in Sheepshead Bay, Brooklyn. At the time, it was rare for a woman to own and run her own business. All the other mothers I knew from the neighborhood were housewives. But in our family, it was the men who stayed home and did the shopping, the cooking, the housework, and the childcare. At times, my mother's secretaries at the dancing school became our two indispensable surrogate mothers, and their families—their children, spouses, relatives—were added to the lineup. This newly organized and creatively defined family kept growing. Even our dentist (no blood relation) was called "Uncle."

I am often surprised when I hear folks saying that my father wasn't a good father, that he rambled, that he womanized, that he didn't bring home the bacon. All true. He certainly was not a conventional father. But what *is* a "good" father?

In the early days, before Huntington's disease stepped in, my father was our basic caretaker when my mother was out teaching or touring with the Graham company. He kept journals of notebooks chronicling all the things we said. He would turn those into song lyrics. Looking back now at those journals, I find it stunning to read how closely he was *listening* to us. How much he was *loving* so many of the things we were saying. And therefore, how well he *knew* us in ways that most parents never do, to the extent that he gave all of us very personal nicknames, which will remain family secrets!

Whenever we complained about how we were being unfairly treated, as siblings often do, we were told: "You are like three different little flowers in three different pots. Some flowers need more sun, some less sun. Some flowers need more water, some less water. You are each different, and need different things to grow." I have to admit that, as a kid, I totally bought that. It made a lot of sense. Everyone's different. Got it.

When it came to daily family life, I learned from the masters: The best way parents can keep control of kids is by not letting them know you're in control. If you want them to clean up, write a song and have them act it out. Thus songs like "Pick It Up" and "Cleano" were born, as we were guided to *act out* the lyrics. When they have to get up in the morning, write a song called "Wake Up," or if it's bedtime, have them act out "Sleep Eye." If they're not getting along with each other or their friends, how about having them sing "Don't You Push Me Down"? Believe me, this is devilishly ingenious. My father, being very childlike himself, understood these particular powers of persuasion. As long as it's fun, kids will do whatever you want. Got it.

Stretching the idea of family even more, one of the first books I remember pulling off the bookshelf was the photo anthology *The Family of Man* sent to my parents by the photographer and curator, Alfred Stieglitz. I loved turning the pages and seeing all the different ways that people around the world celebrated all the same life passages in different ways: births, deaths, weddings, funerals, religious ceremonies. No words. Just pictures. I get it. We are *all* in the book. We are all part of this family of man.

All of this is not to say that our family life was always easy. We grew up in a blue-collar neighborhood where all the other families were pretty much alike and in agreement on most things like religion, politics, and social and cultural issues like race and sex. Pretty much par for the course in the 1950s-60s postwar America. But where little girls wore dresses and little boys suits, my brothers and I wore jeans and flannel shirts. Early mini grunge. Where our neighbors strived for manicured green grass lawns, our yard was basically a mud hole where all the kids in the neighborhood could come to play without being scolded, "Get off my lawn!" At our house, the kids on the block could meet a Black blues musician, a Haitian or Indian dancer, an avant-garde choreographer, or a blacklisted film composer. They could hear Mozart, opera, Gilbert and Sullivan, Rodgers and Hart, Hammerstein, musicals, cowboy songs, folk songs, Peruvian flute music, and John Cage. And this went both ways. Our family got to mingle and share our lives with all the families on our block: the families of sanitation workers, firemen, policemen, construction workers. These families, so different from ours, opened their doors to us.

As a child, comparing yourself to others, your family to others, your lifestyle to others, can often be painful. Being unconventional is not simple, even if in the end you might appreciate the uniqueness of your family. But at the time you don't just float through it without injuries. There are tears; there is anger, confusion, embarrassment, thinking your family is somehow deranged. There is failing to explain to others why your family is different, and even worse, hoping they won't notice how different you *really* are. Got it. Being a different kind of family takes courage and demands strength.

But in the end, I think that when you keep hearing the word *family* used in so many different contexts, seeing so many varieties wearing so many different costumes, you do grow up understanding and accepting the concept of family in an ever-growing way. And when you get to the point where you hear more philosophical, spiritual, or esoteric ideas on family, you're open to it. You get it. It's not something completely new or frightening. When you hear lyrics like "He ain't heavy, he's my brother" or terms like *sisterhood* or *brotherhood*, it's not such a distant idea. You're already prepared. And when you hear phrases like "global citizen" or "We are one," you're not too far from getting it. It's just another natural extension of the word *family*. You've been well fertilized with the seeds of these ideas. And then you can decide if you want to continue to grow them and expand on them.

So what is family? Well, you can answer however you like. You can take the idea wherever you want, with whomever you want. You determine and define *who* your family will be and how it will behave and interact. I've come to believe you simply create the family you want to love.

Family is an art form. It's *your* art form.

(Left to right) Arlo, Joady, Woody, and Nora, Brooklyn, NY, 1950.

I got a few good hard whippings when I was a kid back in Oklahoma. The first few beatings made me cry, not about the hurt of the strap or the stick, but just to think that the whipper really believed in his whip. The next few frailings I cried lots louder, to get the whipper to take pity on me and stop. The last few, I didn't cry at all. I've never been able to really break down and cry anymore since then.

I've heard Marjorie cry plenty of times in our 5 years together. I tell her I wish to my soul that I could just break down and cry a few times a day. I've seen our daughter, 3 1/2 , Miss Cathy, cry like a baby, like a devil, like an angel, cry just like her mommy cries.

Nobody will ever know how much I would give just to have that first gift and clean talent it takes to turn on your tears and cry. No eyes shine quite as bright as your own while you are having a real good cry. It always looked like to me that you can see how honest a person is by watching them cry. But if this is true, then I must not be a very honest man.

Oh, I guess I do cry. I guess I cry inside of my own self somewhere. I suppose I cry down here on paper. Ink and tears run just about the same rip tides.

Do you know what a hoper is? Well, that's what your mama is, a hoper. She has more hopes per square inch than almost anybody else. Hopes about this and hopes about that, hopes about you, about me, about all of the relatives, hopes about lots of people, all people I ought to say. She's what's called a planner. I guess she makes more plans in a day than fascism could tear down in a century.... Sometimes when I found myself running short of plans, well, I'd just go and borrow some of hers, like a neighbor borrowing flour. Every detail of her life is not only a plan, but it is a dream, and the whole plan of a better world is one that she dreams about always. And she dreams it so plain and so strong that everybody who gets close to her notices it, and picks it up like a radio taking music out of the air.

Woody's second wife, Marjorie Mazia, 1943.

Your mama and papa kept trying to talk about you in advance of your arrival and one would say 'she' and the other would answer back 'he' – and they nearly got into an argument because neither of them ever know what you'd be, so both of them then decided to call you 'it' and, naturally, 'it' is already such an overused word – sounds all right when you're talking about the weather, saying, it blew or it rained, but not about a baby. People say, how far is 'it' to the next town, but never say what this 'it' is, they call animals 'it' – and so we didn't want to call you 'it'. So we agreed to call you Railroad Pete – boy or girl – Railroad Pete would be your name until you come in the mail. All of this business of picking a name can come then.

And so, Pete, you see why we call you Pete.

[Marjorie] says you're going to be the World champion Spitter. Now aint that a hell of a thing to look forward to?

The World's Champ Spitter. ...Not just a useless, wishy washy, kind of spitting, either, but an organized, socially significant kind.

Woody's notebooks and diaries are filled with musings, teachings, and cartoons that show his interest in and unconventional approach to parenting.

MAY
22
FRIDAY

	APRIL 1942								MAY 1942							JUNE 1942					
S	M	T	W	T	F	S		S	M	T	W	T	F	S		S	M	T	W	T	F	S

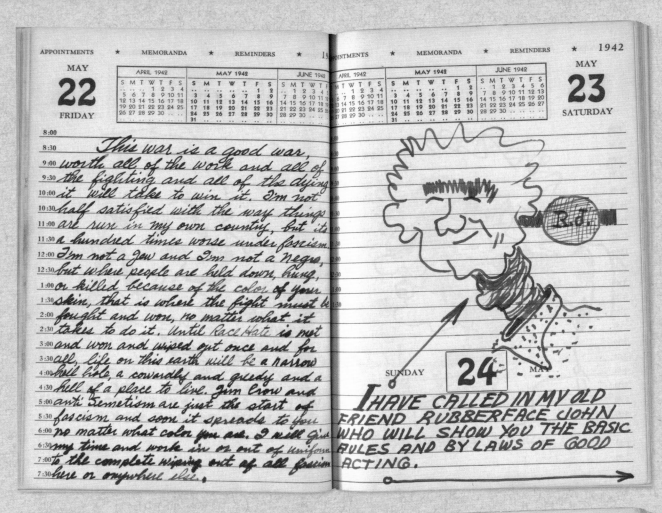

8:00
8:30 This war is a good war,
9:00 worth all of the work and all of
9:30 the fighting and all of the dying
10:00 it will take to win it. I'm not
10:30 half satisfied with the way things
11:00 are run in my own country, but its
11:30 a hundred times worse under fascism.
12:00 I'm not a Jew and I'm not a Negro,
12:30 but where people are held down, hung,
1:00 or killed because of the color of your
1:30 skin, that is where the fight must be
2:00 fought and won, no matter what it
2:30 takes to do it. Until Race Hate is met
3:00 and won and wiped out once and for
3:30 all, life on this earth will be a narrow
4:00 hell hole, a cowardly and greedy and a
4:30 hell of a place to live. Jim Crow and
5:00 anti Semetism are just the start of
5:30 fascism and soon it spreads to you
6:00 no matter what color you are. I will give
6:30 my time and work in or out of uniform
7:00 to the complete wiping out of all fascism
7:30 here or anywhere else.

MAY
23
SATURDAY

SUNDAY **24** MAY

R.J.

I HAVE CALLED IN MY OLD
FRIEND RUBBERFACE JOHN
WHO WILL SHOW YOU THE BASIC
RULES AND BY LAWS OF GOOD
ACTING.

MAY
25
MONDAY

8:00
8:30
9:00
9:30
10:00
10:30
11:00
11:30
12:00
12:30
1:00
1:30
2:00
2:30
3:00
3:30
4:00
4:30
5:00
5:30
6:00
6:30
7:00
7:30

— STUBBORNESS —

MAY
26
TUESDAY

MISTRUST

REPOSE.

SURPRISE

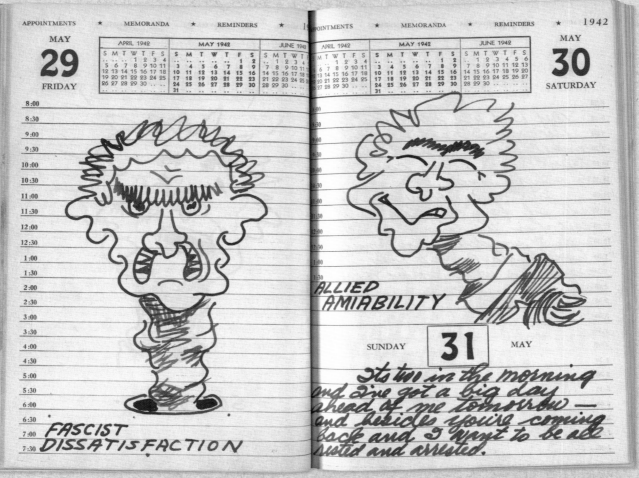

ALLIED
AMIABILITY

SUNDAY **31** MAY

FASCIST
DISSATISFACTION

Its two in the morning
and I've got a big day
ahead of me tomorrow —
and besides you're coming
back and I want to be all
rested and arrested.

Deone Been Up & Starting Down
Woody Guthrie
June 6th, 1947

Looks like now it won't be long
You're a gonna push your way out here amongst us
Gonna pound your way out
Gonna dig your way and climb out of your hole
I'm glad to see Marjorie smile so big and run so fast to town
She'll laugh and tell the Doc
What she told me just now and ten times yesterday
That You've
Done been up and starting down
Done been up and starting down
Growed upwards just about high as her rib bone
Growed upwards just high as her ribs would let you
Growed up that way till you banged your noodoo
And scratched your fanazalam
And bumped your sonorzaler
And whacked your doodah
And hit your head on all of them things
Till you got tired and sick of bumps and bruises
And said to yourself
In there swimming all around
I done been up, done been up, and starting down, down, down.
Grandma felt with her fingers and measured
That first inch that you went down there
Down from Mammy's breats and rib bones
Down from Mommy's roof and rafters
Down from her high parts towards her low parts
Down and around
I felt you kick and sing all around
I felt you thump and beat all around
Heard you laugh and heard you holler
So did all of Marjorie's students
At the big school where she teaches
Down the trolley and bus downtown
They all said and danced and pointed
Everybody around this town
Saying, "Look, look,"
Singing. "Looky".
Up and down half the streets in town
"It's done been up and starting down".
"Done been up and starting down".

Well, the big stir's on around this house here,
Everybody runs in and out
Everybody from the alleys, everybody from the house,
I nailed your bathinette rubber swimmer
Painted my flowers acrost your walls
Washed your playpen and your bed down
With some rags and chemicals
Marjorie washed your walls down prettyo
And she folded up your clothes
Then she set these pots of vines around
To greet you when you come
And she painted these linoleums and she varnished every stick
Of the stools, the chairs, the chest of drawers,
And she works both day and night here like a horse or like a mule
And she tells me every minute or so
She feels good and fine right now
Since you clumb as high up as you could climb
And since you started down,
And it makes us both feel proud
You done been up and started down.

We just hope your downhill trip
Don't tangle your feet up so you slip
Don't cause your eyes to fail you and your nose to hit theground
We want your homestretch trip to be
As fast and good as saife to be
We want you safe and sound
You done been up and started down.　-----30-------

Woody Guthrie

Howdy Little newly Come

Howdy little newly come I'll sing to you my song
I'd like to tell you all about the place you did come from
I'll hold you to my bosom and feel you nice and warm
I'll tell you how you found your way to the world where you are born.

Didie didee didee doe and a die dee die dee dum

Your mommy and your poppy they ate some cake and bread
We drank a glass of brandywine of white and yellow and red
We laughed and sang and hugged and kissed and held each by the hand
We danced away together to your newborn angel's land.

We found honey sweet to make you fat, good bread to make your head,
We took good cheese to make your bones, green vines to make your arms,
with the wind that blows we made your toes, the rain it made your hand,
and this is how we found you in your newborn baby land.

It was my door that you come through to laff and cry in this world
It's my same door I open up for all my boys and my girls
Your daddy and your mother did open their gates so wide
You kicked your way without a scratch from the newborn baby side.

You come from me, I come from you, thats how you and me did come
From milk and honey and bread and cheese and berries and wine and sum
You feel so soft and tender and smooth and warm here to my hand
I feel so glad that you come to me from your newborn baby land.

(30) Sept. 3rd 1947

Woody Guthrie

OPPOSITE: One of Woody's more unique lyrics describes the process of labor and birth.

TOP: Following the birth, he welcomed his newborn child.

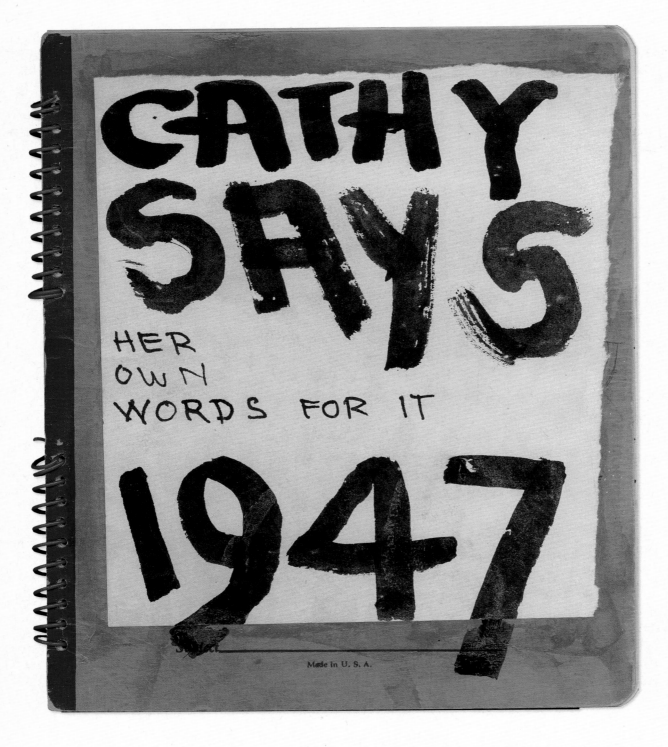

This 1947 notebook documents the words of Woody's four-year-old daughter, Cathy Ann. Throughout the 1940s, Woody spent many days at home caring for his children while Marjorie was away teaching dance and touring as a member of the Martha Graham Dance Company. He found that children's honest expressions were prime material for songs, and he kept notebooks of what his kids said around the house or while walking down the street. He used their thoughts, their daily activities, and their feelings about the world as topics for dozens of children's songs, many of which are still sung by performers, teachers, and children around the world.

WHYO WHY?

Words + music by Woody Guthrie

Chorus:

      Whyo whyo whyo
      Why and why and why?
      Becauxe, because, because, because;
      Good Bye, Goodbye, Goodbye.

Why can't a dish break a hammer?
Why and why and why?
Because a hammer's a hardhead;
Goodbye, Goodbye, Goodbye.

Why can't a bird eat an elefunt?
Tell me whyo why?
Because an elefunt's got a pretty hard skin;
Goodbye, goodbye, goodbye.

Why can't a mouse eat a streetcar?
I'd like to know why and why?
Because a mouse's stummick jist ain't bigga nuff ta
                 hold a street car;
Goodbye, goodbye, goodbye.

Tell me why does a horn make music?
Do you know why and whyyy?
Because the hornblower blows it;
Goodbye, goodbye, goodbye.

Why does my cow drink water?
I can't figure how nor why.
Main reason is because your cow gets thirsty
   just like you or me or anybody else gets thirsty;
Goodbye, goodbye, goodbye.

Why don't you fly up to the man in the moon?
I sure would love to know why?
Because I'm afraid that if I ever was to fly loose and go
   all the way up there to that moon I might not ever be able
     to find my way back down home here agin; that's why I don't
     try to fly up to that man in the moon yonder (etc) adlib.
Goodbye. Goodbye. Goodbye.

Why don't you answwer my question?
Whyo whyo why?
Because I don't know the ansers;
Goodbye, goodbye, goodbye.

           (((The choruse in this song you can
           just throw in whenever you think you
           need it the most))))
        (((((That's what I did)))))))

End

Woody Guthrie

****

MAIL MYSELF TO YOU
WOODY GUTHRIE

CHORUS::

I'M GONNA WRAP MYSELF IN PAPER
I'M GONNA DOB MYSELF WITH GLUE
STICK SOME STAMPS ON TOPPA MY HEAD
I'MA GONNA MAIL MYSELF TO YOU.

I'M GONNA TIE ME UP IN RED STRING
TIE MYSELF WITH RIBBONS, TOO.
I'M GONNA RUN JUMP IN MY MAIL BOX
I'MA GONNA MAIL MYSELF TO YOU.

CHORUS:

WHEN YOU SEE ME IN YOUR MAIL BOX
CUT MY STRINGS AND I'LL JUMP OUT
WASH THE GLUE OFF ALL MY FINGERS
STICK A LOLLIPOP IN MY MOUTH.

CHORUS:

TAKE ME OUT OF MY WRAPPING PAPER
WASH THE GLUE STAMPS OFF MY HEAD
POUR ME FULL OF GOOD HOT MILK
PUT ME IN YOUR NICE WARM BED.

CHORUS:

E N D

call local Union

Stanley -
Hollywood

98261

Mr Koach
MI 1408 *Bklyn*
TR: 5 6195

let Anny Hollywell -
make a fotostatic copy of my
agreemt with Pinto's Songs - oit
Oklahoma Hills -

R. C. A. Building, a magnificent structure of 70 stories, is the tallest building in the Rockefeller Center. There are 27 radio studios in the building, among them the largest in the world. Its observatory roof is an expansive promenade of 200 feet long with an unobstructed view of 50 miles.

MANHATTAN POST CARD PUBLISHING CO., INC.

POST CARD
THIS SPACE FOR ADDRESS ONLY

PLACE
STAMP
HERE

Marjorie Mazia
148 W. 14 St.,
New York
N. Y.

Room 14

WAR FRIENDS, WE'RE GOING LISTEN IN

DEAR MARJORIE: HELLO. HOW ARE YOU? I JUST FOUND SOME OLD PENNY POST CARDS HERE IN THE DESK. THEY WAS USED A YEAR OR TWO BACK TO ADVERTISE ALMANAC DOINGS. SO I'LL JUST WRITE A LETTER ON TOP OF THIS ONE AND SEND YOU TWO MORE FOR NO GOOD REASON AT ALL. I GOT MY MANDOLIN AND BOY IS IT A GOOD ONE? SOUNDS LIKE CHURCH BELLS IN NEW MEXICO. I WROTE A SCRIPT TODAY FOR THE DEPARTMENT OF WAR INFORMATION. IT IS CALLED 'PARADE OF THE STATES' AND TODAY'S IS ABOUT TEXAS. I SAVED YOU BACK A COPY SO YOU CAN READ IT WHEN YOU GET HERE. MY HEALTH IS LOTS BETTER AND I'M BACK AS BAD AS EVER AGAIN. THE LANDLORD JUST COME UP AND BAWLED ME OUT FOR DRIVING NAILS IN OUR NEW ROOM PUTTING UP SOME PICTURES SO IT WILL BE PRETTY WHEN YOU SEE IT AGAIN. LOVE TO ALL. THE SAME AS EVER. Woody.

ART INSTITUTE OF CHICAGO
PERMANENT COLLECTION OF WORKS OF ART
CURRENT EXHIBITIONS · SCHOOL OF THE ART
INSTITUTE ·.· RYERSON LIBRARY (OF BOOKS
ON ART) ·.· ART INSTITUTE LECTURE SERIES
ART INSTITUTE EXTENSION

Howdy
Woody

THE FISHERMAN'S FAMILY
By PUVIS DE CHAVANNES, French, 1824-1898

Cathy Mazia
3520 Mermaid
Bklyn. 24
N. Y.

CHILD SITTING

Watching kids is the highest form of art in the world. It can be as bitter as drink of carbolic acid or as sweet as a warm cup of new milk and wild honey.

I was here with Cathy alone after [the doctor] looked her over from stem to stern. She had a touch of fever and so she did not get out of bed.

Sam, the newspaper man, ran in with his arms full of coloring books, a jar of sticky paste, a big red balloon, another box of crayons, all sent from the candy story by Marjorie on her way to work. Cathy was waving "Bye, Sem." She held up the jar of paste first and told me,

"Deddy, here, opinnit."

"Play with your other things", I told her. "Color all of those nice pictures in your color books there. Cut out things with your scissors. Ahh, that's nice, nice, ah, and ah, and dress all of your dolls up in their clothes, and draw me some good pictures on your paper there with your new crayons. Mommy will feel bad if she comes home and finds old sticky paste all over her sheets and blankets."

I was pacing all up and down the floor all around the bed like a bumble bee lost from his hive.

"That's it. That's a good girl. Old Santy'll fill your stocking and shoes besides with all kinds of nice things. Thats it. Here. I'll put the paste away on a shelf in your room. Here."

"But Deddy, I wanta just paste."

"Color"

"Paste."

"Cut."

"Paste, Deddy, Silly. Don't ya know what paste is?"

"Draw me a nice big, big, big picture."

"I'll paste ya one."

"Dolls."

"My dolls ask me ta paste 'em a s'prize."

"Draw with a pencil."

"But, Deddy, ya cain't paste nuthin' with a pencil."

I sat down at my typewriter here at the head of our bed, rolled in some pages of a ship story I'm writing and paid no more mind to her until sometime later.

She took the phone off the table when it rang and said, "Hullo.... Who?... Laundry?... Nooo. This is me. Cathy.... Cathy.... Who are you?....... Cathy's my name. Stackab-ones. My mommy's name is Marjorie, I'm not any laundry. What's your name?.... Wrong what?...... Wrong number? That's a funny name. He hunged up, Deddy."

"Now you hang up." I kept on writing.

"But, Deddy, I cain't."

"Huhm. Why not?"

"It's stuck to my hand. Lookatit. Deddy, git me loose."

"Lord have mercy on us sinners. Cathy, Stacky Wacky. Jackie Whacker. Cracker Jacker. Rackety Stackity. Look at you. Look at me. Look at that tele-phone. Look. Look. Look at Mommy's and Daddy's bed. Just take yourself a look at that bed."

"Unstick me."

"Didn't I tell you in plain words, Cathy, not to open up that bottle of paste on your Mommy's and Daddy's bed?"

"Unstick my hand from the phone. I hafta paste more."

"More? More paste? Well, I've done all I can do. It's no fault of my own. It's her fault, it's your mama's fault, for ever leaving me alone here in this house with you, anyhow. I've got work to be done. I can't drop everything I'm working on and just spend my days keeping you from tearing the house down. Go ahead. Here's the washrag, warsh-cloth, whatever the devil you call it. Here. Warsh your own paste off of your own hands. I don't care what you do from now on. My work is just as important to me as your mam's work is to her. All right, so she teaches a few people how to flip their heads around in the air and how to dance."

"I danc'd in her big school once, didn't I Deddy" 'Member? You put on my overalls and I carried my dress down in my shopping bag. 'Member? Don'tcha? 'Member, Deddy?"

"I wisht you was with her today."

"The doctor let me look down his mouth with his flashlight an' he said I hadda sore neck an' I said he was fulla mish an' mishmuch, an' he said I couldn't say 'Ahhhhh', 'cause he had a stick stuck down my froat, an' Mommy told me Santy Clawss wood come see me if I stayed home nice an' let Deddy paint my tonsils with that ol' brown stuff, an' I hafta make a paper chain for my doctah, an' for my Mommy an' a cut-out pumpkin with crosseyes past'd for my Deddy, an' I hafta lay my heady down in Mommy's bed cause my bed's too little to hold all my papers an' past'd things. An', Deddy, it's time for you to cook my soup, but don't cook me any soup, 'cause I'm too sick and I don't want any soup, 'cause I don't feel like I like soup. An' I don't like crackers, either. I hafta paste a pumpkin that's gay on Halloween Day on a Chris'mus card white on Thanks-givin' Night."

The whole box of Kleenex tissues were pulled out and pasted on top of one another, like diapers folded flat in a laundry. The color books had paste between their pages. She had cut out chains, pumpkins, baskets, fruit of every kind, masks with eyes, noses, mouths, that look like people you know. She had smeared her cheeks with paste like Mommy does her cold cream, and painted her fingernails with it, the way her grandma showed her.

Everything on the bed was stuck to everything else. I picked up the pasted basket to carry away into Cathy's room and the rest of the mess on the bed all followed me. There was no more paste in the jar, so she asked me for a new package of my typing paper and drew several dozen pictures with her Crayolas. Each page, she made me stop what I was doing and write down with pen and ink what the picture was all about. This took up most of my whole afternoon. Every time I wrote down the next words, she drew another picture, and yelled out some more to be written down. She drew one that was called, "What th' Hell Ya Think This Is?" And one that was called, "You Don't Know What in the Devil You're Talkin' About."

I don't know why I wrote her words down on all of these drawings. It's just a little thing I started doing a year or so ago and now it's a wild thing, a thing of no control, spreading fire, a blaze, a smoke, some kind of a thing like the black market, like gambling, like using dope, it's something that has got so big that I can't stop it by myself. When these days come on which I am left entirely alone in the house with Cathy, Miss Stackabones, I'm whipped, I'm outwitted, out run, out classed, and outmaneuvered. My mind leaves off where hers begins. My ideas stop where hers start in. My brain is no match for her with her sly and slick ways of making me do everything she wants me to.

She sang songs while she drew her pictures after the paste was all gone, and forced me to take down the words as she sang them. I've got several hundred of her songs already written down. I've sold two albums of phonograph records of kids songs just by putting little tunes and guitar notes to her songs she sings. I've written stories of a dozen kind and mailed them away to the papers and the magazines. And still I've not scratched the first crust of top dirt in her garden of the soul.

This is the second day of being at home inside with her cold, and she's up and around and lots better. She is dressed in all of our clothes of this and other years, she has had me tying bow knots all morning long, she has smeared herself all over with lipstick and rouge, stripped her skin naked and danced about the place

late last night

woody Guthrie
4-20- '46

like a windward spirit. The house looks like the big bed did yesterday, only the bed still looks like it did. I've written down a dozen songs today and taken down the names of a dozen more pictures. There're not enough recording companies in the world to make records of all she makes up. Not enough radios or movie studios to catch one tenth of what she floats through every day. And, yet, here I am, a lost man, a sick man, a man that needs help, advice, and good words. She in her room now singing through the wall:

"…. I took some trips
On some foamy ships
An' I'm aimin' ta sail some more, some more,
…. Aimin' ta sail some more."

HOODOO VOODOO

Hoodoo voodoo,
Seven twenty, one two;
Haystacka hostacka,
A B C.
High poker, low joker,
Ninety nine a Zero;
Sidewalk, streetcar,
Dance a goofy dance.

Blackbirdy, bluejay;
One two three four;
Trash back, jump back,
E F G.
Biggy hat, little hat,
Fattyman, skinnyman;
Grasshopper, greensnake,
Hold my hand.

CHORUS:

            Hoodoo voodoo
            Chooka chooky choochoo;
            True blue, how true;
            Kissle me now.

Momma cat, Tommy Kat,
Diapers on my clothes line;
Two four six eight;
I run hide.
Pretty girl, pretty boy,
Pony on a tincan.
I'll be yours and you'll be mine.

CHORUS:

Jinga jangler, tingalingle;
Picture on a bricky wall;
Hot and scamper, foamy lather;
Huggle me close.
Hot breeze, old cheese,
Slicky slacky fishy tail;
Brush my hair and kissle me some more.

CHORUS:

TOP: Cathy Ann and Woody, Coney Island, NY, 1946.

OPPOSITE: Woody with Arlo, Joady, and Nora, Coney Island, NY, 1952

I LIKE TO STAY HOME WITH DADDY
By Woody Guthrie

MY MAMA SHE LEAVES IN THE MORNING
BEFORE THE SKY GETS LIGHT
I NEVER GET TO SEE HER
WHEN THE SUN IS SHINING BRIGHT
    SHE RUNS TO CATCH THE TROLLEY
    AND SHE WORKS IN A FACTORY PLACE
    BUT I LIKE TO STAY HOME WITH DADDY
    'CAUSE HE NEVER DOES WASH MY FACE.

I EAT ANY OLD THING I LIKE TO EAT
AT ANY OLD TIME I PLEASE
BANANAS APPLES ORANGES AND FISH AND PORK AND BEANS
    MY DADDY LISTENS TO THE RADIO
    AND HE HEARS THE HORSES RACE
    YES. I LIKE TO STAY HOME WITH DADDY
    'CAUSE HE NEVER DOES WASH MY FACE.

I BRING IN THE KIDS FROM ALL AROUND
AND WE FIGHT WITH CLAY AND MUD
WE ROLL AND SCREAM AND RIP AND TEAR
UNTIL WE ALL GET TIRED
    DADDY IS READING A MAGAZINE
    HE DON'T WANT TO LOSE HIS PLACE
    SO I LIKE TO STAY HOME WITH DADDY
    'CAUSE HE NEVER DOES WASH MY FACE.

I LIKE TO STAY HOME WITH YOU DADDY
'CAUSE"YOU NEVER DO WASH MY FACE
YOU LET ME DO WHATEVER I PLEASE
AND I SNORT AND RUN AND RACE
    MAMA WILL NEVER KNOW IT
    'CAUSE SHE NEVER COMES ON THE PLACE
    OH I LIKE TO STAY HOME WITH DADDY
    'CAUSE HE NEVER DOES WASH MY FACE.

-*THIS SONG MADE UP 2-24-45, by W.W.WOODY GUTHRIE,
3520 Mermaid Avenue, Brooklyn, 2, New York.

Woody Guthrie
Feb. 19 45
Coney's Isle

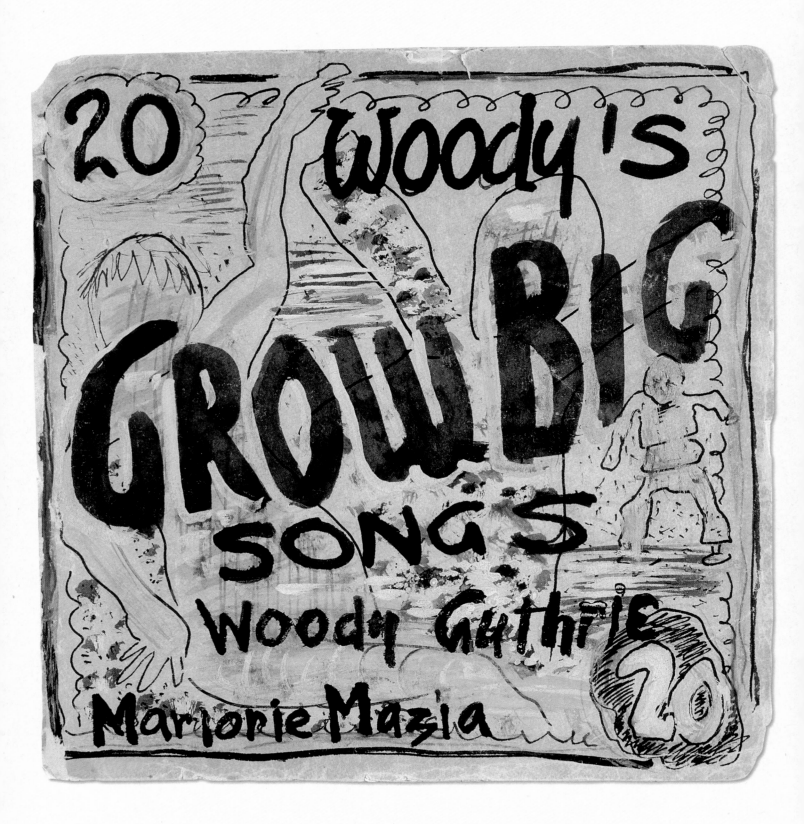

Song
number

1. Wake Up
2. Cleano
3. Mail Man
4. Put Your Finger
5. Dance Around
6. Jigalong Home
7. Merry Go Round
8. Bling Blang
9. Howdy Doo
10. All Work Together

11. Build A House
12. Needle Sing
13. Pick It Up
14. Riding In My Car
15. Race You Down the Mountain
16. My Dolly
17. Little Seed
18. Little Bird
19. Pretty And Shiny-O
20. Sleep Eye

Woody's *20 Grow Big Songs* songbook, with illustrations by Woody and music notation by Marjorie, was created in 1948. Lost for over forty years, it was found on a shelf at Sarah Lawrence College in New York in 1990.

It's too pretty to stay inside,
It's too windy to play outside,
So, what can we do with ourselves on a day like today?
Oh, yes, why didn't I think of it before?
If you'll promise to be real good, and not kick all my paint
off, I'll take you riding in my car.

14. RIDING IN MY Car

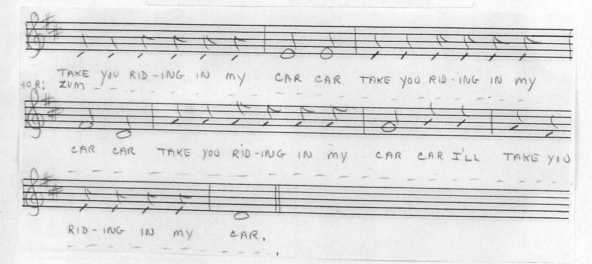

TAKE YOU RID-ING IN MY CAR CAR TAKE YOU RID-ING IN MY
4OR; ZUM ___

CAR CAR TAKE YOU RID-ING IN MY CAR CAR I'LL TAKE YOU

RID-ING IN MY CAR.

I don't want you to use these songs to split your family apart, to give the kids something to do while you do something else. I want to see you throw down your book, your paper, magazine, your worries and your troubles, and to come and join in with the kids.

Let your kids teach you how to act these songs out, these and a thousand other songs. Get the whole fam damily into the fun. Get papa, mama, brother, sister, aunt, uncle, grandma, grandpa, all of your neighbors, friends, visitors, and everybody else in on it.

My songs are not to be read like a lesson book nor a text, but to be a key to sort of unlock all of the old bars in you

```
TAKE YOU RIDING IN MY CAR, CAR,        ENGINE IT GOES, BRRM, BRRMM,
TAKE YOU RIDING IN MY CAR, CAR,        ENGINE IT GOES, BRRM, BRRM,
TAKE YOU RIDING IN MY CAR, CAR,        BRRM, BRRM, CHRRKA CHRRKA, BRRM, BRRM,
I'LL TAKE YOU RIDING IN MY CAR.        TAKE YOU RIDING IN MY CAR.

CLICK CLAEK, OPEN UP A DOOR, GIRLS,    TREES AND HOUSES WALK ALONG,
CLICK CLACK, OPEN UP A DOOR, BOYS,     TREES AND HOUSES WALK ALONG,
FRONT DOOR, BACK DOOR, CLICKETY CLACK, TRUCK AND A CAR, AND A GARBAGE CAN,
TAKE YOU RIDING IN MY CAR.             TAKE YOU RIDING IN MY CAR.

CLIMB CLIMB, RATTLE ON A FRONT SEAT,   I'MA GONNA ROLL YOU HOME AGAIN,
SPREE I SPRADDLE ON A BACK SEAT,       I'MA GONNA ROLL YOU HOME AGAIN,
TURN MY KEY, STEP ON MY STARTER,       BRRM, BRRM, CHRRKA CHRRKA, ROLLY HOME,
TAKE YOU RIDING IN MY CAR.             TAKE YOU RIDING IN MY CAR.

          I'MA GONNA LET YOU BLOW THE HORN,
          I'MA GONNA LET YOU BLOW THE HORN,
          OOORAH, OORAHH, OOGAH, OOOGAHH,
          TAKE YOU RIDING IN MY CAR.


     BRRM, BRRM, CHRRKA CHRRKA, BRRM, BRRM,
     BRRM, BRRM, CHRRKA CHRRKA, BRRM, BRRM,
     BRRM, BRRM, CHRRKA CHRRKA, BRRM, BRRM,
     TAKE YOU RIDING IN MY CAR.
```

that keep the family apart or the school apart. I'm not trying to lure, to bait, to trick, nor to teach the little fellers how to do because the kids have taught me all I ever will know.

Watch the kids. Do like they do. Act like they act. Yell like they yell, Dance like they dance. Sing like they sing. Work like the kids do. You'll be plenty healthy, and feel pretty wealthy, and live to be wise. If you put these songs or any earthly song, on your radio, record player, or on your lips and do like the kids do. I don't want the kids to be grown up, I want to see the grownups be kids.

3520 Mermaid Avenue, Brooklyn, 24, New York   February 27, 1947

The Edgmon Family
Mary Jo, Tinkin Guthrie Edgmon,
Hugh Edward Edgmon
And Pappy Edgmon:

Cathy Ann was burned to death February Ninth in an accidental fire that started from a no good radio wire. She sang and danced in her pads and wrappings at the hospital all night and we think that she would like to see all of us in the whole world go on singing and dancing and working for the best good of all.

Her nursery teachers all said that Cathy was the only completely happy child that they had the pleasure of meeting and dealing with. Marjorie and I always let her have her full vote and voice around our house here. She ran our business and our careers. She decorated our house and she kept the house and both of us in our best of shape. Her drawings, pictures, letters, cutouts and trinkets are still around the house here. We have not had the heart to take them down because these were Cathy's own way of making us think brighter and feel clearer.

We gave her clothing and her toys all away to be given to families that need them more than we do, but we are making all of her letters and writings, paintings, pictures, and poems up into a big bound book as our remembrance to her fine spirit. A lady we know had a tree planted over in the Holy Land in Palestine and named it for Cathy. We thought this was nice and lots better than some big costly stone of marble that would keep three families in debt for a dozen years. She was cremated a few days afterwards and we are going to scatter her ashes down along the sea beach where she loved so many big crowds and mobs of people.

When you write to any of the relatives or friends and tell them the news, tell them that we don't want them, Cathy wouldn't want them to let it get the best of them, but to inspire them on to higher and better works and days and nights of clearest dreamings.

I've got stacks of wires, letters, cards here on my table beside me to answer, so can't write too long a letter now. The snow is still piled up from a big blue norther we're having.

Love and our best wishes to everybody
down your way
                                        Cathy
                                        Marjorie
                                        Woody
                                        And Pete (On his way)...

Marjorie and me are having another
baby sometime in July, around July the Fifteenth.
My birthday is July the Fourteenth. Bastile Day.

This letter to Woody's sister Mary Jo Edgmon describes the tragic death of his four-year-old daughter, Cathy Ann, in a fire in their apartment. Using the Railroad Pete pseudonym, "Pete (coming up)" refers to their soon-to-be-born second child, Arlo. The lyric on the opposite page describes the day of her death, February 9, 1947.

Whistle Birdy

Chorus:
Whistle, ~~whistle~~, whistle birdy;
Try to make me glad;
Whistle, whistle birdy;
Your song makes me sad.
I've lost the best friend
That I'll ever, ever have;
Whistle, birdy, a song
For my Cathy that's gone.

I'd sung for the strikers at Phelps Dodge that day;
Your mommy left a note on our door that did say:
"The firemen were here and the ambulance, too;
We're at Coney Island Hospital waiting for you."
            Chorus:

I saw Mommy and kinfolks and all of our friends;
We cried in the hall and we laughed 'round your bed;
Through all of your bandages you told us funny jokes;
Aunt Clare said you laughed to the end.
            Chorus:

We went a house hunting, your Mommy and me,
For a house that would be good to our family;
We moved in Beach Haven just across the way
From Coney Island Hospital where you laughed that day.
            Chorus:

Words & musi
Woody Gu
49 Mermai
15
October 24th, 1950

Woody, Cathy Ann, and Marjorie,
Coney Island, NY, 1946.

THIS IS MY LETTER I AM WRITING TO MY BUBIE
AND HER NAME IS   *Alisa Greenblatt*
          ALISA   GREENBLATT

     I JUST THIS MINUTE FINISHED READING THROUGH A NINE PAGE
LETTER WROTE IN A REAL FINE AND LITTLE HAND BY MY MAMA
MARJORIE DOWN ON HER HOSPITAL BED AT THE BROOKLYN JEWISH
HOSPITAL.   SHE HOPED SO MANY HOPES FOR ME TO LIVE UP TO
IN THESE NINE PAGES THAT I'M JUST DOWNRIGHT AFRAID THAT
I CAN'T LIVE UP TO ALL OF THEM BY MY OWN SELF, NOT EVEN
IF I WEIGHED EIGHT POUNDS, NOR FORTY EIGHT.
     I NEED LOTS OF HELP.   I NEED LOTS OF HELP FROM LOTS
OF PEOPLE.   IF I DO LIVE UP TO ALL OF THESE HOPES WHICH
MY MOMMY MARJORIE AND MY DADDY WOODY AND YOU AND THOSE
DOCTORS, THOSE NURSES, THOSE BASKETS FULL OF NEWLYBORN
KIDS, THOSE BIG BEDS PILED UP WITH HOPEY MAMAS, I'M JUST
GOING TO HAVE TO HAVE THE HELP OF THE BEST EXPERT HOPERS
THAT I CAN HOPE WITH.
                    THIS IS WHAT MADE ME THINK
ABOUT YOU THE VERY FIRST MINUTE AFTER I RUN MY EYES THROUGH
MAMA'S BIG NINE PAGER HERE.
          YOU KNOW HOW IT WAS DURING THE DAYS THAT YOU
GROWED UP INSIDE OF YOUR MUMMY'S TUMMY AND GOT BIG ENOUGH
TO PUSH YOUR HEAD AND SHOULDERS AND HIPS AND FEET AND
TOES OUT HERE TO PRANCE AND TO DANCE AROUND THROUGH THIS
ODD AND CURIOUS WORLD, YOU REMEMBER HOW YOU HEARD THE
THINGS YOUR OWN MOMMY HEARD?   YOU TASTED THINGS SHE TASTED.
YOU SMELLED EVERYTHING SHE SMELLED.   YOU FELT EVERYTIME
SHE TOUCHED HER FINGER ONTO A DISH OR ONTO SOME HEAD OF
HAIR OF YOUR FOLKS GROWING UP ALL AROUND YOU.   YOU MIGHT
REMEMBER THIS PLAINER THAN LOTS OF FOLKS THAT HAS SORT OF
LET ALL OF THIS SLIP THEIR MIND AND HEART.
     ANYHOW, I KNOW THAT YOU CAN HELP ME OUT WITH ALL OF
THESE BIG JOBS I'VE GOT TO DO, BUILDING SHIPS, RUNNING MY
AIRPLANES, FLYING MY ATOMWAGONS, RIDING MY ROLLERSKATES,
AND GETTING EVERY WORKHAND A JOB AT GOOD WORLDUNION PAY.
THIS IS NOT NO LITTLE MEASLY JOB AS YOU CAN SEE AT ONE
EASY GLANCE.
     THIS IS WHY MY FIRST HOPE RIGHT OUT OF MY HOPINGCAP
IS THAT YOU AND ME CAN SORT OF GET TOGETHER CLOSER AND TO
STICK TOGETHER TIGHTER.   YOU HAD ENOUGH OF MY KIND OF HOPE
IN YOU TO GET YOUR BONES UP AND TO COME DOWN TO THE BIG
HOSPITAL TO TALK ALONG WITH MY MAMA MARJORIE.   YOU HAD A
LOT OF THIS SAME KIND OF HOPE IN YOU WHEN YOU COME OVER TO
MY HOUSE AND HOME HERE AT 3520 MERMAID AVENUE TO HELP MY
DADDY WOODY TO GET HIS HOPES STRAIGHTENED OUT ONCE OR TWICE
EVERY DAY.   YOU'VE GOT MY SAME KIND OF HOPING STRONG ENOUGH
IN YOUR BLOOD AND BOSOM TO HOPE SOMETHING GOOD FOR JUST
ABOUT EVERYMAN, EVERYWOMAN, EVERY LITTLE BOY AND EVERY LITTLE
GIRL YOU LOOK AT WALKING ALONG MY STREET HERE.   YOU SEE, I
HEARD ALL OF YOUR HOPES, HEARD THEM ONE BY ONE, TWO BY TWO,
HEARD EVERY SINGLE HOPE YOU HOPED OVER MY LITTLE RADIO
SENDING AND RECEIVING MACHINE WHICH WAS PARTLY MY MAIN
REASON FOR KNOWING ALL OF THESE THINGS ABOUT YOU AHEAD OF
MY ACTUAL DATE OF SO CALLED BIRTH.   I PUSHED MY WAY OUT
HERE TO GET TO HAVE THIS LITTLE TALK WITH YOU AND TO ASK
YOU TO PITCH YOUR HOPING IN WITH MY HOPING AND WE'LL HAVE
THIS WORLD ON A TWO WAY DOWNHILL PULL, THE OLD WORLD AND
MY NEWER WORLD.
                    YOU KNOW PLAIN ENOUGH AND KNOW ONLY TOO
WELL JUST STEP BY STEP HOW THIS HOPING LIGHT AND LANTERN
OR HOPEFUL CANDLE IN SOME HANDS SEEMS TO BURN OUT AND TO
TURN OFF AWFUL COLD AND DIM AND SAD AND SOUR.   I NEED NOT
TO REMIND YOU THAT YOU'VE BEEN TOO MANY GOOD LIFETEIMES
WASTED BY HOPING THE WRONG THINGS.   YOU KNOW HOW DREARY IT
GETS IN SOME HOUSES AND UNDER SOME ROOFTOPS WHENEVER OUR
OLD HOPES CAN'T BURN AND STAY BRIGHT ALONG WITH THE NEW.
          YOU KNOW THE MAINEST AND HIGHEST SECRET OF ALL OF OUR
HOPING, THAT YOUR MACHINERY FOR HOPES AND HOPERS IS A THING
THAT NEVER GETS OLD, NEVER WEARS DOWN, NEVER FADES OUT, AND
NEVER BLOWS OVER LIKEA STORMY WIND.   THIS I KNOW ABOUT YOU
BECAUSE I FELT YOUR HOPES SHINE DOWN ON ME HERE THAT FIRST
TRIP YOU COME OVER AND CAUGHT ME ALL BUNDLED UP IN A BALL
HERE ON MARJORIE'S AND WOODY'S BED.   WHAT DO YOU SAY, LET'S
YOU AND ME TEAM UP?
          YOUR GRAND SON,   ARLO   GUTHRIE

Feb. 1948 – Arlo about 19 months!

Marjorie, Arlo, and Woody,
Coney Island, NY, 1948.

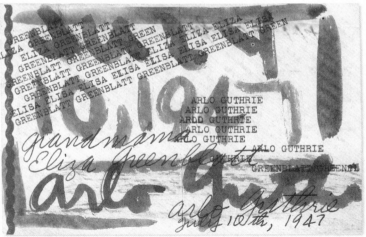

Woody handwrote and hand-painted all the birth notices for his children. Opposite is
the birth letter from Woody (speaking as Arlo) to his maternal grandmother, Aliza
Greenblatt, "my Bubie."

HEADDY DOWN
Woody Guthrie

Honey, lay your head down,
Headdy down, head down;
Zibber lay your head down
Just like mine.

    Headdy down,
    Headdy down,
    Headdy headdy head down;
    Baby lay your head down
    Just like mine.

Old man Zibber See,
Bizzy Bee, Zibby Zea;
Dibuck lay your head down
Just like mine.

    Headdy down, headdy down,
    Headdy headdy headdy down
    Baby lay your head down
    Just like mine.

Joady, lay your head down,
Keppy down, kepula,
Joady, lay your head down
Just like mine.

    (Chorus)

Joady Ben, Joadulah,
Benny, Benny, boombloom,
Joady lay your head down
Just like mine.

    Headdy down, headdy down;
    Joady lay your headdy down;
    Benny, lay your head down;
    Just like mine.

Wink, winka winka wink,
Slipper slopper stinker stink;
Lay your little head down;
Sleepy sleepy sleep.

    Headdy down, headdy down;
    Lay your headdy head down;
    Baby, lay your headdy down
    Just like mine.

Woody Guthrie
1-21- 1949

1-21-49
On the Isle Called Coney

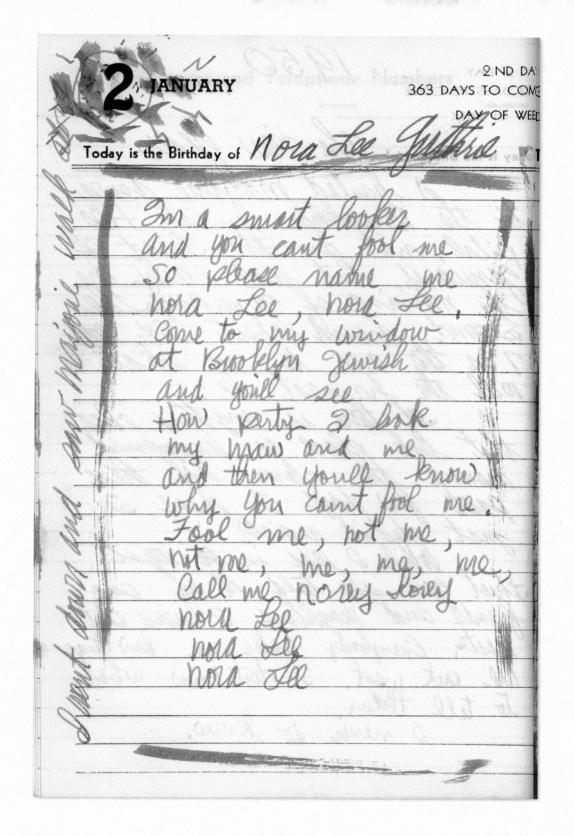

Today is the Birthday of *Nora Lee Guthrie*

I'm a smart looker
and you cant fool me
so please name me
nora Lee, nora Lee,
Come to my window
at Brooklyn Jewish
and you'll see
How pretty I look.
my brow and me
and then you'll know
why you cant fool me.
Fool me, not me,
not me, me, me, me,
Call me nosey losey
nora Lee
nora Lee
nora Lee

"Headdy Down," written on gift-wrapping paper, plays with the Yiddish-isms heard in Woody's Coney Island neighborhood. *Dibuck,* from the Yiddish word *dybbuk,* means a possessed soul, *keppy* is the Yiddish diminutive word for *kepula,* meaning "head," and *Joadulah* uses the Yiddish diminutive ending for a little child's name. Above is the birth announcement recorded in Woody's diary for his daughter Nora Lee.

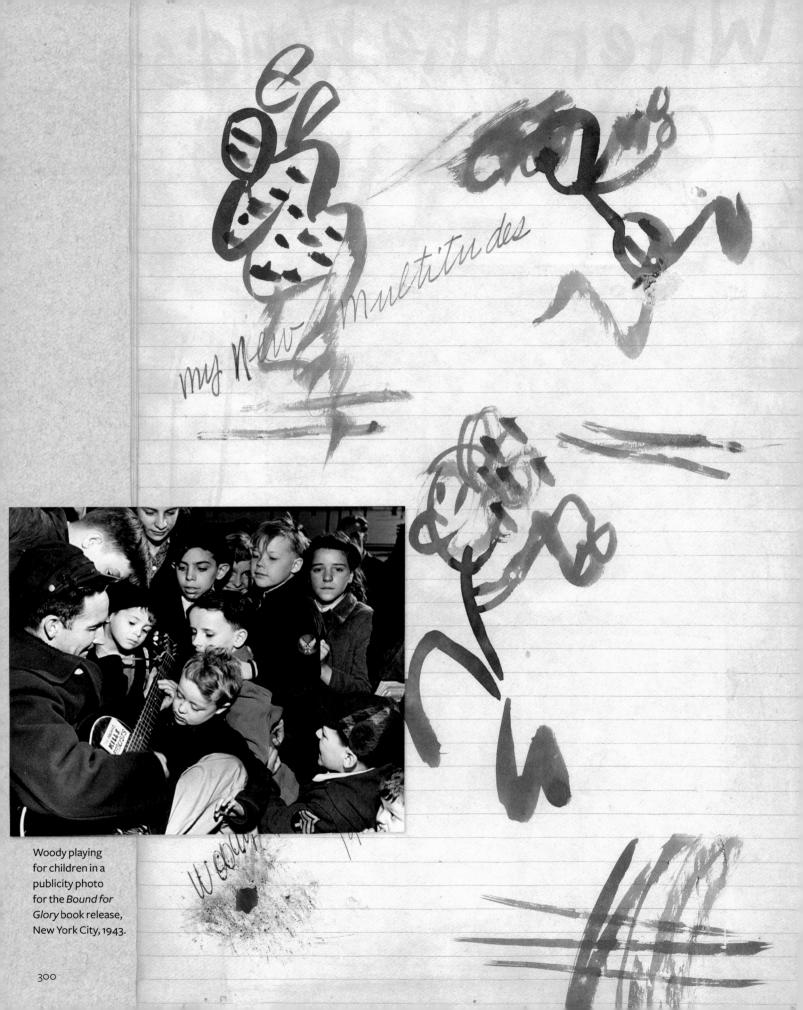

my New Multitudes

Woody playing for children in a publicity photo for the *Bound for Glory* book release, New York City, 1943.

New Multitudes

Woody Guthrie

NEW MULTITUDES

Words & Music allthree by: Woody Guthrie

Gimme my new multitudes;
Gimme my new multitudes;
Gonna win my battle for peace;
Gotta have my new multitudes!

Gimme my new multitudes;
Gimme my new multitudes;
Gpnna build up my old world over;
Gotta have new multitudes!

Gimme my new multitudes;
Gimme my new multitudes;
Gonna make heaven on this earth;
Gotta have new multitudes!

Gimme my new multitudes;
Gimme my new multitudes;
Lets be fertile and multiply;
Gotta have new multitudes.!

Gimme my new multitudes;
Gimme my new multitudes;
 Gpnna build my world with love;
Gotta have new multitudes!

Gimme my new multitudes;
Gimme my new multitudes;
Gonna lose this generation;
Gotta have new multitudes!

                    END

                         Wooody Guthrie.

Something About
this one like
         Woody Guthrie
         Beer Garden Canyone
         Topango Oct 1952

THIS MORNING I AM BORN AGAIN

THIS MORNING I AM BORN AGAIN
AND LIGHT SHINES THROUGH THE LAND
AND I DO NOT SEEK A HEAVEN
I SOME DEATHLY DISTANT LAND.

NO LONGER DESIRE A PEARLY GATE
NOR WANT NO STREET OF GOLD
I DO NOT WANT A MANSION
FOR MY HEART IS NEVER COLD.

THIS MORNING I AM BORN AGAIN
I AM WHOLE AND NEW COMPLETE
I AM OVERCOME ALL OF MY SINS
I STAND ON MY TWO FEET.

I AM LIFE UNLIMITED
MY BODY AS THE SKY
I AM AT HOME IN MY UNIVERSE
WHERE YONDERS PLANETS FLY .

THIS MORNING I AM BORN AGAIN
MY PAST IS DEAD AND GONE
THIS GREAT ETERNAL MOMENT
IS MY GREAT ETERNAL DAWN.

I GIVE MYSELF, MY HEART, MY SOUL,
TO GIVE SOME FRIEND A HAND,
THIS MORNING I AM BORN AGAIN,
I AM IN THE PROMISED LAND.

MARCH 11th, 1939,
This is the date I made this song
up. Los Angeles, California.
I sung it over the air on KFVD.

CHAPTER EIGHT

One Man Religion

BOUND FOR GLORY

ARLO GUTHRIE

*I got me sort of a one man religion. My religion is
so big, no matter who you are, you're in it, and no
matter what you do you can't get out of it.*
—Woody

Woody Guthrie came to his spirituality naturally. He wrestled with it, fought
it, teased it, accepted it, loved and hated it. It was general and also personal.
Ultimately, it was the discovery of his own self and how it fit his perceived version
of reality that was important to him: his truth. He assumed that the uncovering of
truth, and the struggles to do so, were not that much different than the struggles
everyone had to deal with. Not only in his time, but for all time. People are people.

When I was very young, I remember an evening when my father chose to sleep
on the floor instead of a bed. I asked him why. He told me he didn't want to get
soft. He wanted to remain detached from comfort so he could come and go without
distraction. From his friends and peers, I heard stories of him getting a new car,
or guitar, or something of value, only to give it away when it ran out of gas or
needed new strings. He had very clearly learned the first lesson of what we identify
in spiritual life as detachment. The same was true in his relationships (much to
the chagrin of family, relatives, and co-workers). He had learned from a very young
age that attachment to things, people, or places would only lead to the burden of
sorrow. He learned the hard way that the loss of attachments didn't come about
as a chosen spiritual exercise, but as his experiential reality. He learned he could
enjoy almost anything without needing to possess everything.

Detachment did not keep him locked way, isolated on some mountaintop,
but injected him into the lives of others. He enjoyed celebrating and sharing

his experiences with everyone. In our own immediate family, there were unique family celebrations. My father and mother created the Hanukkah Tree—I'm sure we were the only ones in our neighborhood who had such a holiday feature. They were able to step out of the stereotypical holiday and create their own unique celebration because they could. They made the holidays ours, different from the way others celebrated. As kids we knew how to celebrate with others, but we also had our own style.

In the same way, he participated in religious services, civic obligations (such as voting), union organizations, marriages, politics, and a myriad of other functions hosted by others, but he also had his own way. He was able to take religious and civic traditions and make them personal. And through his songs, drawings, books, and everyday conversations, he encouraged everyone to do the same. It was what he called his work.

He believed himself to be unique, and therefore he believed that each individual was likewise unique—one of a kind. And that there was great power in the uniting of individuals with common cause. He sabotaged conformity at almost every opportunity and became belligerent when the uniqueness of others was subjected to conformity.

He realized that, just as no two snowflakes are exactly the same, no two or more people are exactly alike. They were created to be different from the beginning, and any effort to make them exactly the same was a useless and empty effort that ran counter to nature—and to reality. Although he had periods of doubt and frustration, illness and sorrow, he had great faith in himself and his creator that overall his destiny and that of everyone else was *Bound For Glory*.

There's all kinds of living and all kinds of dying. Out in Hollywood they have a place that doesn't do anything but make up lunches for dogs—everyday a different meal, every meal balanced and tested for vitamins. The movie stars shell out $20 a week and every day a shiny white truck drives up and delivers the dogs lunch. That's one kind of dying.

Down in east Arkansas the Negro leader of a share cropper tent colony was beaten to death by a vigilante. He led his people out on a strike and the vigilantes beat the side of his head in. They did it with clubs. They slammed him in the groin and his testicles swelled to the size of footballs. The old man lay on a heap of rags and blankets, and the whole colony gathered around: He told them, "They got our hands tied. Untie us and see what we can do!" Then he died. That's one way of living.

to write me her new set of New Years
Resolutions I'll write down a set of
them my own self:

NEW   YEARS   RULIN'S

1. WORK MORE AND BETTER

2. WORK BY A SCHEDULE

3. WASH TEETH IF ANY

4. SHAVE

5. TAKE BATH

6. EAT GOOD — FRUIT- VEGETABLES- MILK

7. DRINK VERY SCANT IF ANY

8. WRITE A SONG A DAY

9. WEAR CLEAN CLOTHES — LOOK GOOD

10. SHINE SHOES

11. CHANGE SOCKS

12. CHANGE BED CLOTHES OFTEN

13. READ LOTS GOOD BOOKS

14. LISTEN TO RADIO A LOT

15. LEARN PEOPLE BETTER

16. KEEP RANCHO CLEAN

17. DONT GET LONESOME

18. STAY GLAD

19. KEEP HOPING MACHINE RUNNING

20. DREAM GOOD

21. BANK ALL EXTRA MONEY

22. SAVE DOUGH

23. HAVE COMPANY BUT DONT WASTE TIME

24. SEND MARY AND KIDS MONEY

25. PLAY AND SING GOOD

26. DANCE BETTER

27. HELP WIN WAR — BEAT FASCISM

28. LOVE MAMA

29. LOVE PAPA

30. LOVE PETE

SMACK!

31. LOVE EVERYBODY

32. MAKE UP YOUR MIND

33. WAKE UP AND FIGHT

I have hoped so many hopes and dreamed so many dreams, seen them swept aside by weather, and blown away by men, washed away in my own mistakes, that – I use to wonder if it wouldn't be better just to haul off and quit hoping. Just protect my own inner brain, my own mind and heart, by drawing it up into a hard knot and not having any more hopes or dreams at all. Pull in my feelings, and call back all of my sentiments --- and not let any earthly event move me in either direction, either cause me to hate, to fear, to love, to care, to take sides, to argue the matter at all ---; and, yet, there are certain good times and pleasures that I never can forget, no matter how much I want to, because the pleasures and the displeasures, the good times and the bad, are really all there is to me.

And these pleasures that you cannot ever forget are the yeast that always starts working in your mind again, and it gets in your thoughts again, and in your eyes again, and then, all at once, no matter what has happened to you, you are building a brand-new world again, based and built on the mistakes, the wreck, the hard luck and trouble of the old one. . . .

The note of hope is the only note that can help us or save us from falling to the bottom of the heap of evolution because, largely, about all a human being is, anyway, is just a hoping machine.

Woody met up with thousands of homeless people in his lifetime. From his own early days, he understood what it was like to have to make your way alone. "Lost Boy" (a.k.a. "Be Kind To The Boy On The Road") became one of his foundational beliefs.

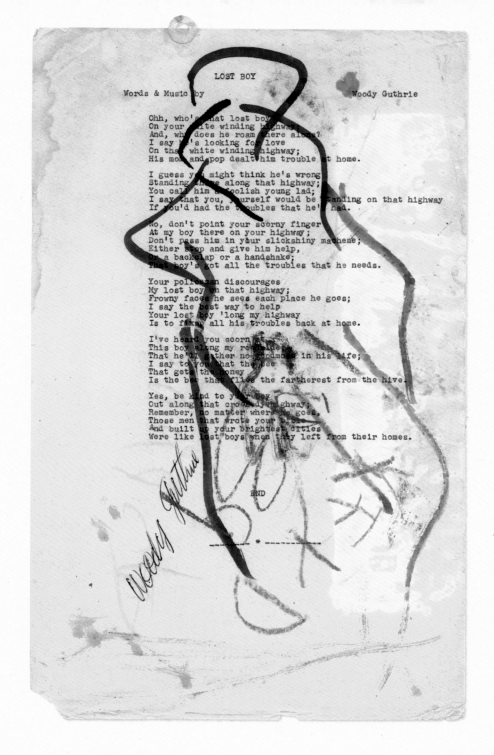

LOST BOY

Words & Music by   Woody Guthrie

Ohh, who's that lost boy
On your white winding highway,
And, why does he roam there alone?
I say he's looking for love
On that white winding highway;
His mom and pop dealt him trouble at home.

I guess you might think he's wrong
Standing there along that highway;
You call him a foolish young lad;
I say that you, yourself would be standing on that highway
If you'd had the troubles that he's had.

No, don't point your scorny finger
At my boy there on your highway;
Don't pass him in your slickshiny machene;
Either stop and give him help,
Or a backslap or a handshake;
That boy's got all the troubles that he needs.

Your policeman discourages
My lost boy on that highway;
Frowny faces he sees each place he goes;
I say the best way to help
Your lost boy 'long my highway
Is to fix up all his troubles back at home.

I've heard you scorn at
This boy along my roadsides,
That he'll gather no goodmore in his life;
I say to you that the bee
That gets the honey
Is the bee that flies the fartherest from the hive.

Yes, be kind to your boy
Out along that crowdy highway;
Remember, no matter where he goes,
Those men that wrote your bible
And built up your brightest cities
Were like lost boys when they left from their homes.

END

Woody Guthrie

I looked up and saw two kids crawl from an open-top car just behind us: a tall skinny one about fifteen, and a little scrawny runt that couldn't be over ten or eleven. . . . I'd seen a thousand kids just like them. They seem to come from homes somewhere that they've run away from. They seem to come to take the place of the old stiffs that slip on a wet board, miss a ladder, fall out a door, or just dry up and shrivel away riding the mean freights; the old souls that groan somewhere in the darkest corner of a boxcar, moan about a twisted life half lived and nine-tenths wasted, cry as their souls hit the highball for heaven, die and pass out of this world like the echo of a foggy whistle.

UNION'S MY RELIGION

Words and Music both by   Woody Guthrie

I just now heard a salty seaman
On this deep and dangerous sea;
Talking to some Army Chaplain
That had preached to set him free:
"When I seen my union vision,
Teh I made my quick decision;
Yess, that union's my religion;
That I know".

                    (And, that I know)

"Yes, I've gotta have a true religion;
That I know.   and that I know.
And, I've gotta finda true religion;
That I know. Yess, that I know.
But, when I think of thugs and deputies,
And see this union blood that flows;
Then, the union's my religion;
That I know.

                    (And, that I know)

"Twas my union saved my mother;
That I know, and, well I know;
It was my union saved my father;
Yes, I know. Yes, yess, I know.
My union saved my sister and brother
From starvation and from whoredom;
'Twas My union saved my people;
That I know.

                    (And, that I know)

"Friend, my union is my religion;
That I know; and, that I know;
My union gives me power;
This I know; and, this I know;
My heart just went wild at prancing
When I seen all colors adancing;
So, my union is my religion;
That I know.

                    (And, that I know)

                        END

                    Made up by me
                    On top of the sea:
                    July 18th, 19&44,
                    It rocked around in my head
                    Just like a ship on the ocean.
                    And all nine of us are
                    Stilla rockin'.

                        WWGee

Woody Guthrie

Union Prayer

Woody Guthrie
9 Jan. 1949

I hear that prayer and praying
Will change this world around
I fold my hands / bow my head
I kneel down on the ground.

I prayed and prayed by nite & day
And then I prayed some more
I prayed till my tongue was dry as dust
I prayed till my knees had sores.

Will prayer change shacks to decent homes?
Will prayer change sickness into health?
Will prayer change hate to works of love?
Will prayer get me my right to vote?
Will prayer give jobs at honest pay?
Will prayer bring stomach full of food?
Will prayer make rich treat poor folks right?
Will prayer take out the Ku Klux Klan?
Will prayer cut down the hoodlum bands?
Will prayer stop the lunchbug hands?
If all of these my prayers can do,
I'll pray till I am black and blue
I'll pray lots more than all of you —
If prayer will bring us Union love,
I'll pray and pray and pray some more.
I'll pray all day from door to door
and tall at nite to pray some more
any prayer with a Union label.

(30)   (30)

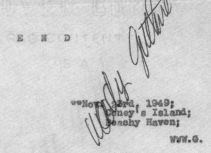

HANNUKA'S FLAME

Words & Music by: Woody Guthrie

Hanuka candlelight, see my flame
Shining on my window's pane;
Come flicker 'cross my glassy glass
And light each lonesome to pass.

If your lifelong heavy load
Brings you down my path and road,
My light of Hanuka shines your way
To ask you in to rest a day.

Hanuka candle dances warm
To help you weather your heavy storm;
Shines like my lighthouse light this night
To bring your worried soul my light.

Now as I light my first and my last
Of all nine candles to guide you past
Through these winds of blowing snows
To take you to your Hanuka home.

If you don't wish to stop inside;
Too bashful proud, or afraid of pride,
I'll send my beam to light your dream
Under your snow where my newgrass hides.

**Nov. 23rd, 1949;
Coney's Island;
Beachy Haven;

W.W.G.

TOP: "Grandpa Tells Hanuka Tales." MIDDLE: "Passover Candles." BOTTOM: "The Lamp That Burned." OPPOSITE: A song about hamantash, a triangular filled-pocket cookie associated with Purim.

Woody's mother-in-law was Aliza Greenblatt, a Yiddish writer and poet. His record producer was Moses Asch, the son of the Yiddish playwright Sholem Asch. Through these two relationships, Woody was introduced to Judaism, spiritually and culturally. He wrote songs concerning the history of the Jews, their traditions, their language, their holidays, and even their foods.

Nosh oh Nosh

Gee oh gee, gosh ohh gosh,
I'ma gonna nosh my homentash!
Nosh oh nosh, homentash,
Help me nosh my homentash!

Soap and water! Wash ohh wash!
Help me nosh my homentash!
Wring my mop dry! squissh and squassh!
Help me nosh my homentash!   (Cho.)

Hanukah gone and Purim's here!
I wish they came ten times a year!
Rattle my rattler! Bifferty bosh!
Help me nosh my homentash!   (Cho.)

I will kiss you pretty and sweet
I'll fix for you some bortsh and beets!
Borscht and beets! Beets and borscht!
Help me nosh my homentash !

Meat ball sour! meat ball sweet!
Lox and beagle is hard to beat!
My broom needs you to give it a push (and)
and Help me nosh my homentash! (Cho.)

Now we dance I hold your hand
We dance to heaven and back again!
You can kiss me girls, but please dont push!
Help me nosh my homentash ! (Cho.)

Here's the secret of my heart
We must meet and never never part!
I need you to do my wash(and),
Help me nosh my homentash! (Cho.)

End

Words & music by
Woody Guthrie
Coney Island N.Y.C.
Jan. 30, 1950.

313

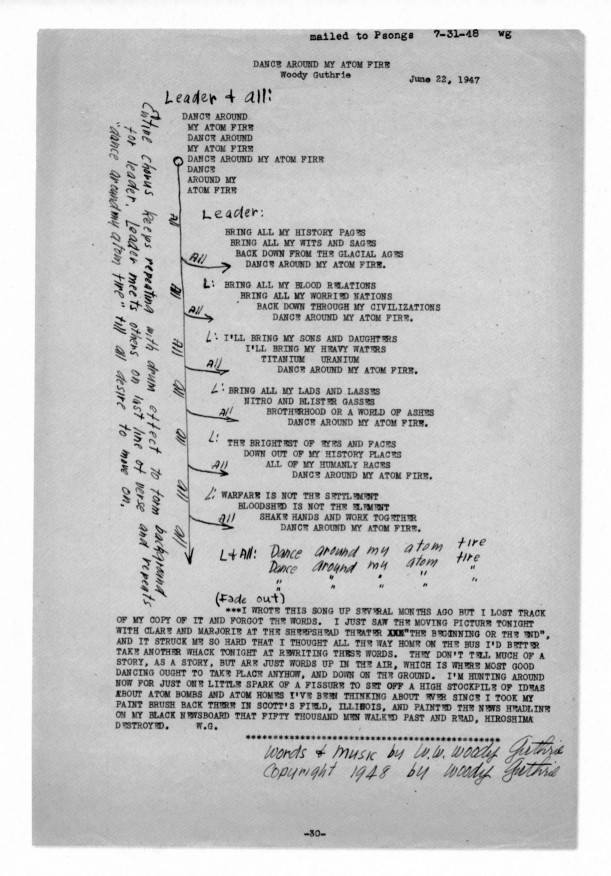

Atomic energy was a real concern in the late 1940s as nuclear weapons became a reality. Woody met with Albert Einstein, and they discussed the subject of atoms in general, from their possible good use to the nightmare of atomic warfare.

World's on Afire

My honey, my sweety pie,
When the world's on afire, fire,
Come lay your sweet head
Here on my bosom.

My angel, my darling,
When that atombomb does come;
Let me be your pillow
While this world's on afire.

When the flames go creeping;
When the smokes go leaping;
Play like we're sleeping
While the world's on afire.

Wildfire will run crawling
Whilst the walls come falling;
Sleep on my bosom
While the world's on afire.

While the skies they're clearing
We'll rise up dreaming;
Build our city from the ashes
Where the world was afire.

When the moon gets brighter,
I'll hug you tighter;
We're gonna build with kisses
Where the world was afire.

End

Words and music by
Woody Guthrie
49 Murdock court apt. 1J
Brooklyn, 23, New York

Oct. 18,
1950

TALKIN' WORLD PEACE

Woody Guthrie

Gonna tell y' what t' do if y' wanta win some peace;
Pray for it in your home; sing peace along y'r street;
Dance in Peace around your block; dance it alla 'round y'r town;
Bark it up tow'rds th' moon; laff it all this world around.
     Stir it up!   Git in that old groove!   Keep it comin'.

'F'ya wanta keep this peace I'm showin' y' howta win,
Y' gotta turn all y'r enemies back inta friends;
Gotta hug an' kiss y'r family, an' y'r brothers an' y'r kin;
No matter what y' fought about n'r color of their skin.
     Lotsa fun once ya cetch onto it.

While y're huggin' 'em an' kissin' 'em y' whisper in his ear
'Bout howta bring ever'body back home fr'm this war;
Bout howta stop this killin' this minnit, right now;
Howta melt our guns back inta garden plows.
     An' dont ever let anybody tell y' Mebbe So, ner Not Now,
     Ner --- Wait ahile ----

'Course ya caint stop no war by talkin' 'round about it;
Caint git much peace justa singin' 'round about it;
Y' wont talk n'r dance much till y'll bump th' right one
Says ya gotta keep this war hot so's he c'n make that Mun.
     That kale. That dough. That geetus. That velvet.
     That stuff. You know, that mazuma. That long green.

When ya find anybody on this war th't's cashin' in,
Spit in their eye 'er mebbe, clip 'em on th' chin;
That's better then lettin' this war spread around
Till these atombombs come an' lay us all in th' ground;
     Spit in their eyes.
     Show 'em you're notta 'fraid ta fight for peace.

Gotta vote somebody inta office knows all them warlord tricks;
Knows my job an' pay an' pension , just howta keep 'em fix'd;
Like Mrs Bass & Mr Vincent and this Ruhe Borough man;
They c'n outfox your killergang if anybody can;
     Pergressive people.
     Only folks that knows th' score 'bout peace 'er war;
     'Er most anything else worth knowin' about.q

END

Woody Guthrie
GEER GARDENO
Topangoe Canyuno
Octobers Last Days
1 9 5 2

- 30 -

My Peace

Words and musical sounds by Woody Guthrie

My peace
my peace
Is all I've got
That I can give to you
my peace
Is all I ever had
That's all I ever knew
I give my peace
To green and black
and brown and red and blue
I guess my peace
Is justa 'bout all
I've got to give to you.

My peace, my peace
Is all I've got
That I could offer t' you
my peace is
Wortha thousan times more.
Than anything I own
I pass my peace
around and about
'Cross hands of every hue;
I guess my peace
Is justa 'bout all
I've got to give to you.

not southern
white peace "S.W.G.R.C.

Woody Guthrie
Topanga Blango
December (25) 1952

39

TICKY TOCK
by
Woody Guthrie

Little hand, big hand
 Long hand, short hand
 Rich man, pore man,
                    Ticky ticky tock
 Hour hand, minute hand
 Fast hand, slow hand
 Worker man, gambler man
                    Ticky ticky tock

Rough hand, fine hand
 Sick hand, well hand
 Angel hand and devil hand
                    Ticky ticky tock
 Smooth hand, blister'd hand
 Robber hand, honest hand
 Living hand and dead hand
                    Ticky ticky tock

Your hand, my hand
 Big hand, little hand
 Lady hand and man hand
                    Ticky ticky tock
 His hand, her hand
 Liar's tongue and coward hand
 Lyncher hand, slave hand
                    Ticky ticky tock

Iron hand, marble hand
 Farm hand, mill hand
 Mine hand, factory hand
                    Ticky ticky tock
 Eating hand, drinking hand
 Saw hand and hammer hand
 Honey hand and money hand
                    Ticky ticky tock

My hand, your hand,
 Warm hand, cold hand,
 Old hand and new hand
                    Ticky ticky tock
 What hand, which hand?
 Come hand, gone hand,
 Good hand and bad hand
                    Ticky ticky tock

Ticky ticky tick tock
Ticky ticky tick tock
Time a gonna git you
Ticky ticky tock.

*Woody Guthrie
love thy self*

                    Coney Island by the clock 5-27-47
--- 30 -----

    This is a little warning song. A warning that your own hand and your own
        time is going t catch up with you. One hand, two hand, three hand and
        four hand, five hand, six hand, seven eight and nine hand. Hands around
        the pillow. Hands around the table. Hands around the block. Hands
        around the whole world. Everybody's hand in everybody elses hand. A
        working man hand and a working woman's hand to show you just how big and
        just how little this world is. Or do you think this world is more than
        one world? Two worlds? Three worlds? Four hands? Five hands? If you
        stick a little brass pin in the skin of just one hand every hand in the
        world feels it and knows you done it. WG.

----- 30 -----

GONNA GET THROUGH THIS WORLD
By Woody Guthrie

WELL I'M GONNA GET THROUGH THIS WORLD
THE BEST I CAN IF I CAN
AND I'M GONNA GET THROUGH THIS WORLD
AND I THINK I CAN.

WELL I'M GONNA WALK IN THIS WORLD
THE BEST I CAN IF I CAN
AND I'M GONNA XXXXXXXXXXX WALK IN THIS WORLD
THE BEST I CAN.

WELL I'M GONNA TALK IN THIS WORLD
THE BEST I CAN IF I CAN
AND I'M GONNA TALK IN THIS WORLD
AND I THINK I CAN.

I AM GONNA WORK IN THIS WORLD
THE BEST I CAN IF I CAN
AND I'M GONNA WORK IN THIS WORLD
AND I THINK I CAN.

IAM GONNA CLEAN UP THIS WORLD
THE BEST I CAN IF I CAN
AND I'M GONNA CLEAN UP THIS WORLD
AND I THINK I CAN.

I'M GONNA LEAVE THIS WORLD BEHIND
THE BEST I CAN IF I CAN
I AM GONNA LEAVE THIS WORLD BEHIND
AND I THINK I CAN.

This song has been on my brain for a long time
but I didn't write it down till this morning.
It was therefore composed and made up by me on this date,
March 21st, 1945, at 3520 Mermaid Avenue, Brooklny 24, N.Y.

Woody Guthrie

Some times
I think
Im a gonna lose my mind
But it dont
Look like
I ever do.

I loved
So many
People everywhere I went
Some too much
and others
not enough.

I dont know
I may go
Down or up or anywhere
But I feel
Like this scribbling
Will stay.

Maybe
If I hadnt
Of seen so much hard feelings
I might not
Could of felt
Other peoples.

So
When you think of me
If and when you ever do
Just say
Well
Another mans done gone
Yep
another mans done gone.

W6

Beluthahatchee, FL, 1953.

MY BATTLE

Show me how
To fight the battle of life
Teach me how to
fight my battles in life
Show me how to
fight my hard times in life
and I'll run away with you

Show me how
to face my share of life
Teach me how to
fight my troublesome fights
Show me how to
win my hard times in life
and I'll run away with you

Show me how
to win my union in life
Teach me how to
win my victory in life
Show me how to
win for all of my people
and I'll run away with you

In 1952, Woody was diagnosed with Huntington's disease, the incurable hereditary illness that took his mother's life. Since many of the symptoms are similar to those of alcoholism—loss of balance, slurred speech and loss of motor control, and erratic moods—Woody's illness took years to identify. His handwriting had always appeared as beautiful penmanship, however, with the onset of Huntington's it became more and more illegible.

You might not quite have
known it
Because maybe I've not quite
shown it
But if you wanta really know
What got me up
And on the go
What patched me up
From head to my toe
What got me ready for my
Battle rattle
Way over here in my rain
And my snow
You wanta know?
Sweet devil!
Sweet devil?
Your smile cured me.
Your smile you threw across
my way here
Saved my neck
and cured my hide
Your big laff got me fired out
And your smile cured me.

(30)

Woody Guthrie
Topanga Canyon
Nov, 1952

IS SPREAD: Sunday hootenanny in Washington Square Park with
a ⎯blin' Jack Elliott, Washington Square Park, New York City, 1955

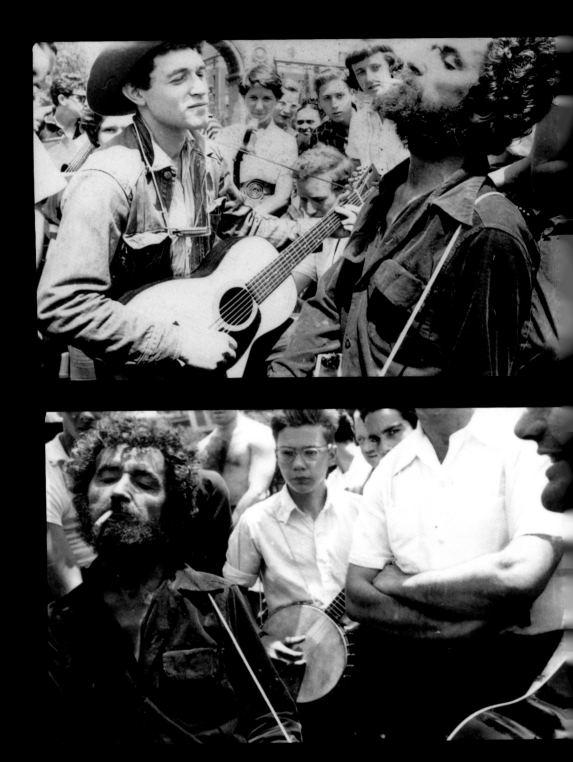

Death and me
Tried to get married
In holy wedlock
But we just argued and fought
and cussed
And raved and tore back
and forth at each other
That we didn't get along at all.
I killed old death.
I killed old Death

(80)

Woody Guthrie
Topanga Canyon
november 1952

I never dread the day that
I will die
'Cause my sunset is
Somebody's morning sky.

MY SOUL'S GOT WINGS

I GOT A HOUSE 'WAY UP IN THE SKY
I GOT A HOUSE 'WAY UP IN THE SKY
LIFE MAY BE DREARY, STILL I CAN SING,
FLY UP TO HEAVEN,
                    MY SOUL'S GOT WINGS

            MY SOUL'S GOT WINGS, LORD,
            MY SOUL'S GOT WINGS,
            MY LOAD IS HEAVY,
            STILL I CAN SING
            CLIMB UP MY MOUNTAIN,
            WALK ON MY SEA,
            GONNA FLY UP TO HEAVEN
            'CAUSE MY SOUL'S GOT WINGS

SO FULL OF JOY DON'T KNOW WHAT TO SAY
KNEEL AT MY BEDSIDE EACH NIGHT TO PRAY
SLEEP ON MY PILLOW, ALL NIGHT I DREAM
GONNA FLY UP TO HEAVEN,
                    MY SOUL'S GOT WINGS

WAKE IN MY MORNING, UP WITH MY SUN,
WORK FOR MY LORD TILL MY DAY'S WORK IS DONE
NIGHT TIME I STOP JUST TO COUNT MY GOOD DEEDS
AND I FLY UP TO HEAVEN,
                    MY SOUL'S GOT WINGS

            *** I COMPOSED THE WORDS AND THIS TUNE
            ON A HOT NIGHT IN JULY, 1939, IN A LITTLE OLD
            SHACK HOUSE I RENTED ON THE BACKSIDE OF A VACANT
            LOT ON CHESTNUT STREET IN GLENDALE, CALIFORNIA.
                    WOODY G.   *******

Pritty   Near

woody Guthrie

1951

I knew that my trail would be a story that whirls, and a song that spins in the middle of the sun, a hunt for the universe on the points of our needles. I knew the tale would be a freewheeler, a quick starter, but a high running, circling chorus that keeps on repeating over and over, and would sing every song to be sung under the one tune and the one name, and would shake under the fires and grates and furnaces, a track that would go everywhere.

Not The End.
Just Resting.
Give Me Time.
I'll Hit 'Em Again.
Your Time Now.

Woody's painted lyric, "So Long It's Been Good To Know Yuh," ca. 1948.

of the people I've met

another places I've been

Some of the troubles

So long

It's been good

to know you

So long

Been a mighty long time

since I've been home

and I've gotta be driftin' along

Music is just a
handy way of
telling whats
on your mind

No mind
No music

Instead of having a book of fifty or a hundred of my best songs and best ballads why not let the book be a story about the road of the man?

Start off with the kid and the songs he heard around him. Go on through family to Texas plains, cattle plains, oil fields, songs of country and ranch dances, my first made up songs, marriage & kids, shack house, fiddlings, jobs of work in liquor store and markets, school, girl friends, and all, on to chamber of commerce banquets, rodes, etc., then hit the road west and find and make up other songs as I go, then jalopy hopping on skid rows and playing on radio in L.A. for Two years, union meetings, churches, etc., onto breakup of marriage, onto N.Y., then onto records, radios, rallies, all over streets, waterfronts, and let the songs be good, bad, fair, medium, or however they are, onto merchant marines, army camp, Second marriage, marjorie, Cathy, Coney Island, more unions, the Daily Worker, Peoples world, almanac tours, and pick a song I made up at every turn. How does this sound?
                                          woody

NOTES AND SOURCES

The bulk of the material in this book originated in Woody Guthrie's family home, collected and saved by Marjorie Guthrie. The collection is now housed at the Woody Guthrie Center in Tulsa, Oklahoma, part of the new American Song Archive.

All original lyrics, manuscripts, correspondence, artwork, photographs, and newspaper articles courtesy of the Woody Guthrie Archive, except for the following collections and repositories:

Barry & Judy Ollman Collection: 42, 96, 97
Gail Knighton: 199
Library of Congress: 151
Mary Jo Edgmon Collection at the Woody Guthrie Archive: 18, 21, 30, 35
Michigan Tech Archives: 121
New York Times: 116, 194: © 1941, 1948 The New York Times Company. All rights reserved. Used under license.
Nora Guthrie Collection: 80, 88, 139, 154, 158, 227, 233, 248, 273, 274, 288, 289, 295, 297
NYU Tamiment Library, courtesy of People's World: 137
Ralph Rinzler Folklife Archives and Collections, Smithsonian Institution: 53, 75, 143, 177, 181, 223, 232, 254, 258, 286, 337

Bound for Glory artwork series: 23, 24, 27, 32, 41, 47, 49, 61, 62, 68, 92, 163, 175, 241, 247, 253

PHOTO CREDITS

Al Aumuller: 160
Lester Balog: 138
CBS Photo Archive/CBS via Getty Images: 234–237
Chicago History Museum/ Archive Photos via Getty Images: 183
Arthur Dubinsky: 326, 327, 333
Sid Grossman © Howard Greenburg Gallery, New York: front cover, 74
Pictorial Parade/Moviepix via Getty Images: 179
Alfred Puhn: 137
Eric Schaal: 3, 55, 76, 80, 156, 206, 300
Eric Schaal/The LIFE Picture Collection via Getty Images: 1, 156, 169
Seema Weatherwax: 44–46, 102